Enigma Books

Salazar: A Political Biography
The Italian Brothers
Nazi Palestine
Code Name: Kalistrat
Pax Romana
The De Valera Deception
Lenin and His Comrades
The Decision to Drop the Atomic Bomb
Target Hitler
Truman, MacArthur and the Korean War
The Eichmann Trial Diary
Working with Napoleon

David Levy

Stalin's Man in Canada

Fred Rose and Soviet Espionage

Enigma Books

Published by Enigma Books, New York

Copyright © 2011 by David Levy

First Edition

Printed in the United States of America

ISBN: 978-1-936274-27-7
e-ISBN: 978-1-936274-28-4

Publisher's Cataloging-In-Publication Data

Levy, David (David Kinder), 1938-
  Stalin's man in Canada : Fred Rose and Soviet espionage / David Levy. -- 1st
ed.

    p. : ill. ; cm.

  Includes index.
  ISBN: 978-1-936274-27-7

  1. Rose, Fred, 1907-1983. 2. Espionage, Soviet--Canada—20th century. 3.
Espionage, Communist--Canada--20th century. 4. Politicians--Canada--
Biography. 5. Communists--Canada--Biography. 6. Russians--Canada--
Biography. 7. Immigrants--Canada--Biography. I. Title.

F1034.3.R67 L48 2011
327.1247/071/092

For my mother and father, Ann and Lionel Levy,
from whom I inherited an interest in history.

"History calls those men the greatest who have ennobled themselves by working for the common good; experience acclaims as happiest the man who has made the greatest number of people happy."

Karl Marx, age 17.

Contents

Stalin's Man in Canada

I.

Balcons and Escaliers...

> ...and there your maisonry
> Of pendant balcon and escalier'd march...
> A. M. Klein

> "...Lithuania, stepmother of mercy!"
> Daniel Ben-Nahum

This is the story of Fred Rose, labor organizer, politician, Soviet agent. We'll call him Freddy, what his pals called him. The story has different beginnings, one of them in Cartier.

The dwellings of Cartier, a one-time working class district in the city of Montreal, consist mostly of brick houses two and three stories in height with flat roofs, balconies, porches and exterior staircases in front and back. The rooms are distributed lengthwise. One proceeds past a double living room, through a hallway to a dining area and a kitchen in the rear. For the houses with three floors, the stairs from the balcony on the second floor to the third floor are inside.

The buildings were erected between 1891 and 1921, at a time when migrants without the means to acquire single-family accommodation poured into the city to labor in its plants and factories.[1]

The exterior staircases have been much criticized as ill-suited to the city's icy winters, though it has been argued that thus constructed the buildings were without the confined noise and odors of apartment interiors and better suited to the city's stifling summers. In the summers, recalled pianist Paul Bley, the iron staircases became everyone's front yards.[2]

In one estimate, Cartier in the 1940s was roughly 45 percent Jewish, 40 percent French-Canadian, the remaining 15 percent a mixed demographic, in another 55 percent Jewish, 35 percent French-Canadian ten percent diverse, and in yet another the Jewish and French-Canadian numbers were judged to be about equal.[3]

The Jews of Cartier were an immigrant community that had fled the pogroms of Eastern Europe. Most were needle-trade and fur factory drones, some small-time shop keepers and factory owners, candy and cigarette jobbers, plumbers, cabbies, carpenters and electricians. The more affluent and better educated, the doctors and lawyers, had arrived from Germany a generation earlier. There were others from Romania and Hungary. The larger number, themselves or their relatives, had come by sea at the turn of the new century from Kovno-Guberniya— *guberniya* meaning province—in northern Lithuania then under Russian control. Departing by ship they traveled from the Baltic port of Memel, now Klaipeda, sailed on to Hamburg, then to Liverpool, across the Atlantic Ocean and up the St. Lawrence River to Montreal.[4] Lithuanian Jews are called *Litvish, Litvaks,* a label they acquired in Poland. There is a claim that *Litvaks* were Ashkenazi Jews who had inhabited the Pale of Settlement and fled to Poland to escape the pogroms that broke out in 1881 following the coronation of Alexander III. *Litvaks* have a reputa-

1. Jean Claude Marsan, *Montreal in Evolution*, McGill-Queens Press, 1981.
2. Paul Bley with David Lee, *Stopping Time: Paul Bley and the Transformation of Jazz*, Vehicle Press, 1999.
3. Robert A. Moreau, "Fred Rose: Une Voix Communiste au Parlement, 1943–1945," M.A. dissertation, University of Ottawa, 1989; Myer Siemiatycki, "Communism in One Constituency: The Communist Party and the Jewish Community of Montreal with Particular Reference to the Election of Fred Rose to Parliament in 1943 and 1945." M.A. dissertation, York University, 1977. In the weeks leading up to the June 1945 election, *The Canadian Tribune*, the party's English-language paper, gave the Jewish population a registered voter advantage of five percent.
4. Betty Kobayashi Issenman, "A Jewish/Japanese Odyssey," *The Wallenberg Bulletin*, Winter 1998.

tion as rationalists, philosophers and artists. When in the 18th century the Hasidic movement and its mysticism spread across Eastern Europe, the *Litvaks*, led by the Vilna Gaon, Rabbi Eliyahu, resisted. As a consequence, though Lithuanian Jews were renowned for their religious feeling and great erudition, Hasidism acquired few adherents among them.[5] Some smile at the *Litvak* hypothesis, certain the *Litvak* numbers in Cartier were not as great as the arrivals from Poland.

There is a vision of the world of Cartier in Esther Trepanier's *Jewish Painters of Montreal.*[6]

It is not a documentary vision. There are no images of the muscled and stoic draught horses that hauled wagons loaded with coal, blocks of icebox ice, loaves of bread, and glass bottled milk through the terrible winter cold and sweltering summers. A mostly snow-less, horse-less modernist painterly world of men and women relaxing on the green wood and cement-framed park benches of Fletcher's Field, Berson's open-air midtown cemetery monument yard, Group of Seven-like empty streets, views of building rooftops, empty rooms, hookers and street beggars, a streetcar, a line of men and women at the door of a soup kitchen in winter, the unemployed, proletarian crowds at nightclubs on the lower Main, tavern and cabaret scenes, Hitler and Goebbels caricatures, a welder, a boy with a violin.

Cartier was dotted with barbotte houses, large and small. Barbotte, barbot, barbouthe, barbooth, barbudi was a dice game Middle Eastern in origin supposedly brought to the city in pre-Seaway times by Greek sailors. The murders of Jews associated with gambling, Charlie Feigenbaum in 1934 and Harry Davis in 1946, were alternatively a source of pride and discomfort. Following the huge Davis funeral at the original Paperman's funeral chapel on St. Urbain Street the *Keneder Adler* newspaper pleaded that the man was "a victim of circumstances. If the police were not corrupt and had not taken bribes, gambling houses would not be able to operate."[7]

---

5. Dov Levin, *The Litvaks: A Short History of the Jews in Lithuania,* trans. from the Hebrew by Adam Teller, Yad Vashem, 2000; Rabbi Yitzchak Kasnett, *The World that Was Lithuania: A Study of the Life and Torah Consciousness of Jews in the Towns and Villages of Lithuania and Northeastern Poland*, Mesorah Publications, Ltd. 1997.
6. Esther Trepanier, *Jewish Painters of Montreal: Witnesses of Their Time 1930–1948,* Les Editions de L'Homme, 2008.
7. Suzanne Morton, *At Odds: Gambling and Canadians, 1919–1969*, University of Toronto Press, 2003.

Unseen as well in the paintings were the *blind pigs*, dives that sold illegal liquor, some located in what appeared to be ordinary residences.

The Jews of Cartier may have had more in common with their French-Canadian neighbors than anyone suspected. The American poet Kenneth Rexroth: "New France was a very peculiar kind of France, and bore more resemblance to Kievan Russia with its Varangian, Kazar, and Bulgar river-borne fur traders than anything to be found in the homeland."[8]

---

8. Kenneth Rexroth, *American Poetry in the Twentieth Century*, Herder and Herder, 1971.

II.

Red in the House

"Arise ye workers from your slumbers…"

The dead voted in every Cartier election. Not only the dead. The voters list included a phantom electorate of men and women who may not have ever existed. An infant of seven weeks was down as a bookkeeper, a girl of five as a spinster. The chief returning officer responsible for the accuracy of the lists, Lazarus Bavich, was a blood nephew of the Liberal candidate.[1]

In February 1943 the Red Army had defeated the Nazis at Stalingrad. In July the greatest tank battle ever, at Kursk in the Ukraine, drove the Wehrmacht from the motherland.

In Cartier that summer it was election time once more, a by-election brought on by the death of long-time Liberal incumbent, Peter Bercovich elected in 1940 with a margin of near on 16,000 votes.

1. Siemiatycki, "Communism in One Constituency." See too Henry F. Srebrnik. *Jerusalem on the Amur: Birobidzhan and the Canadian Jewish Communist Movement, 1924–1951*, McGill-Queens Press, 2008.

On 10 August 1943, the day after Election Day, the newspapers carried stories of mayhem that included photographs of city reporters and campaign workers beaten bloody by gangs armed with brass knuckles, clubs and lead pipes. "Hoodlums" were reported to be "much in evidence" throughout the day. Five men were taken to hospital for treatment. Several vehicles were wrecked. Hoodlum targets were the drivers and scrutineers of the Labor-Progressive Party (LPP) candidate and eventual by-election victor, Fred Rose, described as a "Communist jailed for his activities in the 1930s and a fugitive from the Defense of Canada Regulations during the first two years of the war."[2]

Freddy's main opponent was Paul Massé, the candidate of the right-wing anti-conscription Bloc Populaire. Supporting Massé and the Bloc were Jean Drapeau and Pierre Trudeau. The Liberal candidate in this traditional Liberal seat was the establishment lawyer Lazarus Phillips. The CCF, the Commonwealth Cooperative Federation, a political party founded in 1932 in Alberta by farm and labor groups, was represented by David Lewis born *Losz*. Working for Freddy was future Quebec independentist premier Jacques Parizeau.[3]

The 1943 boundaries of Cartier, says Elections Canada, consisted of that part of the city of Montreal "bounded by a line starting at the intersection of St. Gabriel Street with the center of Craig Street, thence following the centre of Craig Street to the center of St. Lawrence Boulevard, thence following the center of St. Lawrence Boulevard to the center of Pine Avenue, thence following the center of Pine Avenue to the center of Park Avenue, thence following the center of Park Avenue to the center of Duluth Avenue, thence following the center of Duluth Avenue to the center of Esplanade Avenue, thence following the center of Esplanade Avenue to the center of Mount Royal Avenue, thence following the center of Mount Royal Avenue to the center of Hutchison Avenue, thence following the center of Hutchison Avenue to the center of Laurier Avenue, thence following the center of Laurier Avenue to the center of St. Lawrence Boulevard, thence following the center of St. Lawrence Boulevard to the center of Mount Royal Avenue, thence

---

2. "Police Hunting Gang Leaders: 'Terrorism' Charged at Polls in Cartier," *The Montreal Daily Star*, 10 August 1943; "Cartier Casualties Include Newsmen," *The Gazette*, 10 August 1943; "33 p.c. of Vote In Cartier Cast; 1 Arrest Made," *The Montreal Daily Star*, 9 August 1943.
3. *Fred Rose: Un Canadiaen Errant,* a film by Francine Pelletier. Great North Films, 2002.

following the center of Mount Royal Avenue to the center of St. Denis Street, thence following the center of St. Denis Street to the center of Craig Street, thence following the center of Craig Street to the point of departure."[4]

There was a report of a ballot box stolen from the home of a deputy returning officer. Freddy's supporters brought him ballots they said were found on a street near one of the polls it turned out had been in the pilfered box. There was one reported voter impersonation arrest, a couple of hundred cases of double voting. Some polls were short of bibles for the swearing in of poll clerks, some deputy returning officers were not on the job promptly at 8 a.m. to open the polls.[5]

Freddy was rated an effective public speaker. The slick campaign flyers produced by fellow traveling ad man Saul Pomerantz highlighted Freddy's Jewish roots, socialist goals, and criticism of appeasement, what the campaign literature called "the crime of Munich that made Hitler strong." The party put out stories in English and Yiddish associating Freddy with the fabled struggle of the USSR against the mass murders committed by the Nazis in Eastern Europe and anti-Semitic attacks on Jews in the Montreal area. The people of Cartier, declared Fred, "must work together for the victory of our united peoples over the fascist enemy. This is our first task, it is our only hope for freedom to fight for a better world." There was no talk during the campaign of a revolution to destroy the capitalist system. Freddy's sharpest verbal blows were directed at the CCF's David Lewis. Much bad blood flowed between the Communists and their social democrat second cousins.

The campaign peaked with a mass rally at Fletcher's Field, a large park area in the heart of Cartier, in one estimate the crowd numbering 10,000, in another 20,000. "I stand," declared Freddy, "for victory in this people's war. Towards this end I shall fight in Ottawa for a total war effort. This includes a healthy and friendly labor policy, a policy which will make labor a partner in the war, a policy which will utilize the patriotism of the workers for the common good rather than insult the workers' devotion to the nation as does the Minister of Labor…. The aircraft strike is the result of the anti-labor policy of the government

4. The boundaries of Cartier, 1943, *Elections Canada.*
5. "33 p.c. of Vote in Cartier Cast; 1 Arrest Made," *The Montreal Daily Star,* 9 August 1943.

which I ask you to defeat by defeating the candidate of the Liberal machine, Lazarus Phillips. I stand for equality for the French-Canadian people not only in words but in deeds. Wages in Quebec must be equalized with those in Ontario. The slums in Cartier must be swept out. Tuberculosis must be eradicated. The children must be taken from the dirty alleys and given playgrounds. I pledge a bill in the House to that effect. I am also pledged to introduce a bill against anti-Semitism because I consider this scourge a danger to the nation as a whole. I appeal that the Cartier people vote for me because I am convinced this meeting of thousands of citizens is the proof that I represent the will of the people for a new deal, for a change."[6]

Stalingrad apart, the other shadow that hung over the August 1943 Cartier by-election was the uprising in the Warsaw ghetto that began 19 April, *eriv* Passover 1943. It was an event that appeared to have been of little interest to the Jews of the wartime left in fealty to Uncle Joe. As documented in Yisrael Gutman's account of the uprising, *The Jews of Warsaw*: "The Communist press did not devote much attention to the ultimate fate of the fighters, and its articles do not relate to the irksome question of why the Allies and particularly the Soviet Union—which hoped to agitate the populace and induce it to embark upon combat operations—did not come to the aid of the fighters in the ghetto."[7]

The political culture of Cartier was multi-faceted. The left drew its support from workers in the garment industry *aka* the *shmata* trade. The industry was driven by the big department stores and merchandizing chains into a state of vicious competition, cost-cutting at any cost. Wages were low, working conditions appalling. Instead of uniting against the stores to humanize the industry, the manufacturers turned on their employees.[8]

It was a fractious community that pitted Jewish workers against Jewish manufacturers, ethnic identity colliding with a fragile class consciousness. At times unexpected alliances would surface. My mother remembered a hat factory strike she was involved in in which a Jewish boss had persuaded the young female francophone workers to stay on

---

6. *The Gazette*, 9 August 1943. At the time, 20,000 aircraft workers at three Montreal plants were on strike.
7. Israel Gutman, *The Jews of Warsaw, 1939–1943: Ghetto Underground Revolt*, trans. Ina Friedman, University of Indiana Press, 1982.
8. Gerald Tulchinsky, *Canada's Jews: a People's Journey*, University of Toronto Press, 2008.

the job while the Jewish female employees followed the nervous francophone union head, who had a large family to support, out of the shop.

For *United Jewish People's Order* (UJPO) founder Joshua Gershman ethnicity and politics were one and the same: I became a Communist, he said, *because* I am a Jew. The UJPO was Communist affiliated, Gershman himself a party member of long standing. Other UJPO members were declared Communists if not always party members. The larger attraction of the Communist movement was its messianic character heralding a perfect from-each-to-each world. The UJPO ran summer camps, organized public lectures and concerts. Having evolved from the Arbeiter Ring, the Workman's Circle of Bundists, leftists dedicated to the advancement of Yiddish culture, the UJPO supported Montreal's Morris Winchevsky schools. Winchevsky, ne Leopold Benzion Novokhovich, a litvak from Kovno, was a secular Jewish philosopher based in England. Freddy was among the speakers at UJPO youth meetings.[9]

Zionists included adherents of both the left and the right. The Jewish left had, at least until 1945 and the revelation of Nazi atrocities, labeled Zionists in Cartier and elsewhere *fascists* and *Hitlerites*. The name calling may too have been directed at the left-oriented labor Zionist Hashomer Hatzair. The Zionist-inclined Canadian Jewish Congress, standard bearer of the Jewish establishment, was tarred with the term "social fascist." *The Canadian Jewish Chronicle*, a high-profile establishment publication, cheered on Quebec's anti-Semitic premier Maurice Duplessis for his attacks on Communists.

---

9. Irving Abella, "Portrait of a Jewish Professional Revolutionary: The Recollections of Joshua Gershman," *Labour/Le Travail*, 2, 1977. See too Ross Lamberton, "'The Dresden Story': Racism, Human Rights, and the Jewish Labour Committee of Canada," *Labour/Le Travail*, 47, Spring 2001:

"The Jewish Labour Committee (JLC) was founded in 1936, an offshoot of the American Jewish Labour Committee, a trade union umbrella group with roots in the Workman's Circle, a radical left Jewish fraternal organization that had its origins in Eastern Europe. At its peak it claimed about 50,000 members, coming largely from such Jewish-dominated trade unions as the International Ladies' Garment Workers Union, the Amalgamated Clothing Workers Union, and the United Cap, Hat and Millinery Workers Union.

"The JLC was social democratic and anti-communist. In the early part of the century, most socialist Jews in Canada were members of the Workman's Circle, but in the wake of the Russian Revolution the 'left' communists began to move away from the 'right' social democrats. By 1926 the two factions had split completely, with the communists leaving to create an organization called the Labour League and the social democrats remaining in the Workman's Circle. The latter continued to be the social and intellectual home of the JLC labor activists, while the former performed the same function for Jewish communists, even after it changed its name in 1945 to the United Jewish People's. Over the years these two factions remained bitter rivals."

Also, Ester Reiter & Roz Usiskin, "Jewish Dissent in Canada: The United Jewish People's Order," *Outlook,* 30 May 2004.

With the end of the war in 1945 things changed. Freddy became a member of the Congress's Dominion Council and the UJPO achieved representation in the Congress, which the RCMP read as an attempted red takeover of those organizations. The RCMP's equation of Jews and Bolsheviks ever endured despite their own finding that Jewish membership in the CPC never exceeded ten percent.[10]

The 1943 Cartier by-election was observed with much interest as a contest between secular French-Canadian nationalism and Jewish internationalism. Nevertheless, the LPP campaign in Cartier had the backing of high profile French-Canadian labor leaders. There was strong support for Freddy from out of town party bigwigs, J. B. Salsberg, Stewart Smith, Joshua Gershman and others who addressed a huge July crowd at a Feltcher's Field election rally and showed up for the big Mount Royal Hotel victory celebration in September.[11]

To nobody's surprise, the campaign was marked by predictable nastiness. The Bloc candidate referred to the electoral irregularities of Cartier as Jewish rather than Liberal fraud. When David Lewis raised the issue of two prominent Polish Bundists, Henryk Ehrlich and Victor Alter, murdered on Stalin's orders, Freddy denounced Lewis as a notorious Soviet-hater.

A story in *The Gazette* a couple of days after the vote claimed Freddy, Lewis and Phillips had split the Jewish ballots, that it was French-Canadian votes that accounted for Freddy's narrow margin of victory. Lazarus Phillips, the Bronfman lawyer and Liberal candidate finished in third place, Lewis finished fourth. In all the excitement, the party's Yiddish-language *Kanader Yiddishe Vochenblatt* made the delirious claim that anti-Semitism had not only been outlawed in the USSR but had actually disappeared there!

If the election result was clear, the explanation was less so. Was it the Jewish vote or the French-Catholic vote that won the day for Fred Rose and the party? The margin of victory over the Bloc was thin. Massé apparently received no Jewish votes. With a name like Fred Rose, recalled labor leader Michel Chartrand, "we thought he was one of ours!" There was a clear appeal by the party to the francophone voter.

---

10. Tulchinsky

"Avec Fred Rose," said the Comité pour l'élection de Fred Rose in a tract, "vous pouvez construire un Cartier plus heureux." With Fred Rose you can build a happier Cartier.

The Gazette judged Freddy's by-election success in the Liberal strong-hold of Cartier a protest against the policies of Liberal Prime Minister William Lyon Mackenzie King. Phillips contributed a party-like version of the result: "I should indeed be sorry if my fellow Canadians were to draw the conclusion from the result of this election that Canadians of Jewish background are Communists. This conclusion would be entirely erroneous because Mr. Rose drew a considerable number of votes from the French-Canadian and the foreign population."[12]

A francophone campaign worker recalled the francophone vote as significant but not decisive: "When Fred Rose was elected, I worked for him. I did the translation for our little group. But it was not French-Canadians who elected Fred Rose; it was the engaged Jewish electors.... It was in Cartier that there were the largest numbers of Communist party members.... It was a formidable campaign. In the evenings we organized door to door sessions. We saw three or four families each evening. I introduced Fred Rose, we got cards signed. Four hundred people were involved. We also distributed election circulars.... Cartier was a cosmopolitan district in which there were French-Canadians. If they had not voted for him he would not have won."[13]

The explanation, *Saturday Night* magazine speculated, was that over fifty percent of the Cartier electorate was of Slavic and mostly Slavic Jewish origin, the "potent factor at the bottom of the Communist success in Montreal-Cartier."[14]

Among those unhappy over Freddy's election triumph was Maxime Raymond. The head of the Bloc accused Freddy of cheating, of registering transients from outside Cartier. Raymond demanded a royal commission to enquire into Freddy's election win. If, he said, "the Labour-Progressive candidate polled 150 votes more than our man, it is

11. "COMMUNIST PARTY OF CANADA, Federal By-Election, Cartier Division, 1943—Montreal, P.Q." RCMP, Montreal Detachment, 7 July 1943, 9 August 1943.
12. "Massé Will Ask Recount of Votes Polled in Cartier," *The Montreal Daily Star,* 10 August 1943; "Post-Mortem," *The Montreal Daily Star,* 10 August 1943.
13. Marcel Fournier, *Communisme et Anticommmunisme au Quebec (1920–1950),* Les Editions cooperatives Albert Saint Martin, 1979.
14. Jim Wright, "Why a Communist Represents Montreal-Cartier," *Saturday Night,* 28 August 1943.

only because thousands of fictitious names had been added to the voters' lists and thousands of voters had been deprived of their electoral rights." In the initial count there were 5,784 votes for Fred, 5,463 for the Bloc. The recount changed the numbers but not the result, reducing the LPP margin to 150 votes.[15]

Joining the Bloc in disappointment was the poet and essayist Abraham Moses Klein. During the campaign he'd urged David Lewis to adopt a pro-Zionist stand. Alienating the constituency's Labour Zionist groups, he warned, would cost Lewis the election.[16] As it happened, Lewis the Bundist harbored few Zionist sympathies. I could not, he said some decades later, accept the notion that "a Jewish homeland was the answer to the problem of Jewish rights and of anti-Semitism in the world. I could not visualize any Jewish state able to accommodate more than a minority of world Jewry."[17]

In the wake of the Fred Rose election victory, the Quebec premier Maurice Duplessis, speaking at a provincial election campaign rally, spread the word that in return for financing Liberal candidates the fictitious International Zionist Brotherhood had arranged for 100,000 Jewish refugees to settle in the province. An explosion of public outrage flowed into protest meetings. At one of the gatherings Freddy was loudly scorned as *Rosenberg rouge*—Red Rosenberg! Freddy subsequently drew attention to a piece in a Union Nationale publication that, accompanied by a "picture of a Jew," warned that those 100,000 Jews would soon be arriving in Quebec.[18]

The discontent pursued Freddy to Ottawa. It was tradition for two MPs to escort a new member to the Speaker's dais. When the new session of Parliament opened on 27 January 1944, only Saskatchewan MP Dorise Nielsen was willing to honor the custom, announcing to the Speaker that Freddy had been elected for the Cartier constituency in Montreal and demanded to take his seat. Running in 1940 as a Progressive Unity candidate, Dorise was the first Communist to win a

15. "Fraud Charge in Cartier By-Election," *The Vancouver Sun*, 1 February 1944; "Recount Gives Seat to Rose," *The Globe and Mail*, 21 August 1943.

16. Usher Caplan, *Like One That Dreamed: A Portrait of A. M. Klein*, McGraw-Hill-Ryerson, 1982.

17. David Lewis, *The Good Fight: Political Memoirs, 1909–1958*, Macmillan, 1981.

18. Irving Abella and Harold Troper, *None is Too Many: Canada and the Jews of Europe 1933–1948*, Lester & Orpen Dennys, Publishers, 1982; RCMP report, 10 August 1944.

federal election in Canada. She was never re-elected.[19]

It was doubtless a remarkable sight, bouncy, diminutive Fred on the move towered over by Dorise who in her pumps stood close to six feet tall.

Dorise was inclined to support CCF measures, Freddy ever opposed. Before long there was an unpleasant quite audible row between them. That aside, Dorise came to Freddy's defense whenever he was attacked, telling the House on one occasion that Freddy ought to be given credit for speaking up on the issues of the day. But the actual status of their relationship appeared from that point on uncertain. In February Freddy was denounced by the CCF for voting against M. J. Caldwell's call for the socialization of industry. Cartier voters were told that they in fact had been deceived by Fred Rose, who "supported the present system in Canada and lined up with big business. He violated every principle for which he was supposed to stand."[20]

Initially Freddy was not assigned an office in the parliament building which Speaker J. A. Glenn cynically blamed on a lack of cooperation from other members.[21]

Freddy took up Ottawa residence in an apartment at 30 Beechwood that had been the home of Israel Halperin, a party associate.

In his first speech in the House following the January 1944 opening of Parliament Freddy praised the 28 November to 1 December 1943 meeting of the Big Three in Tehran, the first time Franklin Delano Roosevelt of the United States, Winston Churchill of Great Britain, and Josef Stalin of the USSR had met. He hoped, he said, Canada would join these world leaders in the creation of a peaceful postwar world. He probably didn't know that Stalin had arrived for the meeting in what was described as a "prickly and suspicious mood." The source of that mental state was his discovery, through a highly placed mole in British intelligence, of the details of the Quebec Agreement. In August 1943 Winston Churchill and Franklin D. Roosevelt met in Quebec City to discuss war plans. On 19 August they signed a separate agreement dealing with

---

19. "M.P.s Reluctant to Introduce Rose," *The Toronto Daily Star*, 27 January 1944.
20. Faith Johnston, *A Great Restlessness: The Life and Politics of Dorise Nielsen*, University of Manitoba Press, 2006. RCMP reports, 18 February 1944, 16 March 1944, 27 November 1944. Of the CCF Freddy said in the July 1944 issue of *National Affairs Monthly*, its "policies are a mixture of morbid defeatism and featherbrained utopianism." Ivan Avakumovic, *Communism in Canada: A History*, McClelland & Stewart, 1975.
21. "Rose Asks An Office Be Allocated to Him," Associated Press, 24 February 1944.

American-British collaboration on the development of an atomic bomb. The agreement explicitly committed both parties not to communicate information about the bomb to any third party without mutual consent. Not said in so many words, that third party was J. Stalin. On 4 September 1943 a detailed account of the Agreement was on its way to Moscow in a coded radio message. Stalin apparently arrived in Tehran feeling himself the victim of a low blow, a dirty Anglo-American trick.[22]

In March Freddy was on his feet in the House to badger justice minister Louis St. Laurent about the release of two men interned for fascist activity under the Defense of Canada Regulations. A department official had claimed that the two were no longer likely to be a danger. Said *The Glace Bay Gazette*: "On too many instances Mr. St. Laurent and his scarlet-coated watchdogs have used this form of immunity in a manner that can only be condemned. Neither he nor the RCMP hesitated to intern socialists when this "red scare" was on. Yet it needed a public outcry to have Adrien Arcand and former federal Quebec Conservative Party head Camillien Houde interned. Mr. Houde's case was so blatant that not even the red-baiting Louis St. Laurent could escape placing him in an internment camp."[23] Arcand was a journalist who in 1934 founded the National Social Christian Party, an anti-Communist front that urged the deportation of the Jews of Canada to the Hudson Bay region. Richard Bennett, the head of the federal Conservative Party, provided financial support for Arcand's activities, secretly engaging him as his chief organizer for the 1935 federal election.

In a speech in Sudbury, Ontario in April, Freddy addressed the question of unity—in the party, the province and the nation. The example for all to follow, he said, was that of Stalin and "the great country of Russia and its peoples." It was one of his few direct references to the Soviet leader. In June Freddy mounted an impassioned plea for government spending on jobs and security. Among the scenes I

---

22. Moreau. On the Quebec Agreement and Stalin, see Harry Chapman Pincher, "My Life Exposing Traitors," *The Daily Express*, 8 July 2009; also, Chapman Pincher's *Treachery: Betrayals, Blunders, and Cover-ups; Six Decades of espionage Against America and Great Britain*, Random House, 2009. Stalin sought to level the playing field by having the Soviet residential facility that housed the American delegation bugged. See Gary Kern, "How 'Uncle Joe' Bugged F.D.R.," C.I.A. Library, *Studies in Intelligence*, 2003.
23. *Glace Bay Gazette*, 25 April 1944.

have to witness, he said, are old men and women selling newspapers in the city of Montreal on cold winter nights.[24]

He eagerly took time from parliamentary duties to plead the case of a member of the Montreal Aircraft Workers Union, dismissed from his job at the Canadair aircraft plant, with the labor minister, Humphrey Mitchell. The labor minister had asked the RCMP to look into Freddy's "voluminous file" for ammunition to "expose Fred Rose in the House of Commons, should the latter become obnoxious and disagreeable."[25]

In July 1944 *L'Action Catholique* demanded authorities act to block a scheduled LPP meeting in Montreal. The meeting was disrupted by demonstrators, party head Tim Buck forced to seek refuge in a police car. We have, said a *Saturday Night* editorial, "no special sympathy for the Communists or Mr. Buck, since for two years between 1939 and 1941 they were among the most ardent supporters of Mr. Duplessis and his Union Nationale Party in opposition to the war, and merely reaped what they carefully sowed." Freddy said little beyond drawing attention to the rise of violence in provincial politics.[26]

The RCMP continued to devote much attention to the ethnicity of party meeting attendees. The crowd at a gathering addressed by the MP Fred Rose was composed, said a report, of "Russian Jews, French-Canadians, English, Negro and Chinese." The Mounties noted that at a meeting held at the same venue in Montreal in December 1944 approximately one hundred and fifty persons were in attendance, sixty-five percent "of Jewish extraction."[27]

In January 1945 Freddy addressed the issue of Montreal's housing crisis, calling for better homes at lower rents. He pointed out that large numbers of servicemen would be returning from the battlefields of Europe, that 89 percent of the people of Montreal were tenants, that the city would experience a 50,000 home deficit.[28] In May, with the war winding down, Freddy cabled the office of Louis St. Laurent to protest the rumored release from internment of Arcand and some of his Nazi followers. While war raged, Freddy wrote to Norman Robertson, Under-

---

24. "Post War Reconstruction, Jobs and Security" House of Commons debates, June 1944.
25. Extract from an RCMP report on a Labor-Progressive Party meeting in Montreal, 9 November 1943; RCMP report 13 December 1943.
26. "Too Much Violence," *Saturday Night*, 8 July 1944.
27. RCMP report, 10 November 1943.
28. "Housing Situation Said 'Deplorable'," *The Montreal Standard,* 20 January 1945.

Secretary of State for External Affairs, urging him to put the RCMP on Arcand's case. A royal commission, he said, was needed to look into fascist influence in Canada.

In April, with a general election campaign in progress, Jack Esselwein *aka* I. John (Johan) Leopold, Inspector, Assistant Intelligence Officer, RCMP, had reported that though the Communists were known to be firmly opposed to Zionism and the establishment of a Jewish National home in *Palestine*, Jewish Labour Progressive candidates appeared to have reversed that view in favor of a Jewish State. He cited a front-page article in the *Canadian Jewish Weekly*, "Jewish Leaders of the LPP Take a Positive Stand for a Jewish State in Palestine," based on a report to the party's National Jewish Committee from high profile Jewish party member Joshua Gershman. An analysis of the Yalta meeting decisions had persuaded Gershman that the time was ripe for the establishment of a Jewish State in Palestine and the creation of friendly relations with the Arabs. "It therefore seems," Leopold reported, "that Fred ROSE is attempting to appear as a sort of super-Zionist…to mislead, if possible, Zionists into the Communist movement."[29]

Esselwein/Leopold was born in Bohemia in 1890 to Jewish parents, his eastern European background and language skills easing his entry into the Force. The RCMP's British recruits found the short of stature Esselwein "foreign looking." It was a time when immigrants from southern and eastern Europe were suspected of being associated with labor radicalism, and the Mounties were suspicious of men with those backgrounds hired as secret agents. Before long Leopold, who passed himself off as Roman Catholic, achieved a reputation as a clever Communist Party infiltrator. He'd gone undercover in Regina in 1921 to infiltrate Communist organizations. By 1928 when he was exposed by party officials he was the RCMP's leading expert on Communism in Canada.[30]

On the other hand, competition for the Jewish vote persuaded the Liberal Party that heeding the advice A. M. Klein offered David Lewis would win back the seat. The party's candidate to run against Fred Rose

---

29. J. Leopold, "Re: Canadian Jewish Weekly," Memorandum, 25 April 1945.

in the 1945 federal election in Cartier was Samuel Edgar Schwiesberg, a Jewish lawyer and prominent Zionist.[31]

To prepare for the 1945 campaign, Freddy produced and had distributed to Cartier voters a Yiddish translation of a fifty-page anthology of his House of Commons speeches, *Fred Rose in Parliament.*

Apprehensive of a return to Tory rule, and given what seemed the diminished popularity of the Mackenzie King government, the LPP campaign in Cartier shifted focus from local concerns to the need to rally progressive forces. The CCF maintained its opposition to any collaboration with the Communists, which intensified the feud.[32]

The LPP continued to claim great inspiration from the Tehran accords, arguing that a new era of cooperation between the classes was now possible. For Cartier and Fred Rose this meant "grasping the hands of those patriotic forces of the Liberal camp who stand for social progress" in a contest that targeted both the Tories, and their promise of a return to the good old British imperial days, and what Freddy called adventurist "utopian CCF socialism."

Not for the first time there was public confusion over party goals. Was the unity of English and French-Canadians of all classes now no longer an LPP priority?

On the other hand, the 1945 election in Cartier was without the acrimony of the 1943 contest. There were only three candidates: Paul Massé for the Bloc, Samuel Schwiesberg for the Liberals and Fred Rose for the LPP. Said *The Montreal Daily Star* of Fred Rose: "...he is the only man the people can trust to fight for the program of full employment."[33]

The attentions of the RCMP were mostly focused on the activities of labor activists among the factory and sweatshop workers of the land, in particular on the role of Jews in the labor movement. There is this from a February 1945 RCMP Regina file: "It is realized that the notorious leadership given to the Communist Party may be by a substantial minority of Canadian Jews. Nevertheless, such a minority has undoubtedly great influence. It may well be said that Jews are the dynamic

---

30. Steve Hewitt, "Royal Canadian Mounted Spy: The Secret Life of John Leopold/Jack Esselwein," *Intelligence and National Security*, Vol. 15, No. 1 (Spring 2000).
31. *The Canadian Jewish Weekly*, 24 May 1945.
32. "C. P. Activity in Federal Elections," RCMP report, 21 February 1945.
33. Moreau.

nucleus of the Communist Party of Canada. FRED ROSE (Rosenberg) M.P. Norman FREED (Friedenthal), Sam CARR (Kagan) Raymond Arthur DAVIES (Dacinsky), Joseph SALSBERG (a member of the Ontario legislature), and William KASHTAN, are Jews and number one Communists."[34]

In a campaign puppet show children threatened by monsters were saved by a puppet that looked like Fred Rose in the company of one resembling Josef Stalin.[35]

If there was confusion over LPP policy it did Freddy's campaign minimal damage. He received 10,413 votes to the Liberal Party's 8,935, Massé coming in third this time with 6,148 votes. It was a month before the Trinity A-bomb test in New Mexico. Days later Freddy again demanded the arrest and trial of Adrien Arcand for treason.[36]

There was a report by Inspector C. W. "Slim" Harvison of a meeting in a coldwater Cartier flat in August 1945 attended by 35 members of the Federation of Democratic Youth. The flat was the home of Anne and Archie Moss, devoted party workers. Those Cartier flats were not terribly spacious; how the Mosses got 35 adult persons into one is a puzzle. The report is quite detailed about who attended, and what was said. Whether Harvison was present incognito or dispatched a ringer is unclear. In 1944, Anne Moss was a member of the City Council of the Cherbourg Labor Progressive Party in the city of Ottawa and Freddy's stenographer.[37]

All was not bouquets between the party and the unions. In August 40 union leaders, all members of the A. F. of L., were called before a labor court convened by the Montreal Trades and Labour Council to respond to charges that they'd "aided a subversive movement." This followed publication of an ad in a local newspaper that carried their names in support of Freddy's re-election campaign.[38]

That autumn, Freddy again rose in the House to attack the use of reserve army personnel, claiming that during a strike of local police and firemen 1,000 soldiers were kept at the ready in a barracks in Montreal.

---

34. "C. P. Activity in Federal Elections," RCMP report, 21 February 1945.

35. "Re: Federal Election—Province of Quebec, 1945, Subversive Activities Within," RCMP report, 6 June 1945.

36. Election results, RCMP report, 22 July. 1945.

37. "Federation of Democratic Youth," RCMP report, Montreal, 20 August 1945.

38. "Union Men Face 'Trial' for Backing Fred Rose," *Kingston Whig Standard,* 11 August 1945.

The RCMP noted in a report that Freddy, the now twice-elected member of the federal parliament for Cartier, had attended a workers' meeting in Ottawa in support of a strike at the Ford Motor Company in Windsor, Ontario.

The authorities tended not to distinguish between the goals of organized labor and those of the party, between working men and women demanding improved living conditions and party stalwarts preaching revolution. Ditto many in the party. Moreover, neither Freddy nor party head Tim Buck seemed able to see that the party's election triumphs in Cartier in 1943 and 1945 were not portends of greater things to come but flukes of circumstances.

Naturally, the road to election victory in Cartier was paved with some *litvakian* skepticism. A character in Mordecai Richler's *The Street*, no party cheerleader, is sure that "all politicians are dirty crooks," and claims to know for a fact that Liberal Party organizers hire "impecunious McGill students…to go down to the cemeteries with notebooks and compile lists of all those who had died since the last census. Other students were paid to represent the dead at the polls…"[39]

Though he denied it, Freddy told the Russians about the closed Parliament session convened on 25 November 1944 to deal with the redeployment of Canadian forces in Europe following the collapse of the Nazi military campaign. In the summer of 1945, the MP Fred Rose informed the Russians he'd heard it from Ernest Bertrand, the ex-Postmaster General and now fisheries minister that the war would be over in a month, which the Russians judged to mean by 1 September. Bertrand had also told him three days before the last of the anti-Hitler mutinies on 20 July 1944 that "tremendous" events would occur in Europe. As well, Freddy passed on to the Russians information he'd gotten from the journalist Jean-Louis Gagnon that certain German officers had done everything possible to ensure the landing of Anglo-American troops in Normandy. In a conversation Gagnon had with Charles de Gaulle during the latter's stay in Quebec City the French leader complained

---

39. Mordecai Richler, "The Red Menace" in *The Street: Stories and memoirs from St. Urban Street*, Penguin Books, 1977.

about the "extraordinarily slow advance of the Anglo-American troops in France."[40]

Such were the times that not everyone could see that the party's endeavors on behalf of working men and women had an ulterior and limited purpose—essentially to enlarge support in Canada for the USSR. Freddy never challenged the CPC's absolute subordination to the interests of the Stalin regime. As John Manley pointed out in his meticulous study of the relationship of the Communist parties in Canada, the United States and Great Britain to the USSR, those parties all obeyed a distant master: "Set against Moscow's record of uprooting apparently entrenched national leaders, summoning others for political re-education, using Lenin School graduates as a mobile political commissariat, and installing compliant leaderships prepared to accept every twist and turn of the line as the last word in Marxist theory, these three national experiences reveal no significant degree of autonomy of initiative from below....what really mattered was the power to make and break policy in the interests of Socialism in One Country. And as clear-eyed Communists had recognized since 1929, the leaders of that country held all meaningful power."[41]

"The Communist spirit has," said CPUSA trooper Jacob Liebstein, *aka* Jay Lovestone, in 1923, "given tongue to the tongueless millions. The sun never sets on the lands where Communist hearts beat in unison.... The Soviet government stands today as the granite foundation of the Communist system." Six years later Lovestone, a member of a CPUSA delegation in Moscow that was looking to put an end to Stalin's interference in the American party's business, got the word straight from the boss himself. "For scabs," Stalin told him, "there is plenty of room in our cemeteries."[42]

---

40. Fred Rose LAC file document.
41. John Manley, "Moscow Rules? 'Red' Unionism and 'Class Against Class' in Britain, Canada, and the United States, 1928–1935," *Labour,* No. 56, Fall 2005.
42. Thomas Powers, "The Plot Thickens," *Intelligence Wars: American Secret History from Hitler to Al-Qaeda* , New York Review of Books, 2002. "The Communist International," Walter Krivitsky told the House of Representatives, Special Committee to Investigate Un-American Activities in 1939, "that operates in Moscow is nothing more than an administrative body which transmits the decrees reached by the Political Bureau of the Central Committee of the Communist Party." In Gary Kern (ed.) *Walter G. Krivitsky: MI5 Debriefing and Other Documents on Soviet Intelligence*, Xenos Books, 2004.

Note

This research has drawn on the 28-volume Fred Rose file in Record Group 146 (Records of CSIS, the Canadian Security Intelligence Service) volumes 4160–4162 of the *Library and Archives Canada.* The file includes approximately 5,100 pages of documents. The RCMP compiled reports on the activities of Fred Rose from 1928 until his demise in Warsaw in 1983. The information came from ringers who attended party meetings, from a range of publications including the Canadian and American establishment press, *The Canadian Jewish Weekly, The Canadian Tribune,* the English-language party paper, the party's Yiddish-language publications, *Der Kampf* and the *Kanader Yiddishe Vochenblatt,* and others, transcriptions of radio broadcasts, the Canadian government's Igor Gouzenko material, *aka* the "Corby Case," including documents obtained from Igor Gouzenko, Fred Rose's political pamphlets and election campaign material, and House of Commons speeches. There are as well extensive files of Fred Rose press clippings in the Canadian Jewish Congress Charities Committee, National Archives in Montreal and the Jewish Public Library, Montreal, Quebec.

III.

Standing on Guard for the USSR

On 12 July 1945 the Soviet embassy in Ottawa forwarded the news to Moscow: "Debouz was re-elected for a second time as a member of the Federal Parliament. Thus from the Corporants there is one member." The term *Corporant* was a code word for the CPC. Debouz was Freddy's cover name. On 12 August 1943, three days after the Cartier by-election, Pavel Mikhailov, the GRU (*Glavnoye Razvedyvatelnoye Upravlenie*—Soviet military intelligence) *rezident* in New York City informed Moscow in a coded message "FRED our man in Lesovia has been elected to the LESOVIAN parliament. His personal opportunities undoubtedly improving. But warn LION about increasing caution to the maximum."[1]

LION was Sergei Koudriavtzev, a military intelligence officer in the Soviet embassy in Ottawa. Lesovia, meaning *forestland*, was the Soviet intelligence code word for Canada. Freddy was here identified not simply

---

1. Venona decrypt. See John Earl Haynes and Harvey Klehr, *Venona: Decoding Soviet Espionage in America,* Yale University Press, 1999. Thomas Powers has reminded us that the Venona decrypts consisted almost entirely but not exclusively of KGB cables. See Powers, *Intelligence Wars*, 2002, p. 88. Alexander Vassiliev, white notebooks #2, p. 10: "Fred Rose. Communist member of Canadian parliament. Provided leads to Canadians in the US."

as a Communist Party member of the Canadian parliament but an agent of the USSR who provided leads to Canadians in the United States. The message was that if the Russians were careful, Freddy could be of assistance in obtaining pieces of the four kinds of information Stalin was interested in:

> (i) Hitler's plans for the war in Russia; (ii) the secret war aims of London and Washington, especially with regard to planning for a second front in Europe; any indications that the Western allies might cut a separate peace with Hitler; and (iv) American scientific and technological progress, particularly in developing an atomic weapon.[2]

The 1943 Soviet intelligence link to Freddy was caught on VENONA, the American military decryption scheme that began that year to collect Soviet cable traffic. John Haynes, Library of Congress historian and acknowledged authority on VENONA, told me it would have been unlikely for that information to have leaked out to the RCMP much before 1947 when some limited sharing of VENONA data with the RCMP had begun.[3]

The CPC was formed in 1921 out of a Comintern-engineered fusion of the Canadian branches of the Labor Party of America and the United Communist Party of America.[4] Working through the party, Soviet espionage activity in Canada appears to have begun in 1924, which is to say that by the time Freddy joined the party in 1925 its subordination to Soviet interests was pretty much a fact of party life.

Stalin had encouraged a rivalry between state and military intelligence agencies, the NKVD, *Narodnyy Komissariat Vnutrennikh Del*, the People's Commissariat, and the GRU. They were to operate apart, the one acting as a check on the information obtained by the other.

After the June 1941 Nazi invasion of the USSR the Russians became important allies. In 1942 a diplomatic mission was opened in Ottawa

---

2. Robert Louis Benson and Michael Warner (eds.), *Venona: Soviet Espionage and the American Response, 1939–1957*, National Security Agency, Central Intelligence Agency, 1996. Soviet officials had been warned about VENONA by William Weisband, an American Armed Forces Security Agency officer. See Allen Weinstein and Alexander Vassiliev, *The Haunted Wood*, Random House, 1999.
3. In a private conversation at CASIS, *The Canadian Association for Security and Intelligence Studies*, Ottawa, 31 October 2009.
4. William Rodney, *Soldiers of the International: A History of the Communist Party of Canada,* University of Toronto Press, 1968. Up to 1924, the party called itself the Worker's Party.

with the status of a legation, raised to the rank of an embassy in 1944. The first ambassador was Fedor Tarasovich Gusev. The plan was for the mission to serve as an espionage command centre. Before the official opening, Major Vsevolov Sokolov, at the invitation of the Canadian government, arrived in the country in 1941 to organize the spying operation on the pretext of a job with the Canadian Mutual Aid Program to the USSR. Sokolov's superior, Sergei Koudriavtzev, was head of GRU operations in Canada. When Col. Nikolai Zabotin took up residence in Ottawa with the title of military attaché in 1943, Koudriavtzev reassigned Sokolov to Zabotin's network. Zabotin's key responsibility involved accelerating delivery of military technology, including top secret information through the Canadian espionage network, in place when he arrived.

The Russians early on attempted to assess the amount of security control to which their diplomats in Canada might be subjected. Unaware that for a time the RCMP was monitoring telephone traffic between their consulate in Halifax and the Ottawa mission, they used the telephone to pass on messages. In 1943, a government official, concerned that if discovered the activity might become an embarrassment, used his influence to have the practice terminated.[5]

In May 1942 Freddy, an NKVD operative, had approached Maj. Sokolov to offer his services to the GRU. At the time, the Ottawa NKVD chief Vitalii Pavlov and the GRU's Col. Zabotin were near mortal enemies. In September approval, sought via Pavel Mikhailov, the GRU chief based in New York City, was granted. Under Sokolov, Freddy's team included Harold S. Gerson, code-name *Gray* employed at the time by Allied War Supplies, a Crown corporation established to supervise the building of facilities for the production of chemicals and explosives, and Raymond Boyer, *the Professor*, a chemistry professor at McGill University and reputed expert on explosives, and someone named *Green*, never otherwise identified, who worked at a Montreal army tank plant.

The Russians recorded the arrangement in an undated coded message to Moscow: "Previously he worked with the neighbors up to 1924… In May-June 1942 came to DAVY with a proposal to help.

5. Mark Kristmanson, *Plateaus of Freedom*, Oxford University Press, 2003.

DAVY check up [*sic*] on FRED through New York (MOLIER). The neighbors proposed to use FRED. After this in 1942 September FRED contacted DAVY on instructions from MOLIER. MOLIER was sent to work in Ottawa to organize the work. At the present time on the list of parliamentary candidates in Quebec."[6] The "neighbors" was a reference to the NKVD, "up to" apparently a mistranslation of a Russian term meaning *from*.

DAVY was Maj. Sokolov, MOLIER was Pavel Mikhailov, GRU station chief in New York, GRAY was H. S. Gerson. Freddy was given charge of a Montreal group tasked with supplying information on war materiel. Moscow had suggested that Freddy should contact *Primrose*, cover name for British atomic research physicist Alan Nunn May, but Zabotin thought it would be too risky and appointed one of his own men for the task.

There appears to be no record of why Freddy sought out the switch. It was the case that the GRU was better established in Canada than the NKVD, having got hold of the best assets. Freddy may have imagined a larger role for himself as a conduit of important technical information. The thing was that technical nuts and bolts were beyond him, something Zabotin and Sokolov seemed unaware of. Freddy may have been the source of the Russian confusion of the RDX plant outside Shawinigan with the uranium operation at Chalk River. The Rose *forte* was fingering scientists and others who possessed classified military information and turning these individuals over to Col. Rogov whose overriding interest was in uranium isotopes.

Freddy and party organizer Sam Carr, born Schmil Kogan in Tomachpol, Ukraine, in 1906, had participated in the day-to-day operation of the Sokolov network. When Zabotin took over they were withdrawn from the network to help maintain the USSR's friendly public face and re-assigned to the less hazardous tasks of procuring recruits and providing advice. Carr was involved in fake passport work. Zabotin set up two parallel GRU networks, one he ran, the other was managed by Sokolov, the one Freddy worked for.

---

6. Among the documents supplied to the RCMP by Igor Gouzenko, National Archives of Canada, RG 33, Royal Commission 62/62. We note the claim that Freddy's involvement with Soviet intelligence dated from 1924.

In the spring of 1945, Freddy had to explain to Zabotin that he needed a break; he was preparing his re-election campaign, though he didn't tell Zabotin that.

Among Freddy's NKVD chores was the organization of study groups that expounded the principles of Marxism and the struggle of the working class in Quebec, in Canada and worldwide. This was a recruiting tactic. Numbers of men and women in the 1930s, carried along by the appeals of the popular front and the Chinese and Spanish relief committees, were drawn into the Communist fold and from there into the Soviet espionage net. These groups were organized informally not as party activities. The party was at that time illegal.

Freddy had a reputation as a colorful and forceful group leader. Social workers, artists, and accountants attended the study sessions. The meetings, held in people's homes, were not publicized. In the winter of 1936 one such group meeting was attended by Norman Bethune.[7]

In a history of the RCMP entitled "Canada's Security Service: An Historical Outline 1864–1966" there is the claim that "…there was little that the RCMP Intelligence Section did not know about the Communist movement in Canada, its activities, policies, memberships and international connections."[8] The RCMP might have known that a certain number of Jews belonged to the party but, until the Igor Gouzenko revelations in the late summer of 1945, the agency seemed to know next to nothing about the party's role in Soviet espionage. RCMP files bulged with reports on Freddy's work as a labor organizer but contained little about his espionage activity, this despite his frequent visits to the Soviet embassy, his meetings with scientists and civil servants and military personnel all of which would have had hardly anything to do with his involvement in the labor movement.

The RCMP early on identified Freddy as a seasoned campaigner for radical causes but were never overly suspicious of his role as a Soviet intelligence agent. When they labeled him a *revolutionary* it mostly had to do with his work with organized labor, his speeches at rallies, his published pamphlets. Apparently, until the mid 1940s, the RCMP regarded the party as a source of *subversion,* not espionage, which is to say that they

---

7. Wendell MacLeod, Libbie Park and Stanley Ryerson, *Bethune: The Montreal Years, An Informal Portrait,* James Lorimer & Company, Publishers, 1978.
8. Gregory S. Kealey and Reg Whitaker (eds.) *RCMP Security Bulletins, 1919–1945.*

appear to have taken to heart the Marxian line that the organization of the workers was a decisive step on the road to revolution.[9]

The *litvaks* of Cartier had of course no way of knowing that Fred Rose the man many, though how many remains uncertain, twice dispatched to represent them in the federal parliament in Ottawa was not just a formidable labor organizer and prominent party official but a GRU agent. Nothing to say French-Canadian voters were any wiser. In 1940, there was some RCMP suspicion that the party was linked to the activities of the Soviet secret police whose agents were thought to be operating in Canada. Questions were raised about whether Freddy might have been associated with the GRU, but there was apparently little further investigation of these suspicions. Kathleen Willsher, a secretary at the UK High Commission in Ottawa, recalled that she met Freddy in 1935 and that she began turning over information to him for the Russians in 1936.[10]

In 1939 the RCMP chief in Montreal advised his superiors that *The People's Committee Against Antisemitism and Racism* was a Communist front, the proof being that Abe Rosenberg, Freddy's bother, was a Canadian delegate to the organization's World Congress held in Paris in September 1937.[11]

Fishel Rosenberg *aka* Fiszel Rozenberg *aka* Fred Rose was born in Lublin, Poland in 1907, a town with a population of 50,000 or so, about half the inhabitants of Jewish background. *Fodor's* (2007) does not say that Lublin was renowned as a centre of Jewish learning and culture, only that it was "once at the very heart of the Polish-Lithuanian empire."

The Majdanek Concentration Camp sat on the outskirts of the town, according to *Fodor's*, about three miles southeast of the city centre, close enough for the Nazis to have marched the prisoners arriving at the town train station in freight cars to the camp.

Fred Rose stood 5'4", same height as Stalin, had blue eyes and fair hair. The third child of carpenter father Jacob, *aka* Jakow Rozenberg, he

---

9. This might in part explain the thick RCMP file on CCF-NDP leader Tommy Douglas. See "Tommy Douglas: Air secret RCMP files," *The Toronto Star*, 22 December 2010. The file holds over 1,000 pages, some of the contents going back 70 years.

10. In Robert Bothwell and J. L. Granatstein (eds.) *The Gouzenko Transcripts, the Evidence Presented to the Kellock-Taschereau Royal Commission of 1946*, Deneau Publishers & Company, 1980.

11. H. A. R. Gagnon, RCMP. Superintendent, Commanding "C" Division, Montreal.

had two sisters, Ida and Sarah, and three brothers, Alfred, Abraham, and Harold, all born in Poland. A sixth sibling did not survive infancy. Freddy arrived in Canada in 1920 aboard the S.S. *Corsican* with his father and mother, Rachel *nee* Kaufman *aka* Ruchla Laja. Jacob first came to Canada in 1913, perhaps to test the waters, soon after returning to Poland to collect the family but had to wait out the end of the war.

Lublin was then occupied by Russia. A notorious anti-Semite, the Tsar had seen to it that laws were enacted to limit Jewish commerce. For reasons of economics, the likelihood of forced service in the Tsar's army, and the rise of anti-Semitism, between 1890 and 1920 there was substantial Jewish emigration from the territories under Tsarist control, including the Ukraine and Russia, as well as Poland. Family heads travelled to France, England, the United States, and Canada to investigate conditions, then returned to gather their wives and children for the voyage to new homes. Jews who left Lublin rarely returned.

The Rosenberg family settled in Montreal. The following year Freddy became a British subject, Canadian citizenship not a fact of life until 1947. A carpenter by trade, Jacob Rosenberg got a job with a building contractor.

In Lublin, Freddy had attended the *Gymnase Humaniste de Lublin*, a Jewish high school for girls and boys, where he received French language instruction. The school operated out of two buildings close to each other, one for the girls, one for the boys. The facilities were substandard. There was a sports field for the boys that the girls could use. A French teacher at the school named Mme. Lewin was notorious for her unpleasant disposition. The students observed errors in her Polish speech, some Russian words, tried to get even by snickering at her linguistic gaffs. She apparently taught there when Freddy was a student, though it is not certain that she was among his instructors. Freddy's knowledge of French was a skill of great value to him in his political career in Quebec.[12]

---

12. Rose Fiszman-Sznajdman, *My Lublin*, published in Yiddish in Tel Aviv, 1982 by Farlag Y. L. Peretz, in Polish in Lublin, Poland, by Lubelskie, 1989, also in Swedish. For a reading of the pages in Polish and Yiddish referring to the Gymnase Humaniste de Lublin I am grateful to Prof. Michael Rosenbush. Said the author: "The events and facts contained in this book were dictated to me only by my memory, but they are authentic, not less and not exaggerated. Written with fidelity, with devotion to the city and the Jews who lived in it, with nostalgia and compressed with heart pain." This and related information was supplied by

Upon his arrival in Montreal Freddy spoke no English. The family enrolled him in grade six in a public school. His knowledge of French helped with his early education.[13]

At age fifteen young Fishel Rosenberg took a job as a messenger for a Montreal pharmacy. Freddy then went to work with a construction crew, lugging bags of cement at twenty cents an hour. Assured that the new world of radio pointed the way to the future, Freddy traded construction work for employment with E. B. Myers, an American company that produced radio tubes. The job paid him $14 a week.

His Polish *gymnase* French enabled him to represent francophone workers in a dispute with the company's unilingual anglophone bosses over the poor air quality in the room where the tubes were processed. The francophone women who worked in the area occasionally fainted. It was the start of his career as a labor organizer. In 1925 E. B. Myers moved back to the United States. Finding himself out of a work, Freddy found new employment in an electric lamp factory.

Encouraged by brother Abraham, known as Abie (also Abe), for a time a leading party member who had been active in the Bund in Poland, that year at age 18 Freddy joined the Young Communist League and began an apprenticeship in Marxism-Leninism. Before long he became convinced that the Russian revolution was the ultimate model for the transformation of the nations and began to contemplate a world revolutionary movement championed by the USSR.

Freddy soon turned his energies to labor militancy, to the mobilization of workers. Before long he was fingered by the RCMP as someone worth keeping an eye on. Freddy's indulgences, said a 1928 RCMP report, included smoking, drinking, and a little gambling. Talkative, he was inclined to speak quickly in a high pitched voice and a mild Jewish accent. An adept learner of languages, he spoke English, French, Yiddish, Ukrainian, Russian, some Hungarian. Freddy was known to be associated with what the RCMP referred to as "other Jewish Communists in the city." He lived unmarried, said the report, with "a young Jewess." The RCMP observed that Freddy was an effective

Robinn Magid, Lublin Archives Project Coordinator, Jewish Records Indexing—Poland, 1811–1945, source of Fred Rose family information. See too, "Lublin," *Fodor's*, 2007 ed.

13. Corolyn Cox, "First Communist in Commons Was In the 'Battle of Queen's Park'," *Toronto Saturday Night*, 22 April 1944.

organizer and a public speaker who commanded the interest of his audiences.[14]

RCMP tracking of Freddy began during the tenure of Commissioner Cortlandt Starnes. Born in Montreal, Starnes had served in Dawson City and had as a young officer been involved in the repression of Louis Riel's 1885 North-West Metis Rebellion.

In 1928, when written communications within the Force concluded with the archaic formalism "I have the honor to be, Sir, Your obedient servant" Insp. J. W. Phillips, Commanding Quebec District, referred to Freddy in a note to Commissioner Starnes: "I have the honor to advise you that the above named left with Maurice Spector for Toronto on the night of the 1st inst. Our agent states there is some talk of Rosenburg [*sic*] remaining in Toronto. Rosenburg at present is the leader of the Young Communist League in Montreal."[15]

Spector was a leading national party figure. More than likely it was Spector not Freddy that was the prime surveillance target.

Following the 1919 Winnipeg General Strike legislative changes aimed at curbing the activities of the labor movement in Canada were introduced. Section 41 of the Immigration Act, enacted June 1919, permitted officials to deport any alien or Canadian citizen not born in Canada for advocating the overthrow of the government by force.[16]

The RCMP, with Section 41 in mind, began to wonder about Freddy's citizenship. In a December 1928 note to Starnes Phillips raised the question of Freddy's naturalization, adding that Freddy was "the most prominent member of the Communist Party in Montreal."[17] Freddy's citizenship was a matter Canadian officialdom would revisit. For the time being the question was: Could Section 41 be used to put Freddy out of business and on the next boat back to Poland? Starnes wrote back to Phillips to say that he would "make inquiries as to whether (Fred Rosenberg) has been naturalized; but in view of his youth when he entered Canada, it is possible that he claimed naturalization through his father. Please supply me with the particulars of the father,

---

14. Fred Rose files, LAC, 27 December 1928.
15. J. W. Phillips to Cortlandt Starnes, 8 May 1928.
16. David Jay Bercuson, *Confrontation at Winnipeg: Labour, Industrial Relations, and the General Strike,* McGill-Queens Press, 1990.
17. J. W. Phillips to Cortlandt Starnes, 28 December 1928.

including the first name, so that I can make inquiries of the Naturaliza-tion authorities."[18] Two weeks later, Phillips informed Starnes that "there is at present a Jacob Rosenberg, carpenter, living at 36 Duluth St. W. Montreal and there is little doubt but that this man is Fred Rosen-berg's father.... Our files show that Jacob Rosenberg applied for his naturalization papers in November 1925, and received Certificate of Naturalization in March 1926." In addition to the Duluth Street address, Jacob's file contained this information: "...place of birth—Lublin, Poland; married; six children; five years in Canada (from Nov. 1925); Polish Jew; occupation—carpenter; speaks, reads and writes English; etc." It is, said Phillips, "almost a certainty that Jacob Rosenberg and Fred Rosenberg are father and son, but it is a matter that will be checked up at the first favorable opportunity. The name should be as above and not Rosenburg as _____ has been spelling it."[19]

Starnes next wrote to the Under-Secretary of State, Naturalization Branch for confirmation of Freddy's naturalization. By the fact, said the reply, of having their names endorsed on the father's certificate, these children became British subjects. The children's names appeared on the 1926 certificate: Fred born in 1907, Ida born in 1908, Harold born in 1912, Sarah born in 1919, brother Abe and one other sibling, an Alfred.[20]

In July 1929 the RCMP learned that Freddy had resigned his posi-tion as party secretary in Montreal and was leaving for Toronto, that he'd been elected the Young Communist League's National Secretary. That same year he was arrested at a demonstration in Toronto for calling police officers "traitors and scabs," according to a witness, "at the top of his voice."[21] Convicted of disorderly conduct, he was given the choice of a fine of $25 and costs or thirty days in jail. He chose jail.

The following summer, Starnes in a secret memorandum told the Commanding Officer of the RCMP Division in Toronto that he had "received information" that in May a ship, the *Megantic,* had sailed from Montreal heading for Germany with three individuals on their way to

---

18. Cortlandt Starnes to J. W. Phillips, 14 January 1929.
19. J. W. Phillips to Cortlandt Starnes, 28 January 1929.
20. The Undersecretary of State, Department of the Secretary of State to Cortlandt Starnes, 6 February 1929 in reply to the commissioner's letter of 1 February 1929.
21. Lita-Rose Betcherman, *The Little Band: The Clashes Between the Communists and the Political and Legal Establishment in Canada 1928–1932*, Deneau Publishers, 1982.

Moscow: "The leader of the party was a man named Rose or Rosenberg, an electrician.... It appeared that he was going to Moscow to attend the Lenin School, and it is added that subsequently he would either return to Canada or be sent to other spheres as a Communist agitator." Starnes said he'd learned this from a letter forwarded to Scotland Yard in August 1930 by a D. Newman, who identified himself as ship's interpreter on the White Star Liner *Megantic*, claiming that when the ship was in Montreal it was boarded by three young men on their way to Germany via Le Havre. Newman said he learned from a conversation with Freddy, who was one of the three, that "although their Canadian passports are made out for Germany in fact they are going to Moscow the oldest of them apparently the Leader named Rose or Rosenberg an Electrician a known Communist agitator to the authorities in Ontario and Quebec."[22]

In late October Starnes received word from the Toronto Division that Freddy was indeed at the Lenin School in Moscow where he was being trained as an organizer.

In 1930, the party's Canadian coffers were close to empty, the combined CPC-YCL membership only just over 2,000, the number in Quebec close to zero. Moreover, the leadership of the CCF was united in their opposition to any co-operation with the party. The following year, according to the RCMP's secret estimates, ever calculated in terms of ethnicity, Jews comprised less than 10 percent of total Canadian party membership; the count tallied 3,000 Finns, 800 Ukrainians, 400 Jews, and 200 Anglos.[23]

Upon his return home from the USSR in January 1931 Freddy was the featured speaker at a Young Communist League meeting in Montreal. Said a report to Starnes: "Amongst other matters he said he had attended the trials of the eight engineers on charges of sabotage and high treason." Not something Freddy mentioned to a *Montreal Star* reporter. What Freddy did tell the fellow was that the USSR's Five year plan was succeeding "beyond the wildest dreams of its originators," that "all the Collectivist farms are surrounded by great blocks of apartment houses in which the peasants live under model conditions.... They have

---

22. Cortlandt Starnes to G. L. Jennings, 20 August 1930.
23. Tulchinsky, *Canada's Jews.*

hot and cold water and many have telephones…. I visited one colony of murderers who lived together working out their salvation in ideal surroundings, even marrying girls from the neighboring district and having children."[24]

In 1931, Freddy married Frodel "Fanny" Charnous, *aka* Charnes, a Ukrainian woman he met at a Young Communist League event, the daughter of Leib and Leah Charnous.

Freddy's political models were the stone revolutionaries Lenin and Trotsky, organizers, writers, orators, leaders of the masses. His aliases included Moses Rosenthal, Moses Rosenberg, Fred Bosse, Berry West, George Lambert, Fred Dumbrovich.

In an April 1931 pamphlet, "Smash the Embargo," Freddy spelled out his political philosophy. The goal of the Canadian Communist Party was to "lead the Canadian workers to establish a system similar to that of the Soviet Union." The Communist Movement, said the pamphlet, was preparing for decisive battles between the working class and Canadian capitalists, and would lead the workers' fight for "state unemployment insurance paid for by the bosses, for immediate cash relief for the unemployed, for the 7-hour day and 5-day week, for the defense of the Soviet Union and against the betrayers who are found in the ranks of the working-class."

For all that, Freddy and his Soviet masters were hardly ever on the same wavelength, something Moscow understood much better than he ever did. As someone put it, Moscow could not impose policies or duties unpalatable enough for the branch-plant Canadian party to reject. In Canada, the United States, and Great Britain the workplace was to be targeted as the key arena for the promotion of class struggle. What Moscow had in mind was the development of *red* unions subordinated to Soviet interests.[25] The Soviets were actually not much interested in the revolutionary transformation of Canadian society, Cartier's large working class, Jew and gentile alike, was not much of a priority. Seen from Moscow, the key virtue of Canada was its proximity to the United States, regarded as invaluable as a jumping off point for Soviet agents.

---

24. J. W. Phillips note the commissioner RCMP, 12 January 1931; "Russia Seen as Happy and Prosperous Land," *The Montreal Star*, 10 January 1931. Freddy said nothing about the Gulag, established in the USSR, April, 1930.

25. "Memorandum: Re Fred Rose," RCMP, 17 January 1944.

The revolution that happened in peasant Russia rather than in industrial Germany appeared to contradict Marxian prophecy. It occurred to the men in Moscow that their revolution very much depended for survival on the support of a Communist International, a *Comintern*. One obeyed Comintern instructions or faced the consequence. In 1928, leading CPC party member Maurice Spector was expelled for his pro-Trotsky views by John MacDonald, who was himself removed from his position as party head a couple of years later for refusing a Comintern directive to move against "right deviationists" and Trotskyites.[26]

In time, it seemed to Freddy and others that the Canadian working class could not be persuaded to opt for a new destiny based on the pure idealism of building a worker's state. Socialism would not emerge serendipitously in Toronto, Winnipeg, and Montreal. The defeat of capitalism required the chaos of desperate circumstances. The Winnipeg General Strike seemed a one-time thing, the federal authority in Ottawa an inadequate villain, managing after a fashion but hardly ruling.

Freddy was doubtless familiar with Lenin's contempt for the uncertainty of elections, the Bolshevik view that only the party could bring about the revolutionary transformation of society, that party rule needed to be imposed. In Czarist Russia, there was the death and destruction and despair of WWI, the weakness of the tentative Kerensky government, vulnerable, as Lenin knew, to Bolshevik ruthlessness. Freddy was enough of a Leninist to know that crisis was the key to the revolutionary overthrow of capitalism. Hadn't Marx prophesied that the crisis of capitalism would propel the bourgeois industrial universe in the direction of the stateless worker's state?

In Canada, the evolving tension between Quebec and the rest of the county might be the crisis that would do the trick. In anticipation of the VIth party convention in the spring of 1929, there was uncertainty as to whether a future capitalist crisis was in the works. The answer would be delivered by Wall Street a few months later. In the meantime, Freddy pointed out that the pre-convention document, "The Draft Thesis and

---

26. Rodney.

Situation of Our Party," ignored the "French-Canadian Question."[27] In an article in *The Worker* Freddy reminded party faithful that Québécois comprised 27 percent of the Canadian population and 30 percent of the country's working class, that the party was not paying adequate attention to that reality in relation to the time spent on Ukrainians and Finns. At the last party convention, "just a few moments were devoted to the French-Canadians." Moreover, for all who had eyes to see, Quebec had revolutionary importance, something the Finns and Ukrainians in Canada did not. There was the conscription crisis of 1917 that had created great tension between the nation's anglophone and francophone communities. Should the anticipated attack on the USSR be launched by the "imperialist powers," the opposition of French-Canadians to conscription would turn them into potential Soviet allies, a situation that might lead to civil war and ultimately to the triumph of Communism in Canada.

It seemed that nationalism, along with religion, stood in the way of the advance of Communism in the Catholic Church-dominated province. Freddy opposed Québécois nationalism which he regarded as a reactionary force and an obstacle in the cause of the working class.

Freddy may have in a sense taken some inspiration from the philosophy of Lionel Groulx's *Action Française*. In 1922, the Abbé thought French Canada formed a nation, though he didn't give the nation a name. He was responding to the advance of urbanization in Quebec that seemed to threaten French-Canadian survival: the high death rate, low birth rate, the glamorization of promiscuous characters in American movies, the appeal of American jazz in the dance halls, fathers in the taverns, mothers away at work, the mobility of young women.[28]

The Abbé's answer was *social Catholicism*, Catholic doctrine opposed to the trends of urban life that were detracting from established rural values. The situation called for a return to the norms of religion, language and family. Seized by the perception of an uncertain future, the Abbé found himself in the grip of a nostalgia for rural certainties. What he proposed amounted to a serious alternative to the party's socialist

27. Andrée Levesque, "The Weakest Link: French-Canadian Communists Before 1940," McGill University, May 2008.
28. Susan Mann, *Dream of a Nation; A Social and Intellectual History of Quebec*, McGill-Queens Press, 2002.

future. It was a challenge the party in Quebec could no longer ignore. There were those within the party convinced that the crisis of which the Abbé spoke, such as it was, might be put to better use.

The topic re-emerged as an issue for the party in 1934 when the theoretical journal *The Review* published an article that repeated the Abbé's argument that French Canada was a nation and had a right to self-determination "up to separation." In *The Worker* the following year, Freddy weighed in with his perspective on the "French-Canadian problem." French Canada, he said, fulfilled all the conditions for nationhood except one—there was no French-Canadian economy. The party, in other words, recognized that French Canada constituted a distinct entity with the potential for advancing the socialist cause.

That aside, a crisis with much greater potential had appeared on the scene: the Great Depression. In New York City, grown men were picking scraps of food out of garbage cans. Across the ocean, Welsh miners stood single-file in the gutters of London singing for pennies to send home to their starving families. The breadlines and soup kitchens and farm foreclosures coincided with the spread of fascism and the civil war in Spain. An age of chaos and murder seemed to be dawning. Freddy and his Soviet masters appeared to read the despair of the Depression years as a once in a lifetime opportunity to expand Soviet influence in North America, to exploit the feeling, growing in strength, that change was necessary and urgent, that the USSR was the hope of the world and the key to a socialist society that would forever eliminate want and oppression. Desperation gave Soviet communism the magnetism of a religion, a faith to be absolutely embraced, whole-heartedly, unquestioningly. When in the early 1930s news leaked out about Stalin's campaign of genocide by starvation in the Ukraine, *The New York Times* said there was no actual starvation, only disease due to malnutrition.[29]

---

29. Walter Duranty, "Russians Hungry Not Starving," *The New York Times,* 31 March 1933. In 2003, the Pulitzer Prize Committee considered withdrawing the 1932 prize awarded to Mr. Duranty for his reports, but chose not to do so. The committee's statement on the decision, Nov. 21, 2003: "After more than six months of study and deliberation, the Pulitzer Prize Board has decided it will not revoke the foreign reporting prize awarded in 1932 to Walter Duranty of *The New York Times.*

"In recent months, much attention has been paid to Mr. Duranty's dispatches regarding the famine in the Soviet Union in 1932–1933, which have been criticized as gravely defective. However, a Pulitzer Prize for reporting is awarded not for the author's body of work or for the author's character but for the specific pieces entered in the competition. Therefore, the board focused its attention on the 13 articles that actually won the prize, articles written and published during 1931. In its review of the 13 articles, the Board determined that Mr. Duranty's 1931 work, measured by today's standards for foreign reporting, falls seriously

In January 1931 Freddy and four party associates were arrested on a Section 98 charge of sedition and sentenced in June to a year in prison. Their crime was having urged 300 unemployed workers to organize and demand government assistance. The gathering was broken up by 150 police officers. Said a November RCMP report: "Fred Rose. Jew, born in Lublin, Poland...has been convicted in both Toronto and Montreal courts as a result of Communist activity; is under a year's sentence on a charge of sedition in Montreal, the case at present being in appeal." The appeal was unsuccessful and Freddy spent time in Bordeaux Jail, outside Montreal. "For years," said the RCMP, "Rose has been one of the leading Communist agitators in this district."[30]

Section 98 had been inserted into the Criminal Code following the Winnipeg General Strike of 1919. Any association, it stated, "whose professed purpose was to bring about any governmental, industrial or economic change within Canada by use of force, violence or physical injury to person or property, or by threats of such injury, or which teaches, advocates, advises or defends the use of force, violence, terrorism, or physical injury to person or property to accomplish such change, or for any other purpose, or which shall by any means persecute or pursue such purpose or shall teach, advocate, advise or defend, shall be an unlawful association." Attending meetings, distributing literature, and speaking out could land one in court. In effect, it meant that the Communist Party was banned in Canada, whoever did what people do at party meetings could be found guilty of a crime.

In August 1932 party head Tim Buck and seven other party members were arrested at the party's Toronto offices. In a November trial, the eight were found guilty of advocating the violent overthrow of the existing order and sentenced to hard labor at Kingston Penitentiary. The chief witness for the Crown was John Leopold who testified that

short. In that regard, the Board's view is similar to that of *The New York Times* itself and of some scholars who have examined his 1931 reports. However, the board concluded that there was not clear and convincing evidence of deliberate deception, the relevant standard in this case. Revoking a prize 71 years after it was awarded under different circumstances, when all principals are dead and unable to respond, would be a momentous step and therefore would have to rise to that threshold. The famine of 1932–1933 was horrific and has not received the international attention it deserves. By its decision, the board in no way wishes to diminish the gravity of that loss. The Board extends its sympathy to Ukrainians and others in the United States and throughout the world who still mourn the suffering and deaths brought on by Josef Stalin."

30. J. W. Phillips to the Commissioner, 17 June 1931; the loss of the appeal was reported in *The Montreal Gazette,* 19 May 1932. See too Morris Wolfe, "Hard Labour," *Canadian Forum,* December 1991; *The Worker,* Vol. 11, No. 523, 1932.

Canadian Communists were financed by Moscow and were planning to smash the existing order by force. While Buck was in the Kingston pen, a riot erupted. Eight gunshots were fired into Buck's cell. Pressed to explain, Hugh Guthrie, the justice minister, admitted in the House of Commons that shots had indeed been fired into the cell but not with the intention of causing him any harm, just "to frighten him."[31]

In that heady time an unemployed Ukrainian worker named Nick Zimchuk was shot dead by police for resisting eviction. The authorities, aware that the party intended to exploit the incident for political gain at a huge public funeral, planned to steal the body and make sure there would be no funeral. The party had revealed their plans to the local newspapers and radio stations. Some party men were pressed into service to guard the corpse overnight. Joshua Gershman had this recollection: "I used to be very friendly with Fred Rose...who was at the time the leader of the Communist Party in Quebec. We had been the ones in charge of organizing this demonstration and so the police used to follow us wherever we went. So we decided to go not far from the funeral parlor where the dead body of Nicholas Zimchuk was lying, we decided to go into a steam bath, a Jewish steam bath on Colonial Avenue. Two minutes later the police arrived and we spent the entire night from midnight till six in the morning. We spoke with them, drank with them, and even joked with them. They were sure that something was going to happen, then they'll take away the body and there would not be the demonstration. But we fooled them. The whole thing was a hoax. While they were watching us in the steam bath, the body remained in the funeral parlor. In any case we had a real army of people to defend the body there too. The funeral was one of the biggest demonstrations Montreal ever had, over 10,000 people participated in that demonstration. Many people were arrested, police interfered. But he was buried and I think I was the only speaker at that funeral...."[32]

In 1933, 60 percent of the Canadian work force was unemployed, a quarter of a million people on government assistance were getting help with clothing, food, rent, heating. Average annual income for those fortunate enough to find employment was $785.

---

31. Morris Wolfe, "Tim Buck, Too," *The Canadian Forum,* December 1991.
32. Abella, "Portrait of a Professional Revolutionary."

In July RCMP reports claimed to identify a "Russian Jewess" named Rosenberg, no Christian name, alleged to be bringing "certain material and instructions for the conduct for [*sic*] the Communist Party of Canada" but at the time living in Russia where she was in charge of a railway station. Described as forty years of age "Miss Rosenberg was one of the Young Communist leaders in Montreal and was expelled from the Baron Byng High School for the Communist propaganda she was making amongst the students."[33]

In 1934 a Finnish police official told *The New York Times* that the USSR had established an espionage operation in the United States and Canada that it employed many trained agents, Americans and others at all levels of society.[34] With other priorities on their plate, the RCMP seemed content to file the clipping away and return to business as usual, chasing down the Jewish labor leaders who had organized a dressmakers strike.

It was about that time that Freddy seemed to have concluded that conditions for a Leninist coup did not yet exist in Canada. Given the evident disunity among the exploited classes, a government takeover on the Bolshevik model was not in the cards. On the other hand, uniting the conflicting elements in a common revolutionary cause might be achieved through electoral politics. The debates over the political direction of the Jewish and French-Canadian citizens of Cartier appear to have persuaded Freddy that with the Depression shaking the population's faith in the establishment, the party's entry into the corrupt electoral contests of Cartier might be a step in healing the breach with the CCF and appealing in a more traditional fashion to the constituency's working class Jewish population as well as attracting Québécois to the cause. What Freddy and the party would discover was that Depression misery was an inadequate long term solution to overcoming the ethnic and class frictions in Cartier and the country.

The issues that framed the Cartier elections in 1943 and 1945 had begun to surface a decade earlier. In 1935, when Freddy became Quebec party head, party membership in Quebec hovered at around 1,500. Freddy was faced not only with the French Canada question but also

---

33. C. F. Hamilton, Director of Intelligence to Officer Commanding, RCMP. "C" Division, Montreal, P. Q. 17 July 1933.
34. "Finns Say Soviet Had Spy Ring Here," *The New York Times,*" 29 April 1934.

with the tensions between the CCF and the party, and the competitive appeal of Zionism for the Jewish population. At a meeting in Montreal in January 1935, labeled in an RCMP report a meeting of "the Communist Party of Canada, Jewish Branch" Freddy pointed out that the CCF had in the past ignored the appeal of the party for a United Front. Freddy's brother Abe complained that Jewish party members had always taken it for granted that the Jewish masses were with them, that as a consequence there were few Jewish workers in the party. That the "fascist Zionist" groups had been organizing and as a result the influence of the Zionist organizations on the Jewish masses was far greater than the influence of the party ever was, that Zionists had gained thousands of converts, and that Zionist organizations did not support the party and work was needed for the party to gain a better foothold among the Jewish masses.[35]

To draw attention away from this apparently intractable reality, Freddy continued to pepper his public statements with boilerplate attacks on fascist governments supported by the bourgeoisie, elected minions in league with the predatory capitalists of St. James Street, Montreal's Wall Street, union stool pigeons, etc.

In 1935, the message from the Comintern directed the CPC to switch gears and join the *Popular Front Against Fascism*. For the CPC that meant Canadian finance capitalists and home grown Nazis like Adrien Arcand.

In the spring of 1935, Freddy announced his decision to run as the Communist candidate in the federal election in Cartier. It was a move the RCMP followed with great interest. Freddy opened his election campaign with a mass meeting at the Mount Royal Arena that drew a crowd of 5,000 and featured Canadian party head Tim Buck. Freddy spoke out against provincial government attacks on the unemployed and mass arrests by Quebec Provincial police of on-to-Ottawa protest marchers. The decision had been made with the full backing of party leadership. The campaigns in 1935 and 1936 were marked by the energetic partici-

---

35. G. F. Fletcher, "Communist Party of Canada, Jewish Branch, Montreal, Que., RCMP "C" Division. Montreal to the Commissioner, 27 January 1935.

pation of Joshua Gershman, Stanley Ryerson, Emile Godin, David Kashtan, and Stewart Smith.[36]

At a May Day rally he addressed an Arena crowd of 3,500 over one-third, said an RCMP report, French-Canadian. The party, he declared to applause, had at last caught the attention of French-Canadians, that fascism was on the move in Quebec where police terrorism was worse than anywhere else in Canada, that the authorities were attempting to eliminate the right to strike and picket. Addressing Depression anguish Freddy spoke out against the cuts in Montreal of benefits to the unemployed and prophesied a dark future in which those benefits would be eliminated altogether.[37] What he didn't say, and perhaps didn't need to say, was that the great foe of the party in Quebec was not capitalism but the Roman Catholic Church.

The RCMP noted that of the 400 people at a meeting sponsored by the Central Unemployed Council in June, most "were foreigners," 15 percent French-Canadians. At a campaign rally attended by between 5,000 and 6,000 people in July, Freddy urged the formation of a united front of the working class.[38]

Tensions persisted within the labor movement. That month it was announced that Freddy was without the support of the Labour Party, unhappy over his refusal to stand aside for a straight Labour Party candidate.[39]

He was, he explained to supporters at a campaign meeting, sorry to say that at a time when unity was most needed, the Zionist organizations backed by the Jewish Zionist Labour movement had taken a definite stand against unity, that the *Poale Zionist* labor party preferred to support Liberal Peter Bercovich against a real working-class candidate, that Bercovich did not support Jewish workers and had made no attempt to stop the publication of anti-Semitic newspapers in Quebec.[40]

In the 14 October Cartier vote Freddy placed second losing to incumbent Liberal Samuel William Jacobs who beat him by more than

---

36. "Communist Party of Canada, French Branch, Montreal," RCMP, 9 April 1935.
37. "Communist Party of Canada," RCMP, Montreal, 2 May 1935.
38. "FRED ROSE, Unemployed Movement, Montreal, Que.," RCMP, 20 June 1935; "Communist Party of Canada," RCMP, Montreal, June 1935; "Unemployed Movement," RCMP, Montreal, 24 July 1935.
39. "Communist Party of Canada," RCMP, Montreal, 12 September 1935.
40. "Communist Party of Canada," RCMP, Montreal (Secret), 23 December 1935.

10,000 votes. Freddy had labeled Jacobs a person with ties to the under-world and a tool of the Bronfmans, prohibition era booze barons.[41]

With a provincial election day approaching in November 1935 in the St. Louis riding, the provincial designation for Cartier, the party held a mass meeting, presided over, in the words of an RCMP report, by "a young Jew." Freddy was praised for having led a strike of textile workers at Cowansville upon his release from jail, his political opponents were denounced as supporters of fascism, the conflict between fascists and Communists taking place in Spain likely to be replayed in Quebec.[42] Freddy polled a mere 578 votes

Today, Freddy told 1,000 people at a Lenin memorial meeting in Montreal on New Year's Day, 1936, that the Soviet Union ranked first in Europe in industry and at the completion of the second Five-Year Plan may even surpass the United States. It was an absolutely fantastic claim that nevertheless drew a huge round of applause.[43]

A week earlier he'd informed a party meeting of a "gradual swing of the masses toward the "Left," that though the people of Quebec voted Liberal in the federal election, the French-Canadian masses wanted a change from the reactionary policies of the provincial government.[44]

The party's approach to the question of Jewish settlement in British mandate Palestine was the topic of a meeting in July 1936 chaired by Freddy's brother Abe. When it came his turn to speak, Freddy said that francophone party supporters were outperforming the old Jewish party members, they were organizing not only in Montreal but gaining influence in some small towns, also in Quebec City, Trois Rivières and Sherbrooke.[45]

In November brother Abe speaking in Yiddish told a mass gathering estimated at seven hundred celebrating the 19th anniversary of the Russian Revolution, "attendance composed mostly of Jews and foreigners... practically no French-Canadians present," that there was in

41. "Communist Party of Canada," RCMP, Montreal, 24 January 1936.
42. "Labour-Communist Compromise Fails," *The Montreal Gazette,* 14 July 1936.
43. "C. P. of C., Montreal, Que," RCMP, 22 July 1936.
44. "Results as seen by ridings in Quebec General Elections," RCMP, 18 August 1936; "C. P. of C., Montreal, Que. (Quebec Provincial Elections)," RCMP, Montreal, 17 July 1936.
45. "C. P. of C., Montreal, Que. (Provincial Elections)," SECRET, RCMP, 13 August 1936.

Russia "absolutely no racial discrimination "that anti-Semitism had been "stamped out of Russia."[46]

As the eyes of conservative Quebec gazed across the sea at the profiles of Hitler, Mussolini, Franco and Salazar, the province was witnessing the rise to power of the Trois-Rivières pharaoh Maurice Duplessis. Quebec devotees of Marshal Petain, who urged fellow Frenchmen to strive to recover the Greco-Roman values of the past, claimed that Jews were devious businessmen, rapacious anti-Christian entrepreneurs, who exploited good Christian folk. On the other hand, Jewish immigrants said *Le Devoir*, ignoring the absence of logic or consistency, included large numbers of Communists.[47]

In the vanguard of Quebec anti-Semitism was an intellectual elite that included members of the St. Jean Baptiste Society and Catholic Church officials. Through the 1930s, expressions of anti-Semitism in the province were open and unsubtle. Said Abbé Groulx: "The Jewish problem could be solved from one end of Quebec to the other. There would be no more Jews left here."

Le Devoir, May 1935: "If you ever buy bread that was made by a Jew, don't eat it before you've carefully examined every slice. If you find little black spots don't put it in your mouth. Those little black spots are crushed cockroaches. The Jewish bakers raise these small bugs. They weigh more than flour and they don't cost anything."

In those Depression years, the Church looked with great displeasure at the appeal of the party and its Jewish leaders in Catholic Quebec.

In Quebec a patronage scandal involving Liberal leader Alexandre Taschereau gave the 17 August 1936 Quebec provincial election to a Duplessis-engineered coalition that united Conservatives and the Action Liberal Nationale, provincial Liberal Party dissidents, in the right-wing Union Nationale. Duplessis saw that he needed Church backing if he was to prevail. "Duplessis declare la guerre au Communisme," said a 17 October headline in *L'Action Catholique*, Duplessis declares war on Communism. In March 1937 comprehending the fragility of his 1936

---

46. "C. P. of C., Montreal, Que. (November 7th Celebration)," RCMP, 8 November 1936.
47. Esther Delisle, *The Traitor and the Jew: Anti-Semitism and the Delirium of Extremist Right-Wing Nationalism in French Canada from 1929–1939*, translated by Madeleine Hebert, with Claire Rothman and Kathe Roth, Robert Davies Publishing, 1993. See too Eric Scott, *Je Me Souviens: The Esther Delisle Story*, 2003, a documentary film.

political triumph, Duplessis responded to pressure from the Church by enacting the anti-Communist *loi du cadenas*, the padlock law—"an Act to Protect the Province Against Communist Propaganda." The legislation gave authorities the power to lock up any building the Attorney-General, Duplessis himself, determined was employed in the dissemination of Communist propaganda, and to seize any and all literature deemed Communist. The timing may have seemed right. That summer, Freddy along with Norman Bethune and party philosopher Stanley Ryerson had addressed a mass rally in support of the anti-fascist Spanish Republican cause at the Mount Royal Arena.[48]

Duplessis let it be known that he was responding to the expressed concern of Jean-Marie-Rodrigue Cardinal Villeneuve. It was unofficially understood that the target of the legislation were Jewish intellectuals newly arrived in Quebec from Europe and Jews active in the labor movement. A few months later, *Le Devoir* published a letter from the heads of the Spanish clergy alleging the murder of thousands of priests by Republican elements during the Civil War. The letter spoke graphically of executions involving mutilation, eyes plucked out, tongues cut out, slaughter by axe blows. The mayor of Montreal cancelled a party meeting at the Mount Royal Arena following a threat of violence from University of Montreal students. In November, in the wake of anti-Communist statements from the Cardinal, Duplessis used the padlock law to order the provincial police to shut down the communist news-paper, *La Clarité*. A couple of small printing businesses were seized. A prominent Quebec communist, Jean Peron, was padlocked out of his home and quantities of subversive literature stored there were carted off. The terms of the law were broad enough to allow its use against minority organizations, including the Jehovah's Witnesses and Jewish groups. Duplessis's police could on a whim lock up any facility they chose. Padlock targets included numerous gambling houses whose locks were then removed in exchange for payoffs. One-time party activists excitedly recall pamphlets flushed down the toilet to prevent their discovery by police.

---

48. Conrad Black, *Duplessis*, McClelland & Stewart, 1977.

On 27 January 1950 the *Sûreté du Québec*, the provincial police force, padlocked the Morris Winchevsky Cultural Centre, the UJPO head-quarters in the heart of Cartier.

It seemed to the Canadian prime minister William Lyon Mackenzie King, whose government refused entry into Canada of boatloads of Jews desperate to escape the Nazis, the better part of political wisdom to take no action to overturn the padlock law even though it appeared to be in violation of federal law.[49]

Padlock law aside, for the party it was business as usual. Addressing the 450 delegates and several dozen visitors in the gallery at the October 1937 Eighth Dominion Communist Convention in the Masonic Temple in Toronto, Tim Buck drove home the importance of engaging in muni-cipal politics. This would, he said, be the route to winning concessions from the "capitalist government." It would be a means to create a real mass struggle and the cementing of some form of unity with the CCF. Freddy addressed the situation in Quebec. Denouncing the Duplessis government, the new approach in Quebec, he said, had produced excellent results, that there were over 50 delegates from Quebec, more than at the previous convention. In the fight for the basic interests of French-Canadians, the party, he said, was prepared to co-operate with sections of the Roman Catholic clergy and work with the Catholic trade unions.[50] Among the proceedings was the establishment of a National Control Commission to keep tabs on the activities of party members. Vigilance committees were set up to investigate the activities and com-plaints of party members. That same month Freddy was appointed commission secretary. One of the most powerful bodies in the party, it was a secret group charged with the task of monitoring the membership, identifying rumblings of discontent, weeding out spies and fascists and Trotskyites. For Freddy, it meant a move to Toronto. In November, just prior to the move, Freddy attended a mass gathering in celebration of the nineteenth anniversary of the Russian revolution. The RCMP had a man there. One indication of how closely Freddy's movements were

49. Abella and Troper, *None Is Too Many*.
50. "Working Class Unity Vital, Says Tim Buck," *The Clarion,* 14 October 1931.

being observed was that the report noted that the crowd contained few new faces.[51]

To celebrate the Toronto move, the party organized a banquet for four hundred at Montreal's Café St. Jacques. There were references to events that had transpired in the wake of the padlock law, among them the shutting down of the party's French-language paper, *La Clarité*.[52] An interview with Freddy in the November 1937 issue of the Yiddish language *Der Kampf* published in Toronto noted his role in attracting French-Canadians to the party. But this was likely more to the credit of the Depression and an early stage in the decline of Church influence. In 1933 there had been but fifteen French-Canadian party members, 50 the following year, and in 1937 roughly five hundred, including many long-shoremen, not to mention numerous party sympathizers.[53]

In the summer of 1938, Freddy was the key draw at a rally held in Vancouver under the auspices of the party, seven hundred in attendance. Much of his talk was devoted to an attack on Quebec's padlock law. Freddy's pamphlet, *Spying on Labour*, drew attention to RCMP ringers planted at Labour Congress conventions, *stool pigeons* holding union positions, misusers of funds, moral degenerates and drunkards who should be exposed and driven from the factories and mines, and Trotskyite-Fascist union busters.

In the fall, the party announced that Freddy would be their candidate in a forthcoming Cartier by-election, a consequence of the death of Liberal incumbent Sam Jacobs who had beaten Freddy for the seat in 1935.[54]

Following a campaign speech Freddy broadcast on CBC radio in October 1938, *The Montreal Daily Herald* commented that since Freddy's words urging voter support for a Communist candidate in the 1938 Cartier by-election, namely himself, constituted Communist propaganda perhaps the CBC premises should, in accordance with the "loi de cadenas" [*sic*] be padlocked as well as every home with a radio in it whose owners tuned in to the speech.[55]

---

51. F. J. Mead to the Commissioner, "Fred Rose (Rosenberg)," 25 October 1937.
52. F. J. Mead to the Commissioner, "Fred Rose (Rosenberg)," 14 November 1937.
53. *Der Kampf,* Vol. XIII, No. 671, Toronto 19 November 1937. As summarized by MHA at RCMP headquarters.
54. "Communist Party to Enter Candidate," *The Ottawa Morning Journal,* 1 September 1938.
55. "A Pretty Kettle of Fish," *The Montreal Daily Herald,* 20 October 1938.

Soon after, in line with popular front policy ordered by Moscow, the party ordered Freddy to withdraw his candidacy. The Liberal Party candidate Peter Bercovich was the acclaimed winner. The party sought an accommodation with the CCF, but determined to guard their distance *nyet* was the CCF response.[56]

The padlock law nevertheless was a catalyst in maintaining the solidarity of party members in the context of the Depression, the rise of fascism in Europe and the Adrien Arcand led local brownshirts. On the other hand, the law turned out, at least temporarily, to be inadequate provincial politics. Duplessis's Union Nationale election machine was defeated in 1939 by Adelard Godbout's Liberals. Re-elected in 1944, the Union Nationale government remained in power until Duplessis's death in 1959. In 1957, the padlock law was struck down by the Supreme Court of Canada on a legal technicality.

In June 1937 Canadian Prime Minister Mackenzie King arrived in Berlin to spend time with German chancellor Adolf Hitler. In April the Luftwaffe had destroyed the Spanish town of Guernica, killing hundreds of Spanish citizens. In 1933, the Jews of Germany became sub-humans, *Untermenschen*. Thugs blocked shoppers from entering Jewish shops, marked the following year with yellow Stars of David, *Juden* scrawled on windows. Violence would not be long in coming. For the time being, Jews were obliged to sit on designated seats on buses and trains. The bullying of Jewish school children was encouraged. In 1935, the Nuremberg Laws stripped Jews of German citizenship. Violence was rounding the corner.

This was all a reality the Canadian prime minister was likely to have been aware of but one he chose not to share with his diary.

In a lengthy diary entry, Mackenzie King did note that he first met with Hermann Goering who opened the conversation by thanking him for the bison Canada had sent the Berlin Zoo. Goering raised the question of improving trade relations. Germany, he said, needed raw materials and wheat which it was prepared to exchange for finished goods. When Goering wondered about the absence of a Canadian

---

56. "C. P. of C., Montreal, Que. (Federal By-Election, Cartier Div'n)," 24 October 1938. See too John Manley, "Communists Love Canada: The Communist Party of Canada, the 'People' and the Popular Front, 1933–1939," *Journal of Canadian Studies*, 36, 4 (Winter 2002.)

legation in Berlin, the Canadian prime minister explained it was simply a matter of finding the right people for the job. Germany, he told Goering, "had many problems which had to be understood; that she was showing restraint in dealing with some of them; also that it was not for any country to interfere in the particular policies of other countries."[57]

The meeting appeared in part to echo the 1933 conversation the Duke of Windsor, then the Prince of Wales, had with the Kaiser's grandson. It was, said the prince, no business of Great Britain to interfere in German internal affairs for Jews or anything else. Crowned king in January 1936, the Prince's abbreviated reign as Edward VIII ended with his abdication in December. There was an exchange of letters between Hitler and the Duke. In October 1937 the Duke and Duchess of Windsor arrived in Berlin as Hitler's guests, the Duke twice favoring Adolf with a Nazi salute. The couple subsequently spent time at Hitler's home in Berchtesgaden in the Bavarian Alps. Were the Nazis using the visit of Mackenzie King to lay the groundwork for the Duke's visit and the possible neutralization of Britain?[58]

Mackenzie King seemed pleased that the meeting with Hitler, which he referred to as an "interview," lasted one and a quarter hours, though scheduled, he was told, for a half hour. It began with him informing the Führer about his "old associations" with Germany, that he'd been born in Berlin, Ontario, that he'd lived in Berlin, Germany, an untruth. He spoke to Hitler of the "constructive work of his regime," that he "hoped it would be possible to get rid of the fear which was making nations suspicious of each other, and responsible for increases of armaments." Hitler, according to the diary entry, said that Germany's difficulties had grown out of the enmity of the Treaty of Versailles, that Germany had no desire for war, that war would obliterate European civilization. But there was the danger of Bolshevism and Communism, that England did not realize how serious it was, that if Germany had not acted as she had, conditions in Germany today would be the same as those of Spain.

Mackenzie King gave Hitler a *de luxe* edition of his biography. Hitler's gift was a "red square box with a gold eagle on its cover" containing a photograph of himself inscribed to his Canadian guest. "He is

57. "W. L. Mackenzie King's Diary, "29 June 1937, National Archives of Canada, MG 26 J Series 13.
58. Anthony Cave Brown, *"C": The Secret Life of Sir Stewart Graham Menzies, Spymaster to Winston Churchill,* Macmillan Publishing Company, 1987.

really," said Mackenzie King of Hitler, "one who truly loves his fellow man… There was a liquid quality about his eyes which indicates keen perception and profound sympathy. Calm, composed, and one could see how particularly humble folk would have come to have profound love for the man. As I talked with him I could not but think of Joan of Arc. He is distinctly a mystic." Hitler, he confided to his diary, was a reasonable man who "might come to be thought of as one of the saviors of the world."

The following year the prime minister told a Jewish delegation that Kristallnacht might turn out to be a blessing.[59] Not long after war had broken out, he informed his diary that the war was, in effect, all Britain's fault, that Hitler "would have gone to great lengths in trying to avert war had the British met him in the early stages, and that [Hitler], personally, did not wish to see a great loss of life." Hitler, it has been observed, was a brilliant diagnostician of weaknesses in others.

Mackenzie King was not without apologists of his own. King, said Canadian historian Col. C. P. Stacey, "was attracted to Hitler because he thought he saw in him a fellow mystic." In another view, the man was praised as "the best Prime Minister Canada ever had."[60]

In the 1940s, at a time when Jewish labor organizers were a popular target, the Duplessis government, in league with the Catholic Church, identified orphans, many abandoned by unwed parents, as mentally ill in order to claim payments from a federal government that provided financial support for medical facilities but not orphanages. There was much physical and sexual abuse of these children robbed of their childhoods by a practice that continued into the 1960s. The remains of child victims of medical experiments conducted at these institutions run by the Church, with the knowledge of provincial and federal authorities, now lie in an abandoned cemetery.[61]

---

59. Abella and Troper, *None Is Too Many*.
60. C. P. Stacey, "The Divine Mission—Mackenzie King and Hitler," *Canadian Historical Review*, Vol. 61, 1980; and Charlotte Gray, "Crazy Like a Fox," *Saturday Night*, October 1997. See too Kirk Hallahan, "W. L. Mackenzie King: "Rockefeller's 'other' public relations counselor in Colorado," *Public Relations Review* 29 (2003). This is a study of Mackenzie King's role as a counselor to John D. Rockefeller, Jr., in the 1913–1914 Ludlow, Colorado coal strike. On April 20, 1914, the Colorado National Guard shot and killed 19 strikers. Mackenzie King, a Rockefeller labor lawyer, provided public relations advice including instruction on testifying at government hearings.
61. "The Duplessis Orphans," *CBC* Archives.

Until 1942, Freddy belonged to a network of NKVD illegals—agents without the protection of diplomatic status—run out of New York City by Gaik Badalovich Ovakimyan, the Soviet Consul. A science Ph.D., Ovakimyan was sent to the United States in 1933 as deputy head of the NKVD's scientific-technical intelligence section. He worked undercover as an engineer for the *Amtorg* Corporation founded in New York City in 1924 to handle trade between America and the Soviet Union. The FBI referred to him as "the wily Armenian" though the bureau was not absolutely sure he was Armenian.[62]

It is unclear whether Freddy had ever met Ovakimyan. Ovakimyan's espionage network came to light in the course of a British government investigation of the activities of Mikhail Borovoy, *aka* William "Willy" Brandis, *aka* Brandes, a key figure in the Woolwich Arsenal scheme. Brandis had arrived in England in January 1937 bearing a fraudulent Canadian passport.

Standing five foot seven, the charming blue-eyed Ovakimyan spoke German and French, in addition to Russian and English, and was an avid reader of English literature. His specialty was industrial espionage. Ovakimyan, whose network of agents extended into Mexico, coordinated the assassination of Leon Trotsky. He was visited in New York City for instructions at least twice by the assassin, Ramón Mercader.

As head of the NKVD's American desk Ovakimyan had received bomb material from Klaus Fuchs through Harry Gold. In April 1941, suspecting that the FBI was closing in, Ovakimyan had his household goods and automobile loaded onto the steamship *Annie Johnson*, a vessel operating under *Amtorg* charter, bound for Vladivostok via the Panama Canal. Before he could join his possessions on board, on 5 May 1941 the Soviet spy chief was arrested by the FBI for violation of the Foreign Agents Registration Act. There was no trial. In a problematic deal,

62. Robert J. Lamphere, *The FBI-KGB War: A Special Agent's Story*, Random House, 1986, edition revised 1995; see too John Earl Haynes and Harvey Klehr, *Spies: The Rise and Fall of the KGB in America*, Yale University Press, 2009, Christopher Andrew and Vasili Mitrokhin, *The Sword and the Shield: The Mitrokhin Archive and the Secret History of the KGB*, Basic Books, 1999, Weinstein and Vassiliev, *The Haunted Wood*; David Dallin, *Soviet Espionage*, Yale University Press, 1955 and Nigel West, *Mortal Crimes: The Greatest Theft in History; Soviet Penetration of the Manhattan Project*, Enigma Books, 2004, for the Ovakimyan–Fred Rose connection; and "The Canadian Case in Retrospect," The Security Service (MI5), 15 November 1949. A research assistant at the Armenian Research Center in Dearborn, Michigan told me in a 28 February 2006 email about a book supposedly published in Armenia in 2005 with much information on the USSR's Armenian agents including Ovakimyan. To date the book's author and its location remain an unknown to all interested parties.

Ovakimyan was exchanged for several Americans held in the USSR. He finally departed the United States from San Francisco aboard a Soviet ship on 23 July 1941, never to return.[63]

Obsessed by betrayal real and imagined, Soviet authorities in 1940, had denounced Ovakimyan as a Trotskyite and recalled him home to Moscow to be shot, his impressive recruiting successes apparently evidence of disloyalty. There was too his apparently excessive reliance on his subordinate Jacob Golos. Ovakimyan ignored the order, saving himself by remaining in New York. By the time he did get back home, the danger had passed, the FBI arrest having restored his good standing. Following the departure of Ovakimyan in the summer of 1941, Vassily Zarubin took over as legal station chief.

Ovakimyan's right hand man in America was the Russian-born Yasha Raisin, *aka* Jacob Golos, a key Freddy NKVD contact in the United States. A political agitator from the age of eight, Raisin, code-named SOUND, took on the name *golos*, meaning voice in Russian.[64] Standing two inches shorter than Freddy, Golos spoke English with an Eastern European accent. Golos and Ovakimyan had been observed meeting in restaurants. Golos was an illegal—*nelegal'ny sotrudnik*—an agent who operated without diplomatic cover. Two of the shooters involved in the first attempt to assassinate Leon Trotsky were linked to Golos.

In the fall of 1942, Golos was given charge of a cell of engineers, known as the XY Line, whose prime goal was the penetration of the Manhattan Project, an operation the Soviets code-named ENORMOUS.[65] Julius Rosenberg was the contact person between Golos and the cell.

An American party member from 1919, Golos returned to the USSR in the early 1920s, was back in the United States in 1923, off again to the USSR a few years later, and back in the United States in 1929. As a NKVD illegal who ran a network of American agents, his cover was his position as head of *World Tourists*, a Comintern managed agency involved in arranging travel between the United States and the USSR. In

---

63. "Gaik Badalovich Ovakimyan," in *The Shameful Years: Thirty Years of Soviet Espionage in the United States*, Committee on Un-American Activities, US House of Representatives, 1951.
64. Haynes and Klehr, *Spies*.
65. Nigel West, "The XY Rezidentura" in *Mortal Crimes*.

1932, Ovakimyan had instructed Golos to set up *World Tourists*, located at 175 Fifth Avenue, an operation Golos ran until his death in 1943. As chief of CPUSA-NKVD liaison a key Golos responsibility was acquiring travel documents from American volunteers in Spain to assist in the covert travel of CPUSA and Comintern personnel, and money laundering. As head of the CPUSA's Central Control Commission, Golos was also the enforcer of the Stalinist party line, a function comparable to Freddy's within the Canadian party. The commission's chief role was to hunt down traitors and Trotskyites. In 1938, there was a Moscow plan to purge Golos, who was suspected of assisting Mensheviks and Trotskyites enter the USSR. By 1940, the NKVD was convinced Golos was himself a closet Trotskyite. The appearance of the FBI at *World Tourists* with a search warrant redeemed him. The FBI arrest had the effect of saving his reputation and perhaps his neck. Concern over his loyalty finally faded after the vindication of Ovakimyan.

Golos worked with Ovakimyan from 1938 to 1941. Following the arrest and departure of Ovakimyan, his responsibilities were assumed by Iskhak Abdulovich Akhmerov, who headed the illegal station. Golos was in touch with most if not all of the top NKVD people in America, including Vassily Zarubin, chief of the legal station and Akhmerov's superior, as well as with other station officers in New York City.[66]

Golos was, in other words, a big fish. For a few years Ernest Hemingway was in contact with NKVD agents, Golos among them. Golos never met Hemingway, who was headed for China with his wife Martha Gellhorn, but did arrange for party people to meet the writer, code named *Argo*, in China. It was Hemingway the journalist that interested recruiter of journalists Golos.[67]

The specific circumstances of Freddy's involvement with Golos and the Ovakimyan network and when that involvement in fact began remain unclear. The important thing was that the connection linked Freddy to the executive offices of Stalin's North American operations and in time to Elizabeth Bentley, Golos's lover and girl Friday.

---

66. Private communication from John Haynes. Iskhak Akhmerov arrived in the United States with false papers in 1935, went home in 1939, returned in 1941. A covert resident, he operated as a clothing industry figure under various aliases. Elizabeth Bentley knew him as *Bill*. His Soviet code names were MAYOR and ALBERT. He was succeeded by Joseph Katz. The KGB regarded Akhmerov as one of their most successful agents.

67. Haynes, "Hemingway, the Dilettante Spy," in *Spies*.

Soon after Bentley was hired as a secretary and research worker by the Italian Library of Information in New York City, a branch of the Mussolini government's Propaganda Ministry—*Ministero della cultura popolare*—she went to the CPUSA with an offer to spy on the service for the party. The party decided to turn her over to Golos, who was introduced to her as *Timmy*. Their first meeting in October 1938 took place in a restaurant. Bentley was not immediately impressed with Golos, not with his stature or his worn brown shoes. But love can change everything and as the meal progressed *Timmy* seemed to grow taller, better looking, more powerfully built. Suddenly, she noticed "broad shoulders and firm hands, eyes that were startlingly blue, his hair bright auburn, and I was intrigued by the fact that his mouth was very much like my mother's." Weren't the well-worn clothes a marker of the party's indifference to the externals of dress? Bentley said she felt attracted to *Timmy's* simple, direct manner, to his quick, intelligent mind. He seemed to her a driven man who somewhat oddly reminded her of her New England parents.[68] They soon became lovers, though this needed to be kept secret from the party.

Initially Bentley brought Golos material from the Library. Golos was not pleased by her methods that included listening in at closed doors, and searching through wastepaper baskets. That, he told her, was not the way to operate. "No one does it except in mystery novels. Concentrate on impressing the Library with the fact that you are trustworthy, so that more and more they will take you into their confidence."

Timmy, Bentley learned, was involved with Mexican Communists who were part of the Russian Secret Police assassination squad dispatched to Mexico to liquidate Leon Trotsky. Working with Golos, Bentley became involved with other agents, among them the Silvermaster group, named for Odessa-born Nathan Gregory Silvermaster, who had a job with the Agriculture Department. The group delivered quantities of government documents the Soviets, ever interested in major US policy formulations, would complain were of limited value.

She remembered phone calls received from a Julius and testified that Golos once picked someone up named Julius and dropped him off

---

68. Elizabeth Bentley, *Out of Bondage*, Devin Adair, 1951. See too Lauren Kessler, *Clever Girl*, Harper-Collins, 2003, and Kathryn S. Olmstead, *Red Spy Queen*, University of Carolina Press, 2002.

somewhere, perhaps in Queens. She told the FBI, perhaps coyly, that she saw the fellow from a distance and could not provide a positive ID. She remembered that Golos had a contact named Julius but it was never clear to her that Julius Rosenberg was the man in the car.

The Rosenbergs were a subject that grew in interest. In the fall of 1942, perhaps December, Bentley recalled that Julius was the leader of a Communist cell of engineers turned over to Jacob Golos to be developed in industrial espionage. Julius was to be the contact between Golos and the group. Bentley, in a November 1945 FBI interview said she "received 2 or 3 telephone calls from Julius telling me he wanted to see Golos and relayed the messages to Golos.... My last contact with Julius came shortly before the death of Golos [1943] after the latter had turned the group over to someone else. Golos told me the reason Julius had desired to see him was that he had lost his Russian contact and wanted to enlist Golos's aid in getting re-established."

Golos would tell his CPUSA sources, perhaps uneasy about the possibility that their information was going directly to the Russians, that the material they supplied in fact served the cause of the American party. In 1943, in the months before the death of Golos, Vassily Zarubin, New York City NKVD station chief, had received instructions from Moscow to take control of the Golos CPUSA network. Might this have included Freddy and his Canadian recruits?

Golos, who was opposed to CPUSA members being turned into agents, now came under pressure to cooperate. It was a very different situation from the one in Canada where Freddy seemed to see little if any distinction between CPC sources and Russian operatives. Golos's relations with the Russians began to deteriorate. The struggle, Bentley reported, was a bitter one: "Yasha would come home night after night looking like a beaten man.... What could have happened to shake a strong man like Yasha who was afraid of nothing? .... It was much later on that I realized Yasha had been deliberately driving himself beyond his physical endurance because for him death was a merciful solution to his dilemma. The movement had been his entire life...."

One late afternoon, feeling suddenly ill and out of breath, Golos took refuge in Bentley's apartment. Hearing a gurgling sound coming from the sofa where he'd collapsed, it occurred to her that her Yasha might be dying. She called the medics. After they arrived and pronounced Yasha dead, she kept her cool and sent them out to move their ambulance which was illegally parked so she could go through Yasha's pockets and destroy incriminating papers including the coded phone numbers of his agents. A lengthy grilling by police followed. Very early the next morning, she hurried over to the *World Tourist* office and removed party documents, including a sealed envelope, from his safe. She stuffed the documents in a suitcase and burnt them all, including the unopened envelope, in her apartment fireplace.

Elizabeth Bentley had acted more as Golos's second in command than his courier. This "clever girl" as the Russians called her took over the Golos network after his death. What the Russians liked about Bentley, who claimed descent from a Mayflower pilgrim and a Declaration of Independence signatory, was that she was, in their words, "pure Aryan" with none of the Euro-Hebraic taint of so many of their American stooges. After the death of Golos, Akhmerov, the New York *rezident* became her superior. At their initial meeting she told him she shared the Golos objection to a NKVD takeover of CPUSA assets.

Before long Bentley quarreled with her Russian controllers. Afraid she'd been marked for assassination and/or fingered by the FBI, on 23 August 1945 she went to the FBI office in New Haven, Connecticut. She didn't have much to say and wasn't taken very seriously. She went back in October. In November she sat for a series of interviews, providing what the FBI believed was substantial information. The Bureau realized Ovakimyan had been deported before they had any idea what he was up to. For about a year, Bentley worked under FBI control as a double agent.

The Soviets had offered Bentley money and gifts to prevent her from turning, unaware she'd already gone over. She might have feared exposure by the defection of *Daily Worker* editor Louis Budenz. Was she threatened by the Soviets with assassination over a money matter? Had she grown disenchanted with their demands and threats? While Golos was alive, he'd dealt with these people and spared her the details. In the months after his death, she had to endure hearing a Russian refer to her beloved Yasha as a *traitor* because he'd resisted the pressure to turn over his American contacts. Mostly, it was the fear that the FBI was on her trail that led to her defection.

In November 1945 Bentley participated in fourteen interview sessions with FBI Special Agents Harold V. Kennedy and Joseph M. Kelly. In one of them she reported that: "…sometime in the summer of 1939… I was instructed by GOLOS that I would receive mail from Canada at my address at 18 Grove Street, New York City. GOLOS told me that if I received any letter from Canada it would be for him and I was to deliver it to him. I recall that I received mail from Canada at about this time, about one letter a week. These letters kept coming from Canada over a period of about six months. I subsequently learned that some of the letters that were sent from Canada that I delivered to GOLOS came from either TIM BUCK or FRED ROSE. I am not certain which one."[69]

Some of the mail went to her apartment, most to another address. She said she'd received letters from Freddy for Golos in 1939 and the early 1940s, but claimed never to have read any of them. It was about the time Golos extended his passport work into Canada. Could that have been among the topics discussed in the letters? Canadian party man Sam Carr had been involved in the passport business, perhaps Freddy was too. What might they have needed to discuss during the period of the Hitler-Stalin pact, 1939–1941, and following the Spanish Civil War that required weekly reports from Canada? Was Freddy receiving orders that could be entrusted to the mails? Clearly there had been discussion between Golos and Freddy to establish that mail link. Golos desired distance, not wanting Freddy's letters coming to his address. Diligent tradecraft? Did he write back? Might there have been discussions over the telephone? Bentley didn't say. It is not clear whether such questions were ever put to her. The Golos-Freddy connection pre-dated 1942, when Freddy was still working for the NKVD. Perhaps the letters from Freddy were among the contents of the sealed envelope Bentley destroyed in her apartment fireplace. She never said. Was Freddy aware she'd gone over to the FBI?

Bentley in an FBI interview session in November 1945 said:

---

69. Harold Kennedy, "Statement of Elizabeth Terrill Bentley," *FBI*, March 1946.

Another individual who I met in this work was HAZEN SIZE [*sic*], who I later found out was a Canadian Communist and who comes from a wealthy family in Canada who are alleged to own the Canadian telephone system. I also recall that FRED ROSE...sent one of his contacts, a Royal Canadian Air Force pilot, to see Golos and explain to him that HAZEN SIZE was presently associated with the Canadian Film Board [*sic*] in Washington, D.C., and was probably an individual whom GOLOS wanted to contact. Subsequently this flier introduced SIZE to GOLOS and myself in New York City. I do not recall what conversation GOLOS had with SIZE, but as a result of this meeting GOLOS told me to contact SIZE when I made my periodic visits to Washington D.C.

I first contacted SIZE in Washington in the late spring of 1943 and continued seeing him until the spring of 1944. SIZE furnished me with information that was principally gossip he overheard in the Canadian and British embassy and could be characterized as the names of prominent British individuals who were coming to the United States as well as matters pertaining to Canada's policy as far as the war and other matters were concerned.

Apparently the result of faulty memory, details Bentley supplied could be subject to change. Bentley claimed that in 1943 and 1944, Hazen Sise, National Film Board (NFB) officer at the Canadian embassy in Washington, D.C. and a friend of Lester Pearson supplied her with information obtained from Pearson that was passed on to Soviet intelligence operatives. Bentley said that Sise was a link between her and an unsuspecting Pearson, posted to the embassy in 1942, becoming ambassador in 1944. She claimed Sise, who'd served in the Norman Bethune blood transfusion unit in Spain in 1936 and 1937, was a known Communist, that Sise, a high-rent guy, and Pearson moved in the same circles, that she had regular meetings with Sise who gave her the impression that Pearson was a left-winger. She also said she believed that Pearson was a friend of NFB head John Grierson, who in her view was a Communist, an allegation that did much damage to Grierson's career. The FBI determined that Sise had briefly worked for Russian intelligence after leaving Spain.

In 1949, Sise denied knowing or ever meeting Bentley, or at any rate, could not recall meeting her. For reasons that remain unclear, the FBI re-opened the Sise file in 1970. Sise died in 1974. Bentley claimed she met Sise in the Flatiron Building, 175 Fifth Avenue in New York City, with a Royal Canadian Air Force officer, young, blond and Jewish, whose name she was unable to remember. The officer, who had a note of introduction from Fred Rose, introduced Sise to Golos. She recalled first contacting Sise in Washington in the late spring of 1943, and that he furnished her with gossip overheard in the embassies of Canada and Great Britain including the names of British officials who were to arrive in the United States and some details of Canadian policy with regard to the war. She said that in October 1943 Freddy was in New York with a journalist and a person from the International Labour Organization named Eric to discuss the establishment of an espionage operation to supply information from Canadian civil servants. Perhaps the reference was to Eric Adams, an engineer in the employ of the Canadian Industrial Development Bank, who had visited the USSR with his wife.[70]

In 1972, the RCMP's S. M. Chadwick reported on an interview with a Rodney J. Stewart, a lecturer in Political Science and History at the University of Toronto who was researching a book on Norman Bethune. Stewart was interested in RCMP files on Bethune and the Committee to Aid Spanish Democracy. The Force was curious about what he might have learned about Hazen Sise, someone he'd interviewed in 1970 and 1972. The first meeting at Sise's home in Montreal lasted seven hours. Stewart did not find Sise, who was planning to do a book of his own on Bethune, to be overly forthcoming. Stewart described Sise as "a very vain and circumspect person; very suspicious and a loner."[71]

Until 1944, Canadians arrived in New York with notes for her from Freddy. After the death of Golos her new espionage boss, Akhmerov, refused her request to travel to Canada to meet Freddy and enlarge the link. She said her Canadian contacts included Freddy's "current girlfriend" a small thin woman in the women's army corps. In her autobiography, *Out of Bondage,* Bentley claimed Sise had been "sent to us highly recommended by Tim Buck and Sam Carr" which contradicted an earlier statement that it was Freddy who'd recommended Sise to

---

70. John Sawatsky, "Pearson's Friend Was a Soviet Spy," *The Montreal Gazette,* 8 January 1982.
71. Sgt. S. M. Cadwick to S/Insp. A. M. Barr, "Re: Rodney J. Stewart—Toronto, SECRET," 23 June 1972.

Golos. In a 1945 FBI interview she said her contact with Sise began in the spring of 1943, in 1951 she said it was a year earlier.

In 1951 Bentley told a US senate committee that she and Golos had frequent contact with Freddy.[72]

In her 1948 HUAC testimony, Bentley had been less forthcoming:

> Mr. Stripling: Miss Bentley, you say you first met Mr. Golos in October 1938?
>
> Miss Bentley: That is correct.
>
> Mr. Stripling: Did your acquaintance with him in connection with the activities of *World Tourists* increase to any degree, or was he a casual acquaintance of yours?
>
> Miss Bentley: At first he was the only person to whom I gave information about the Italian Library of Information and its Fascist activities. After I left there in the spring of 1939 I continued to have him as my contact. I suppose now because he thought I was valuable material that could be used in the future. I did odd jobs for him like collecting material in the library for use in what he said were articles in the *New Masses*, or receiving mail at my address for him, and that sort of thing.
>
> Mr. Stripling: Do you recall whether or not you ever received any mail from Mexico addressed to Mr. Golos?
>
> Miss Bentley: Oh, yes.
>
> Mr. Stripling: Addressed to you but to be delivered to Mr. Golos?
>
> Miss Bentley: No. Canada, not Mexico.
>
> Mr. Stripling: Did any of that mail come from Fred Rose?
>
> Miss Bentley: I can't state of my own knowledge, Mr. Stripling, because I didn't look inside the envelopes, but I suspect it may have been.
>
> Mr. Stripling: Do you recall what year it was you transmitted mail from Canada to Mr. Golos?
>
> Miss Bentley: Yes. I can tell you almost exactly. It was 1939, 1940.[73]

The FBI believes that in 1948 HUAC staff would have known about Freddy from the 1946 Royal Commission hearings. According to a

---

72. Pat McCarran, Chair, Subcommittee to Investigate the Administration of the Internal Security Act and Other Internal Security Laws of the Committee on the Judiciary United States Senate, 14 August 1951 in James Barros, *No Sense of Evil*, Deneau Publishers, 1980. The Bentley claim in her McCarran testimony that Hazen Sise told her Lester Pearson *knew* Sise was a Communist "and was willing to help" seems preposterous. Likewise, her claim that the NFB's John Grierson was "extremely close" to the party and wanted to get "as many persons into the Party as he could."

73. House Committee on Un-American Activities, 30 July 1948.

Bureau source, as far as anyone knows, apart from Golos himself, no one has ever read Freddy's letters to Golos.

By the time of his death even Bentley's *Yasha*—and there was no one more loyal or dedicated to the Soviet cause—had begun to wonder whether the great socialist struggle had not been hijacked by goons.

A June 1948 story in the *Toronto Daily Star* reported that Bentley told the FBI she once met Freddy when he was in New York City, apparently after the death of Golos. Following his return to Canada, Freddy sent her messages urging her to come to Canada and work for him, apparently unaware that she was now running her own spy ring.[74] She in turn claimed to have limited knowledge of Freddy's party activity. Bentley said Freddy kept sending her letters asking her to visit. In June 1944 she asked her NKVD controller, Akhmerov, *aka Bill,* to approve a trip to Canada. The response was negative.

How to explain the fact that Freddy who had become a GRU man in 1942 seemed to be maintaining the Golos NKVD connection? Would Maj. Rogov and Col. Zabotin have approved of the Bentley relationship? Did Ovakimyan's departure in 1941 have any bearing on the move? Could Freddy have been risking his espionage career for romance?

In *Out of Bondage*, Bentley's account of her life in and out of the party, she recalled a New York City visit in the summer of 1939 of "a number of leading Canadian Communists." There was no mention of Freddy by name. The instruction from Golos: "I want my meeting with them to look as natural as possible. So we will take them out to lunch or dinner, and you keep their wives occupied while I transact my business with the men."

Bentley did not identify any of the Canadian visitors nor, perhaps anticipating the next question, what this "business" was about. "He never told me, and I never asked. I think I had some vague idea that he was a liaison man between the American Party and the Canadian one....on numerous occasions we entertained the visiting Canadian functionaries. Two of them I remember quite clearly: Sam Carr and Tim Buck, the head of the Canadian Party. The latter I got to know quite well, because he stayed in New York longer than the others....a rather likeable man with a yen for Russian food and 'Vat 69' Scotch whiskey."

---

74. "Spy With Me Said Rose Plea to U.S. Blonde," *The Toronto Star,* 22 July 1948.

As Bentley pointed out in her autobiography, Stalin was after information: "What the Russians wanted to know was practically limitless." That included information on potential Communist recruits, on American government attitudes, officials who might be helpful, military production statistics, aircraft performance tests, troop sizes and allocation, developments on the B-29, and the explosive *RDX*.

The Moscow espionage bureaucrats who seemed to delight in running their stable of espionage serfs on the American estate were imagined by some to possess near inhuman smarts. The impression is inaccurate. According to John Haynes: "A persistent popular and media myth holds that the KGB was a near superhuman organization, staffed by skilled officers carrying out sophisticated schemes designed by clever Moscow overlords who had a long-standing plan on how to subvert the West."[75]

In time, Bentley grew to understand how really dangerously erratic the men running the Soviet show were, under pressure and coerced by ideology, both attracted to and repulsed by displays of madness. By a certain irony their great fear, as she explained in the autobiography, "was that an agent might crack up and land in a psychiatrist's office. If we detected any indication of such a possibility, he was dropped like a hot cake. One case I remember was that of a man whom I shall call Harold Sloan, a young Canadian whom I contacted for over a year and a half while he was working for the Canadian government in Washington.... He had been sent to us highly recommended by Tim Buck and Sam Carr, leaders of the Canadian Communist Party, and had a long and excellent record as a Party member in Canada, including a period of service in the Spanish Civil War. For a long time he functioned efficiently, giving us information which he obtained from his friends in the Canadian Legation. Then he began to have trouble with his wife and became moody and nervous to the point where he insisted he was going to consult a psychiatrist. When it became increasingly evident we could not keep him from going to pieces, I was ordered to stop contacting him."[76] Harold Sloan was a veiled reference to Hazen Sise.

---

75. John Haynes, *Spies.*
76. Elizabeth Bentley, *Out of Bondage.*

Within Soviet intelligence ranks one's fate might have absolutely nothing to do with one's effectiveness. Ovakimyan was suddenly declared a Trotskyite and ordered home to face a firing squad! At one point, Stalin wondered whether Kim Philby was a double agent. Bolshevik bureaucrats who absolutely refused to trust the evidence of their own eyes and ears had only paranoid twitches to fall back on. What seemed to count most in Moscow's ruling circles was being in receipt of a constant stream of reports from abroad, bolstering the impression that much was transpiring in one's faraway sphere of operations even if, as Bentley pointed out with reference to Sise, the information might be next to useless. The foreign agents, *useful idiots* devoted to the Soviet system, likely didn't understand that they might be little more than survival fodder for Moscow schemers.

In 1951, FBI officials became concerned over discrepancies in Bentley's interview statements and events described in *Out of Bondage*. In the autobiography, she claimed that Hazen Sise was recommended to Golos by Sam Carr and Tim Buck. In a 30 November 1945 FBI interview she'd said Sise was put in contact with Golos by a letter from Fred Rose who she described as "the Canadian Communist who most frequently corresponded with Golos." She did not, she said, ever see the letter.

The mentoring of Golos seemed to have prepared Bentley to move almost effortlessly from the arms of the KGB into the embrace of the FBI.

In time it was clear to her that for the American party's Moscow bosses, the party was little more than a tool to serve Soviet interests. The international Communist movement, she decided, was in the hands of the wrong people, that it was the terrible strain of dealing with those people that had killed her *Yasha*: "My faith in my old Communist ideals was gone now...never again will I be able to think and feel and live with such intensity..." Bentley remembered how pleased Joseph Katz *aka* Jack, one of her American comrades, was with a Christmas gift she'd given him. She discovered that after her defection Katz took on the assignment to assassinate her, but for whatever reason never carried it out.

Elizabeth Bentley hardly looked the part of the irresistible seductress. Said *The Daily Worker* following her defection: "They call her the blonde spy queen, but her hair's really a dirty brown."

She remains a key source of what we know about Freddy's link to the Golos-Ovakimyan network. There is no reference to it in any of Freddy's public musings or private correspondence. Golos as far as we know, never spoke of it.

Bentley's claims were, as we know, without documentary confirmation. How credible were they? Was the "clever girl" cooking the details to hustle a book? Curiosity about the discrepancies in her FBI testimony and the autobiography, led CIA historian Hayden Peake to conduct an exhaustive investigation. He concluded that there was no evidence "of a major embellishment of fact or contradictory stories designed to increase marketability." There were in her account minor errors of detail, but nothing to suggest "a cleverly crafted pattern of deception."[77]

A former RCMP counter-intelligence specialist surmises that as an NKVD illegal Freddy's duties consisted of the recruitment of promising information sources, the transmission of funds to the CPUSA, and assistance with bogus documentation for Soviet illegals seeking entry into the United States and beyond.[78]

In 1931 Vladimir Jabotinsky told a Dutch journalist that German nationalism would overwhelm Europe and that the nations of Europe would not unite against the Nazi threat which would lead to the extermination of their Jewish communities.[79] Freddy's misguided response was to join the struggle on the side of men who had always held their Jewish populations in contempt.

---

77. Hayden B. Peake, "Afterword," Elizabeth Bentley's *Out of Bondage*, Ivy Books, 1988. In her statements reporting Hazen Sise's claims about Lester Pearson and John Grierson, Bentley seems to have been repeating things Hazen Sise told her.
78. Private communication.
79. Pierre van Paassen, "As I Remember Him," *Outpost,* December 2004.

IV.

Passports...

Few things in Canada were of greater interest to the Russians than Canadian travel documents. A key CPC chore, apart from recruiting information sources, involved obtaining papers to enable *illegals* to enter and remain in the United States. Montreal, given its geographical position and its status as an international port, was a key point of entry and departure for Stalin's American illegals. Vancouver played a comparable role on the west coast. Assisted by members of the CPC, Soviet agents generally found Canadian passports easy to obtain.

With the arrival of Col. Nikolai Zabotin in Ottawa the pressure from Moscow to obtain Canadian passports increased.

An MI5 document dealing with the Igor Gouzenko defection, "The Canadian Case in Retrospect" confirmed that Freddy's role as an NKVD agent came to notice in the late 1930s through his connection with the Ovakimyan network operating with forged Canadian documents and passports acquired by Soviet agents in the United States and Europe. What the Russians liked about Canadian documents—birth certificates, naturalization papers, passports—was that Canada was not just a convenient jumping off point for dispatching agents into the United States but a land of immigrants who spoke imperfect English.[1]

Ordered to a meeting in Moscow by Comintern chairman Nikolai Bukharin, the CPUSA's Benjamin Gitlow, a member of the Comintern Executive Committee, said he "rushed to Canada and made arrangements to obtain a Canadian passport under a fictitious name with which to travel to Russia." The inside front and back covers of *I Confess* (1940), Gitlow's account of his life in the party, display facsimile reproductions in Russian and English of his "Certificate for the Entry into the USSR" 4 May 1927, issued by the "Official Agency of the U.S.S.R. in Canada" a Soviet trade office located in Montreal. There was at the time no Soviet legation in Canada: "The Official Agency of the U.S.S.R. in Canada hereby certifies that the bearer HAY James ------ 35 years old native of Toronto, Canada ---- Commission Merchant by profession is a citizen of Canadian [*sic*] travelling to the U.S.S.R. , accompanied by _____ Valid until August 4, 1927." The document was signed by one L. Gerus, Official Agent of the U.S.S.R. in Canada. Gitlow provided no details of the passport transaction. Among the attractions of a Canadian passport was that it had a shelf life of five years and could be renewed for another five. According to Gitlow, the Soviets operated fake passport factories in Berlin and Moscow where genuine passports acquired by the intelligence service were copied. Legitimate and fake travel documents were distributed to agents for travel across the globe.[2]

Suspicion raised by anonymous tips in the early 1930s led to RCMP investigations and the discovery that some members of the CPC were attempting to obtain the birth certificates of deceased Canadians, a procedure called *tombstoning*.[3]

The notebooks of Alexander Vassiliev, a KGB/SVR man with unique access to the archival records of agency espionage activity in America, tell us that Jacob Golos was able to get hold of Canadian pass-

---

1. William E. Duff, "New Man in London," in *A Time for Spies: Theodore Stephanovich Mally and the Era of the Great Illegals*, Vanderbilt University Press, 1999.

2. Benjamin Gitlow, *I Confess: The Truth About American Communism*, E. P. Dutton & Co., Inc., 1940; also Rodney, *Soldiers of the International*.

3. Steve Hewitt, "Strangely Easy to Obtain: Canadian Passport Security, 1933–73, "*Intelligence and National Security*, Vol. 23, No. 3, June 2008. The Russians zeroed in on Haileybury, a small northern Ontario town, where fires had destroyed all local records making it more or less impossible to check up on the legitimacy of the documents carried by individuals claiming citizenship. See also Nigel West, "*Conspiratsia*: The Pre-War Networks" in *The Illegals: The Double Lives of the Cold War's Most Secret Agents*, Hodder & Stoughton, 1993.

ports in Ottawa in the 1932–33 period.[4] The scheme for having Canadian passports issued to Soviet agents with fake names appears to have begun earlier. Gitlow's brief account suggested an arrangement that apparently was, at the start of Soviet espionage activity in North America, fairly routine. The formal RCMP investigation of Soviet passport activity in Canada didn't begin until years later.

Neither Golos, who in 1927 was in Russia, nor Freddy, then a twenty-year old member of the Communist Youth League, could have had anything to do with Gitlow's Canadian passport. The arrangement *en place,* such as it might have been, that obtained the document for Gitlow may have been part of the scheme that facilitated the traffic in Canadian passports between Spain and Moscow in the 1930s.

Canada's Mackenzie-Papineau volunteers on their way to Spain routinely turned their passports over to Comintern representatives in Paris.[5] The assassin of Leon Trotsky, Ramón Mercader del Rio, *aka* Jacques Mornard, held a fraudulent Canadian passport in the name of *Frank Jacson.* The CPC had assisted in obtaining a revoked naturalization certificate for a *Frank Jacson* that was used to acquire the Jacson passport. The passport number belonged to a Tony Babich, a naturalized Canadian citizen born in Yugoslavia. Babich, a party member who had travelled to Spain to fight on the Republican side with the Mackenzie-Papineau Battalion, was killed in action on the Aragon front.[6]

At the time, the FBI did inform the RCMP that passports held by those killed in the Spanish Civil War were being collected by agents of the Comintern and forwarded to Moscow, that in the majority of instances, the passports were secured from the volunteers when they reported to the officers of the International Brigades in Paris and never returned. Apparently, the Soviets had also managed to arrange for

4. John Earl Haynes and Harvey Klehr, "Alexander Vassiliev's Notebooks: Provenance and Documentation of Soviet Intelligence Activities in the United States." Unpublished. "*Sound* had an opportunity to obtain Canadian passports. *Sound* was the cover name of Jacob Golos." By 1937 Golos had expanded his passport work into Canada. See Weinstein and Vassiliev, "Love and Loyalties, II: Elizabeth Bentley and Jacob Golos," in *The Haunted Wood.*

5. Hewitt, "Strangely Easy." Walter Krivitsky: "Even when a man was discharged, he was told that his passport had been lost. From the United States alone about 2,000 volunteers came over, and genuine American passports are highly prized at OGPU headquarters in Moscow. Nearly every diplomatic pouch from Spain that arrived at the Lubyanka contained a batch of passports from members of the International Brigade." Gary Kern, *A Death in Washington,* Enigma Books, 2003.

6. William Rodney, "Passport to Murder," *RCMP Quarterly,* January 1954.

assistance in acquiring passports from an unidentified employee of the Canadian passport office in Ottawa.[7]

Elizabeth Bentley recalled Golos showing up at her apartment one evening with packages to be chucked in the fireplace, one containing "a heap of red passports stamped with the official seal of the United States of America." Why was Yasha getting rid of perfectly good passports? They were not, he explained to her, genuine, that "World Tourists sent a lot of Americans to Spain to fight during the Civil War and they all traveled on fake passports."[8]

In September 1945, the FBI fingered a GRU illegal working as a lecturer at the University of Southern California (USC) in possession of a doctored Canadian passport in the name of Ignacy Samuel Witczak.[9] The real Witczak was a Mackenzie-Papineau recruit who had emigrated to Canada from Poland in 1930 to do shoe repair and farm work in Leamington, Ontario, becoming a naturalized citizen in 1936. Unmarried, he left for Spain in 1937 where he was relieved of his Canadian passport by a Polish brigade officer.

Thought to have been killed in the fighting, Witczak returned to Canada from Spain in February 1939 but never applied for a new passport, though he did obtain a replacement of his lost naturalization papers. In 1945 it was discovered that a forged passport had been substituted for the original issued to Ignacy Witczak in *External Affairs* files. That document had come into the possession of a man and a woman who gave their names as Ignacy Samuel Witczak and Bunia Witczak and who had apparently arrived in Canada from France, claiming they were Canadian.

The false Witczak was a Soviet agent named Zalman Vul'fovich. Litvin code name *Mulat*. He arrived in Los Angeles in possession of the fake Witczak passport document issued in 1937 valid with renewal for a decade.

When he became aware that the FBI had begun to keep an eye on him Litvin *aka* Witczak, who'd received a *cum laude* Bachelor of Arts degree at USC in 1942 and a Master of Arts degree in political science in 1943, hastily departed the California scene. On 21 November 1945 he

---

7. Richard Hirsch, *The Soviet Spies: The Story of Russian Espionage in North America*, Nicholas Kaye, 1948.
8. Bentley, *Out of Bondage*.
9. Robert Lamphere with Tom Sachtman, *The FBI-KGB War*, Mercer University Press, 1995.

suddenly "vanished on a barren stretch of beach of the Pacific Ocean in southern California." In 1952, the United States Congress described him as an important Soviet spy. Witczak and his wife were mentioned in at least three deciphered *Venona* messages. Documents Soviet defector Igor Gouzenko turned over to Canadian authorities who passed them on to the FBI put the Bureau on Litvin-Witczak's trail.[10] An investigation of the deception revealed an elaborate procedure for obtaining fake Canadian travel documents. The original Witczak document was issued to a single man 5' 9" in height who gave his occupation as farmer and his birthday as 13 October 1906. The application of the imposter in the files listed a merchant 5' 8" born 13 October 1910, to which the name of a wife, Bunia, had been added by a different typewriter. In the file were photographs of a man and a woman, neither certified as the regulation required. Moreover, the false Witczak application bore no initials which it would have if it had been handled by passport office staff. Nor was there an index card, another standard piece of the application procedure. The passport number for the couple belonged to some other person. Detectives thought the switch had been the work of Passport Office clerk W. M. Pappin. Pappin was subsequently tried and acquitted. The actual identity of the person or persons in the Passport Office who performed the deed has never been determined.[11]

Jacob Golos was linked to the Witczak passport switch as was Canadian party organizer Sam Carr who had obtained the bogus Witczak passport renewal in 1944 for the sum of $3,000. Indicted in connection with the Witczak affair were Henry Harris, a Toronto optometrist and Dr. Samuel Soboloff, a Toronto physician whose signature appeared on the false Witczak passport application. In 1946, Harris told the royal commission investigating Soviet espionage in Canada that he was well-acquainted with Sam Carr and knew Freddy "casually" but did not know Pappin, or anyone else in the passport office. Soboloff claimed that he in fact had no personal knowledge of the man he'd vouched for, that

10. Hirsch, "Two Ignacy Witczaks" in *The Soviet Spies*. Also, "Section V, The False Passport," in the Royal Commission on espionage report. For a comprehensive account of the Witczak affair that identifies GRU man Litvin see Mike Gruntman *Enemy Amongst Trojans: A Soviet Spy at USC*, Figueroa Press, 2010.
11. Hirsch.

he'd signed the application as a favor for Sam Carr, a patient, friend and public figure.[12]

In June 1937, Fred Rose joined Norman Bethune on the platform at a mass meeting of 15,000 at the Mount Royal Arena in Montreal to show support for the 1,600 young men of the Mackenzie-Papineau Battalion the party had sent to fight in Spain. A few months later, the party's national convention in Toronto opened with the unveiling of a monument to the fallen heroes to the singing of the *Internationale* and national Spanish tunes. A Spanish war veteran spoke. Canadians were declared good soldiers held in high regard by Spanish commanding officers.[13]

Freddy had arranged for one Lucien LaTulippe to travel to Europe in 1937, gave him five dollars and told him to get a passport. LaTulippe remained in Spain till April 1938.

William Harvey Hall was a Canadian who travelled to New York City to sign up with the Abraham Lincoln Brigade. Upon his return to Toronto he was "approached by Fred Rose of Montreal who congratulated him on his decision." When he left for Spain he was given a "comradely send off by Rose." Arriving in Spain in late 1936, Hall and his "fellow compatriots were challenged by Spanish authorities and their passports confiscated and stored in an area outside Madrid." Hall was wounded in Spain. Upon his return to Canada Hall didn't seem to have anything to say about the fate of his passport.[14]

Could Freddy and Norman and the other party officials have not been aware of the Soviet passport scam? That same year there was a report of NKVD agents at a party in Moscow celebrating the arrival of bundles of passports from Spain, among them the one belonging to Witczak.[15]

In August 1946, *The Gazette* carried a story claiming that in 1936 Freddy had been involved along with a cabinet minister, Postmaster General Ernst Bertrand, in obtaining a fake passport for a Russian agent,

12. "Claim Moscow Paid $3,000 for False Canada Passport," *The Toronto Daily Star,* 16 September 1946; "Endorsing Passport Said 'Gross Stupidity', Soboloff Fined $500," *The Globe and Mail,* 14 September 1946; "Reports Falsified Records," *The Welland-Port Collborne Evening Tribune,* 30 July 1946; "Forged Passport Sensational Item." *The Winnipeg Free Press,* 16 July 1946; testimony of Henry Harris, *Royal Commission,* 1946.
13. "C.P.C National Convention, Toronto, 8–12 October 1937," RCMP, 18 October 1937.
14. RCMP report on interview with William Harvey Hall, Kitchener, Ontario, 2 November 1972.
15. Dick Sanburn, "Case of the Bogus Passport," *The Ottawa Citizen,* 23 July 1946.

Mikhail Borovoy *aka* Willy Brandis/Brandes. In his statement to the House on 13 August 1946 Bertrand said that in September 1936 Borovoy came to see him in the company of Aaron Marcovich "and another gentleman whose name I gave to the police" claiming his father, one Schulem Brandis, was naturalized in 1913, and that Brandis said he was a Hebrew teacher married to a Mary Stern. Believing all to be *kosher*, Bertrand, at the request of Aaron Marcovich, had signed a letter of recommendation in support of the Borovoy application for naturalization in the name of Brandis. Borovoy said he'd lived in Montreal from the time he entered Canada at age eight. Marcovich later admitted that Mrs. Schulem Brandis was in fact his wife's aunt! Bertrand denied in a public statement the suggestion by John Diefenbaker that Fred Rose had been a co-signer of the recommendation for naturalization: "Fred Rose's name does not appear in the file. I did not know him except long after September 1936... I never heard of Fred Rose in this affair." But how to explain Bertrand's statement to the *Gazette* that he'd known "the spy" Borovoy for five years as a resident of Canada when the man had only been in the country for little more than two weeks? Borovoy received the naturalization papers in the name of Willy Brandis on 15 September 1936 and a British passport the following October. The next day the *Gazette* reported that Freddy along with Bertrand was involved in securing the documentation for Brandis.[16]

In 1938, Borovoy/Brandis/Brandes was arrested in England in connection with an attempt to infiltrate the Woolwich Arsenal. The British and Canadian investigation of the false Brandis/Brandes passport pointed a finger not directly at Fred Rose but at Iosif Vulfovich Volodarski also Volodarsky and Wolodarsky, *aka* Armand Labis Feldman, and in turn at Freddy's link to the Ovakimyan network.

A 1940 RCMP report noted there were indications that Freddy might have been connected through his party affiliation with secret police of the Soviet Union and the 1938 Woolwich Arsenal business. The names of all the other individuals had been deleted from the docu-

---

16. Richard Jackson, "Bertrand Admits Signing Letter for Wm. Brandes," *The Ottawa Morning Journal,* 14 August 1946; "Bertrand Admits Passport Aid; Says He Was Deceived by Brandis," *The Montreal Gazette,* 14 August 1946. Said a 13 August 1946 RCMP report on the *Journal* story: "It can now be stated that William Brandis formerly known as Steinberg in New York City, is the Russian 'master spy' for whom *Fred Rose,* now an M.P., and a present member of the Cabinet acted, to obtain false citizenship and a false passport."

ment as released. There was a reference to "a mysterious [name deleted] whose activities in gathering military secrets in England resulted in the prosecution of four employees of Woolwich Arsenal in February 1938 and who is definitely known to be a Soviet Military Espionage agent. [Name deleted] is a man who has long dabbled in politics and has political connections; Fred Rose introduced [name deleted] to [name deleted] though there was no apparent reason why [name deleted] should be introduced to [name deleted] for he was only in Montreal a week or two and has never been heard of since; he was an elderly man, very short, Jewish, and had a mouthful of gold teeth."[17]

The notaries Adolph Stark and Aaron Marcovich, fake document specialists, were among Freddy's political associates in Montreal. An RCMP report dated 12 October 1940 claimed that a person arrived in Montreal from the United States and with the help of "several local 'shysters,' obtained a false birth registration certificate, and on the strength of this document a Canadian passport." Might this person have been Borovoy-Brandes/Brandis? The names of all involved were deleted. These "shysters" so-called may of course have been involved in saving the lives of individuals fleeing the Nazis, and who received little sympathy or assistance from Canadian officials. The document continues: "Investigations have shown that Fred Rose, well-known Communist, had been responsible for the beginning of the whole of these negotiations, since he had introduced [name deleted] to the various persons concerned."[18]

Freddy's role in the Brandes/Brandis affair remains cloudy. Apparently Volodarsky was the architect of the operation that produced the Canadian document for Borovoy. A key Ovakimyan operative, Volodarsky was born in the Ukraine in 1903. Trained as an engineer, in the 1920s he worked in the Soviet petroleum industry. In 1930 he was sent to London where he was put to work by the OGPU. Arrested in 1932 by Scotland Yard for espionage activity, he was deported to the USSR. Back home he joined the OGPU and was posted to the United States in 1933 as an illegal to study the American oil industry.

17. Fred Rose, *RCMP report,* 1 April 1940.
18. *RCMP report,* 12 October 1940. See too *The Shameful Years: Thirty Years of Soviet Espionage in the United States.*

Volodarsky's main cover was as Armand Labis, born in Paris in 1901, the year he said his parents emigrated to Montreal. In 1936, he secured a Canadian passport in the name of Abraham Feldman, the family name of his wife's mother. The marriage document carried the name Armand Labis Feldman, the identification on a bogus Canadian passport in his possession. In New York City, Ovakimyan had Volodarsky set up the *Round-the-World Trading Company* as an NKVD cover.

Ovakimyan had ordered Volodarsky to drive Borovoy, dispatched to the United States in 1936 by Moscow for a special assignment in England, to Montreal where the documentation scheme was organized with the assistance of Volodarsky's Montreal contacts, Adolphe Stark and Aaron Marcovich apparently via Fred Rose.

Investigation of the Brandes/Brandis passport led to Volodarsky. The NKVD obtained word of an FBI hunt for Feldman who, as did Ovakimyan, wisely resisted a recall to purge-obsessed Moscow. In April 1938, fearing that the FBI was closing in, Volodarsky-Feldman looted *Round-the World* accounts and quietly departed New York City, moving first to New Jersey with his wife and small child where he bought a small farm and did stock market trades. Sensing he needed to leave the United States, he moved to Montreal where he got a job in a small hotel, the Hotel Alberta. Volodarsky was located by the RCMP soon after the start of World War II. Fearing the Russians were closing in and wanting to avoid deportation to the USSR, he decided to cooperate, providing information about work he'd done for the NKVD including his efforts in obtaining fake Canadian passports. The RCMP passed the information he provided on to the FBI, i.e., that Ovakimyan was the senior NKVD officer in the United States. Based on that information, Ovakimyan was arrested by the FBI in May 1941 which apparently redeemed him in the eyes of his Moscow accusers who had marked him for execution.[19]

Volodarsky might have had some involvement with Ovakimyan's Montreal network of NKVD illegals. In the United States, he'd arranged payments to illegals under cover of the *Round-the-World* trading company. In an alternate version of his career, Volodarsky was identified as a

---

19. Haynes and Klehr, *Spies*. See too Duff, *A Time for Spies* and "The Canadian Case in Retrospect," *MI5 Archives*, 1951.

double agent who reported to the FBI on the Golos and Ovakimyan meetings and the activities of Elizabeth Bentley. In that version Volodarsky required no prodding to spill the beans about the Freddy-Ovakimyan link directly to the FBI.

In 1946, roughly four months after Elizabeth Bentley's November 1945 FBI interviews, Volodarsky was questioned by two Canadian royal commission officials, Roy Kellock and Gerald Fauteux. The Canadians seemed aware of Volodarsky's connection to Ovakimyan and Freddy's link to the Ovakimyan network.[20] Did they know what Bentley had told the FBI? An RCMP source: "I cannot specifically recall this particular piece of information but my best guess would be most probably it would have been. Perhaps not immediately but afterwards as the Bureau analysts and investigators ran down each lead GREGORY—Bentley's NKVD/KGB code name—provided. Our relations with the Bureau on this subject were particularly close at this time as we were all following up the Gouzenko revelations which we were sharing with them—so I have no doubt that they would have reciprocated."[21]

All of which may allow us to reconsider Fred Rose's role in the Volodarsky-Borovoy scheme. Given the dysfunctionality of some Cold War intelligence operations, agencies apparently on the same side might or might not opt to cooperate. Even today it can be difficult to understand who knew what at what level of authority *within* an agency, likewise the character of the sharing mechanism.

In the course of the 1946 Canadian interview Volodarsky explained that the NKVD, the People's Commissariat of Internal Affairs, had been established by decree on 11 July 1934, that it contained the Department of State Security, known as the OGPU or the All Union Department of Political Administration, created in 1922 to succeed the CHEKA, the Extraordinary Commission to Combat Counterrevolution, Speculation and Sabotage organized in December 1917. Volodarsky told the commissioners he worked for OGPU in New York until 1 May 1938.

He otherwise seemed to be encouraged to play dumb. He claimed he arrived in the United States in 1933, sent by the Soviet petroleum corporation. His job was to collect information on American oil industry

---

20. Jozef Volodarsky/Wolodarsky, *Royal Commission* interview, 26, 27 April 1946.
21. Private communication.

practices. He was, he said, subsequently contacted by a Soviet Secret Service operative. He allowed that he met Freddy and an OGPU agent, who went by the name "Stern," in a cafeteria in New York City at 57th & 6th Avenue in 1936, the meeting set up by his pre-Ovakimyan boss Simon Rosenberg. Freddy was apparently present to assist Volodarsky in contacting Stark to arrange for Canadian naturalization papers.

The identity of this "Stern" remains a mystery. A former RCMP counter-intelligence specialist who knew Volodarsky and is familiar with the force's Volodarsky file told me it did not appear to be either of two men named "Stern" associated with the party and Soviet espionage, neither Alfred K. Stern, a sugar daddy for left-communist causes whose party connections were minimal until 1940, and certainly not Moishe Stern, the GRU chief in the United States. Other experts have no best guesses. The interviewers for their part asked few questions and seemed simply to want Volodarsky to confirm Freddy's OGPU/NKVD connection.

We of course have only Volodarsky's account of the 1936 meeting. Did commission interrogators Kellock and Fauteux allow Volodarsky to tell the story sideways? To perhaps conceal the fact that the key person at the meeting in fact was *Freddy* with whom he was to arrange documentation for Borovoy/Stern. We need to keep in mind Borovoy's marriage to a Mary Stern on 9 September 1936, and the inclination of agents to use the family names of in-laws. Why assume Volodarsky was telling these two the truth instead of what he thought they wanted to hear?

Stern was, Volodarsky claimed, supposed to help him to obtain Canadian naturalization papers. Volodarsky said of Stern that he "spoke decent English I would say with an east side New York accent. He may have been Canadian or American....was a short Jewish fellow about 5'2" I would say with gold teeth. He had a very sloppy way about himself, unkempt in a way, offhand..." Volodarsky conceded that Ovakimyan was his superior, and that he'd gone to Montreal to meet Stark who was for the sum of $400 going to arrange for naturalization papers. There is nothing of what Freddy might have said at the meeting. At one point Freddy excused himself to make a phone call. Volodarsky claimed to be unhappy about Freddy's presence. Did he think this was something the commission interrogators wanted to hear? Stern, he claimed, said Freddy was a friend of his. As Volodarsky described it, the Stern-Freddy-Stark relationship is unclear.

A 15 October 1938 Scotland Yard report on the Borovoy/Brandis/Brandes investigation said that "…about three years ago Fred Rose (Rosenberg)…brought a man named Stern to Stark's office to ask if Stark could use his political influence to bring a family into Canada from Poland… This would indicate that Fred Rose…is also connected in some way with the conspiracy." Meaning the Woolwich Arsenal caper. In the summer of 1938, an investigation was conducted in Montreal to determine the identity of Willy Brandes. A Yard report dated 30 August 1940 said that: "…a man named Aaron Marcovich of Montreal told us that he believed Brandes had come to Canada in an automobile from New Jersey by the way of Niagara Falls, Ont. with, [or] with the help of, a man named Armand Labis Feldman. Both Brandes and Feldman had contacted Adolph Stark of Montreal. Adolph Stark told us how Fred Rose, one of the leading Communists of Canada, had introduced him to a man named Stern who had in turn introduced Feldman who in turn had introduced Brandes." A Yard report dated 3 April 1941 said that Feldman "claimed he was introduced to Fred Rosenberg [*sic*] by Stern."

Kellock and Fauteux didn't seem to care what Volodarsky knew or had done so long as he confirmed the existence of a long-time link between Freddy and OGPU/NKVD. All the while Volodarsky insisted that he was just a technical person, an innocent eager to escape Soviet clutches. He claimed he saw "Stern" in New York a half dozen times.

John Haynes, an authority on the KGB in America, responding to the question about whether "Stern" might have been a pseudonym for Jacob Golos stated: "Golos is a possibility but parts of Volodarsky's description don't match Golos. Golos was Russian, didn't come to the U.S. until his adulthood. While his English was by all reports excellent, it was not that of a native speaker. Hard to think that Volodarsky, a Russian, would not have recognized a fellow Russian from his speech…. Volodarsky may not have been entirely candid. It is clear that he left out a good deal about his activities and it is possible he may have misled on some matters."[22] Volodarsky didn't explain, at least not in that session, why or how he'd obtained a travel document in the name of Armand Labis Feldman, and was apparently not asked to. Perhaps a deal had indeed been cut: Volodarsky would incriminate Freddy and the rest of it would be forgotten. It was now 1946, both Stark and Marcovich were dead and the events Volodarsky was describing had occurred a decade earlier. Volodarsky said he met Freddy only that one time, that "Stern" was an Ovakimyan man, that he himself now lived in Montreal, that his son was a member of the Black Watch.

Might the Stern presence at the 1936 meeting have been a Volodarsky invention? The man was after all not the straightest of shooters. Odd that none of the experts are able to identify Stern.

Clearly, the RCMP had been suspicious of the party's role in Canadian passport traffic. From the 1930s through the 1960s, the Force pressed for passport reform. In 1951 an operation called *West Wind* was set up to look into the appropriation and use of Canadian passports by Soviet illegals. Passport applications from 1 January 1936 to 20 June 1940 were reviewed.[23] But by then virtually all the prize Soviet horses had galloped off into the sunset...

---

22. John Haynes, private communication.
23. Private communication.

V.

The Pact

Freddy and Canadian party head Tim Buck appeared to put all their faith in the Marxian magic history machine: capitalism goes in one end, the dictatorship of the proletariat comes out the other. Obstructing the process is the great socialist nemesis, *fascism*. As J. S. Wallace explained at the Anti-Fascist Conference in Verdun, Quebec, in October 1933 with Freddy, a member of the conference executive, in attendance: "Fascism is the medium by which the Capitalist class smashes workers' organizations and kills workers."[1]

In a 1938 pamphlet, "Fascism Over Canada: An Exposé," Freddy attempted to point out the inroads fascists had made in the country particularly in the province of Quebec. The pamphlet's prime target was Adrien Arcand and his National Social Christian Party: "The fascist leaders are plotting to destroy the democratic institutions which enable people to defend their interests against the greedy multi-millionaires." Tarred with Arcand were ministers of the Duplessis cabinet who "do not hide their fascist affiliations."[2]

---

1. Gregory S. Kealey and Reg Whitaker, *R.C.M.P. Security Bulletins: The Depression Years, Part 1, 1933–1934*, Canadian Committee on Labor History, 1993.
2. Fred Rose, "Fascism Over Canada: An Exposé," New Era Publishers, 1938

In September 1943, the party held a banquet at the Mount Royal Hotel in downtown Montreal to celebrate Freddy's Cartier election win. In speeches in English and French the defeated Bloc Populaire Canadien was roundly vilified from the head table as a fascist party. Banqueters were told that the French-Canadian population of Quebec was a "great reservoir for the Labour-Progressive Party." Put another way, Freddy and the party were playing the political game, giving full credit for the election win exclusively to Cartier's francophones, saying nothing about the riding's large bloc of Jewish voters. Elaborating on the theme, Buck rose to declare Freddy's election triumph the beginning of a surge of progressive political action. When it was his turn to speak, Freddy promised to bring legislation to the floor of the House to outlaw anti-Semitism, to improve wages and working conditions, and to grant equal rights to the nation's French-Canadian population.[3]

The place of French-Canadians, Freddy told the cheering crowd, was with the Labour-Progressive Party, that Quebec premier Maurice Duplessis would have come to terms with Hitler. But time, he said, was running out, fascists were gaining support from people fed up with the old line parties. For Freddy and his party colleagues, fascism was a rubric that pointed in every direction, at Italian devotees of Il Duce in Italy, at Hitler's Nazis, at the forces of Franco in Spain, at Blocists, local bosses and landlords, at virtually anyone out of step with the Red march of history.

In an October 1942 pamphlet "Hitler's Fifth Column in Quebec," Freddy repeated the allegation that Bloc member Jean Drapeau, the future mayor of Montreal, was a Nazi agent.[4] Drapeau was having none of it. He hired lawyer Guy Favreau and sued Freddy and the publishers of the English and French versions of the pamphlet claiming $999.00 in libelous damages and costs.

There was indeed, said one of Freddy's lawyers, G. Papineau Couture K.C., a fifth column in Quebec which presented a danger to the country. Speaking in his own defense, Freddy claimed that the successful conduct of the war was jeopardized by the principles advocated by Drapeau, in particular, his opposition to the dispatch of a Canadian

---

3. "Buck Party Marks Victory in Cartier," *The Montreal Gazette*, 20 September 1943.
4. Fred Rose, "Hitler's 5th Column in Quebec," Progress Books, 1943. A protégé of the Abbé Lionel Groulx, Jean Drapeau was elected mayor of Montreal in 1954.

force overseas and the conscription of Canadians for service abroad. His research for the pamphlet, he said, included an examination of Hitler's *Mein Kampf*, the speeches of Henri Bourassa, and many newspapers. Drapeau claimed that the paragraphs were without justification and asked that they be struck from Freddy's defense plea. Freddy replied that as a responsible citizen, author and journalist, he was privileged to write what he had written and published which did not exceed the limits of fair comment. Whatever Freddy's credentials and good faith, Drapeau countered, they did not justify libel.[5]

The case was finally settled out of court in February 1946. Drapeau was awarded costs of $500 and agreed to accept damages of $100, a sum he donated to the Montreal Lawyers' Benevolent Association.

It might have seemed a startling act of finger pointing to anyone who remembered Freddy and the party's backing of the Molotov-Ribbentrop Pact *aka* the Hitler-Stalin Pact, officially *The Treaty of Non-Aggression Between Germany and the Soviet Union*.[6] A case, said the RCMP, of the pot calling the kettle black.

Party membership cheered when in September 1939 war was declared on Nazi Germany. Tim Buck urged all-out support for the war effort to defeat Hitler. In July Freddy was pressing the government to investigate "fascist and Nazi activity" in Canada. On 19 September he denounced "the Trotskyite helpers of Hitler."[7]

The next day Stalin via a Comintern resolution spelled out the Soviet position: "The present war is an imperialist and unjust war for which the bourgeoisie of all belligerent States bear equal responsibility. In no country can the Communist Parties or the working class support the war…. The Communist Parties which acted contrary to these tactics must now immediately correct their policy." The message from Moscow

5. "A Member Prosecuted for Libel," *La Presse*, 30 November 1943. Translation of a Clipping by MHA at RCMP Headquarters; "Drapeau Asks 10 Deletions," *The Montreal Daily Star*, 30 November 1943; "Details Asked in Libel Case," *The Montreal Daily Star*, 7 February 1944; "Fred Rose Defense in Libel Suit Under Attack by Jean Drapeau," *The Montreal Gazette*, 29 March 1944; "Libel Suit Settled by Rose, Drapeau," *The Montreal Gazette*, 2 December 1946.
6. Anthony Reid and David Fisher, *The Deadly Embrace: Hitler, Stalin and the Nazi-Soviet Pact 1939–1941*, Norton, 1988. See also, Geoffrey Roberts, "The Soviet Decision for a Pact with Nazi Germany," *Soviet Studies*, Vol. 44, No. 1, 1992.
7. Freddy may not have immediately understood that the game had changed. An RCMP report dated 19 September 1939 had Freddy attacking "the Trotskyite helpers of Hitler" in a party publication.

was clear: the war against Hitler was an imperialist war that needed to be opposed.[8]

The pact guaranteeing the neutrality of the USSR in the wars Hitler had set in motion, caught the members of the CPC, uninformed about the secret negotiations and the agreement to partition Poland, off guard. Negotiations had as well produced a secret protocol that designated spheres of influence among the sovereign nations of Eastern Europe, including Finland, Romania, Lithuania, Latvia, Estonia, as well as Poland. Party faithful felt themselves trapped. The shock some felt over the pact was great. But neither Freddy nor other party leaders were prepared to offer much if any opposition. The price for doing so was expulsion or worse. Party leaders, regardless of their citizenship, could be called to Moscow to face harsh discipline including prison terms. In December 1940 some comrades were expelled from the party for what was termed "undisciplined activity" and "disruptive actions."[9]

Freddy soon recovered. In support of Stalin's message he mounted an altogether unlikely gallery of villains. The people, he said in the pamphlet *1940: A Review*, "...are not falling for the 'new world order' promised by Hitler, Mussolini, Konoye, Churchill, Bevin, Morrison, Roosevelt, Mackenzie King, Coldwell and David Lewis." In the decade that followed, the CCF's M. J. Coldwell and David Lewis ignored these verbal assaults and attempted to assist Freddy when he was overwhelmed by difficult circumstances.[10]

The RCMP reported him declaring in October 1939 that the Soviet German alliance was the finest thing that could have happened, that the Russian annexation of Eastern Poland was a great advantage in furthering "The Cause," that the British Empire would be smashed.[11]

Earlier in the year, Camillien Houde, the mayor of Montreal, had been arrested by the RCMP and interned at Camp Petawawa for inciting

8. Cited in Norman Penner, "For and Against the War," in *Canadian Communism: The Stalin Years and Beyond*, Methuen, 1988.

9. Ivan Avakumovic, "From an 'Imperialist' to a 'Just War'" in *The Communist Party in Canada*, McClelland & Stewart Ltd., 1975; "Section Bulletin," 9 December 1940, an otherwise unidentified party document. Avakumovic found that there was occasional tepid party resistance, condemnations of "German imperialism" and "German capitalism." Attacks on the British government were more frequent along with the claim that the party was opposed to "a victory of either side in this imperialist war."

10. Fred Rose, "1940: A Review," 1940.

11. From "Extract from memorandum submitted by the Royal Canadian Mounted Police recommending the detention of certain persons under regulation 21 of the Defense of Canada Regulations (June 1940).

the male citizens of Quebec to have nothing to do with the National Registration Act, the federal government's conscription legislation. The sympathy of French-Canadians, he said, was on the side of Italy not England.

Perhaps Fred Rose ought to have been taken into custody. But where was he? In March 1940 the RCMP reported he was in Montreal, of all places. What could he have been doing there? The March report was confirmed in May. In June Freddy was said to be living in the city at 3683 Hutchinson, apt. 49, the home of party members Bella and Frank Brenton. The RCMP note added that Freddy was suspected of holding a secret position in the 3rd International, that there was every indication that he might well be a member of the Russian Secret Police.[12]

To make good on his plan to attack the USSR, Hitler needed Soviet grain and raw materials; Stalin required German machinery, arms and equipment to fend off the attack. The destruction of the Soviet state was a sworn Nazi goal. Stalin's disastrous campaign in Finland might have inspired Hitler to imagine that in his scheme to acquire *Lebensraum* in the East, grain from the Ukraine, and Russian petroleum the Red Army would be a pushover.[13]

"I know how much the German nation loves its Führer," said Stalin. "He is a fine fellow. I should therefore like to drink to his health."[14] Whereupon Freddy and the party apparently wasted little time raising their glasses. Freddy likely had no idea that the polyglot von Ribbentrop had friends in Montreal, that he'd arrived in the city in 1910 and soon landed a job with the Molson's Bank, worked for a time for an engineering firm and at one point set up a wine and champagne importation business in Ottawa.

With the Soviet signature on the pact, Stalin called for a reduction in Soviet intelligence operations in Germany while at the same time pressing his German agents to obtain the secret of Hitler's political ascent.

Among those angered by the agreement was Benito Mussolini who sent Hitler a letter of rebuke for abandoning his anti-Bolshevik

---

12. Notes in RCMP files, 23 March 1940, 1 May 1940, 4 June 1940, 13 June 1940, and 12 October 1940.
13. Anthony Reid and David Fisher, *The Deadly Embrace*.
14. Christopher Andrew and Oleg Gordievsky, *KGB: The Inside Story of Its Foreign Operations from Lenin to Gorbachev*, Hodder and Stoughton, 1990.

campaign. Many Nazi Party members too were disgusted. A somewhat similarly concerned Mackenzie King wrote Hitler a long letter, but received no reply.

Apparently Stalin interpreted the 1938 capitulation to Hitler at Munich as a blow directed against the USSR. After Great Britain, France and the United States rejected his proposal to join in a collective security alliance, it seemed that, with the situation in Europe heating up, Hitler was his best bet.

In the months leading up to the signing of the pact, Hitler was constantly high on amphetamines. Near the conclusion of negotiations, he dispatched a man named Heinrich Hoffman to Moscow whose chore it was to get a photograph of Stalin's head. The *Führer* wanted to study the size and shape of Stalin's earlobes to determine whether Jewish blood flowed in the Bolshevik kingpin's veins. Alas, Joe passed the test; following a diligent study of the photographs, Adolf pronounced Joe's ears pure Aryan.[15]

Once informed the document held the required signatures, Hitler boarded a special train named *Amerika* to take him to the Polish front. The pact von Ribbentrop and Molotov signed in Moscow on 24 August 1939, lasted for 669 days, a couple of months under two years.

A week later 1.5 million German troops crossed into Poland. Thousands of Polish Jews and German communists were delivered into the clutches of the Gestapo. In March 1940, on Stalin's orders the NKVD shot and buried 22,000 Polish officers in the Katyn Forest, taken prisoner when the USSR invaded Poland.

In 1940 Soviet troops occupied northeastern Romania, Estonia, Lithuania, and Latvia. In Latvia, arrests and deportations soon followed. Of the 17,000 Latvians deported, about 12 percent were Jews, more than twice their proportion in the population. The Soviets deported 6,000 from Estonia. Soviet military bases were established in Lithuania, the largest and most populous of the Baltic States, and 17,500 Lithuanians deported.[16]

Hitler was guaranteed the tons of supplies of grain, petroleum, rubber, copper, tin, nickel, tungsten, and molybdenum, he needed to

---

15. Anthony Reid and David Fisher *op. cit.*
16. Timothy Snyder, *Bloodlands: Europe Between Hitler and Stalin*, Basic Books, 2010.

conquer Denmark, Norway, France, Belgium, and the Netherlands, all of which coincided with Nazi preparations to attack the USSR itself. In return Stalin received advanced aircraft and navy vessels. For Hitler the pact, as he had calculated, neutralized the Soviet military in the East while he sent his armies westward.

As he had promised, Stalin transferred to the Nazis many imprisoned German radicals, among them Margarete Buber-Neumann, a leading voice of German Communism. In the early afternoon of 8 February 1940 she was among a group of men and women, thirty in all that NKVD officers led to a bridge over the River Bug at Brest-Litovsk. They included German and Austrian Communists and some left-wing socialists who'd settled in the USSR in the 1930s to escape the Nazi regime. They were arrested soon after their arrival. On the bridge it was bitter cold. The prodigals bundled in fear were to be handed over to the SS. Some died in concentration camps of maltreatment, some were shot, some converted to Nazism. After six months in a Gestapo prison in Berlin, Buber-Neumann was placed in the Ravensbruck concentration camp.[17]

Stalin now stepped up his campaign to assassinate Trotsky.

That Freddy and the CPC stood four-square behind the Comintern resolution has been challenged. Norman Penner found the claim in Merrily Weisbord's *The Strangest Dream* (1983) that at a meeting of the party's Central Committee at which the message from Moscow was discussed, J. B. Salsberg and Fred Rose opposed the Comintern's position but, pressured and outnumbered, they acquiesced, had no basis in fact.[18]

Kim Philby knew but Freddy may not have that what Stalin feared most was not the Hitler regime but a coup in Germany that would replace the Nazi regime with one pro-Western and anti-Soviet.[19]

On the afternoon of 7 September 1940, the London Blitz began. For two hours German planes dropped incendiary bombs on the city, departed then returned to drop more a few hours later. There were in all 71 major bombardments. The CPC maintained its silence while 18,800 tons of high explosives rained down on the British capital. The death

---

17. Tzvetan Todorov, "The Achievement of Margarete Buber-Neumann," in *Hope and Memory: Lessons from the Twentieth Century,* trans. David Bellos, Princeton University Press, 2003.

18. Penner, *Canadian Communism: The Stalin Years and Beyond.*

19. Genrikh Borovik, *The Philby Files,* Little Brown, 1994.

toll numbers vary, but were certainly many thousands. The Blitz continued until 11 May 1941, ceasing with Hitler's order to move the bombers east in preparation for Operation Barbarossa, the assault on the Soviet Union that began the following month.[20]

In the USSR, Hitler's *fascist hyenas* became *the German authorities.* Sergei Eisenstein's *Aleksandr Nevskiy* (1938) was shelved and Eisenstein ordered to mount a Bolshoi Theatre production of the operas of Wagner. Once banished, German literature returned to Soviet library shelves.

There were Jewish Communists who backed the pact, some uneasily, some enthusiastically, among them the UJPO's Joshua Gershman: "If not for the pact the Soviet Union would not have been in the position they were….they would not have been in the position to help us… to defeat Hitler."[21]

There were those in the party, Freddy among them, who argued that Britain and France, were the true scallywags, that they had forced Stalin into a pact which bought the USSR time to muster a defense against Nazi forces, that the Nazi attack on the USSR in the summer of 1941 proved that Stalin had not become a Nazi ally.

There were Jewish Communists who claimed the pact and the portioning of Poland that followed was a blessing for Polish Jews, that the Soviet troops that occupied eastern Poland halted Hitler's eastward march, that it was in Jewish interest to oppose the imperialist war against Hitler.[22] Odd as it may seem, Jewish Communists had in effect become Nazi allies.

On 1 September 1939 German planes began bombing Polish cities. Captured Polish troops were murdered, civilians shot in large numbers. In Poland, the Wehrmacht discovered large communities of religious Jews, something they would not have encountered in Germany where a mostly assimilated Jewish population constituted *less* than one percent of the total. Jews made up ten percent of the population of Poland. Forty-

---

20. Daniel Swift, "Bomb proof," *The Financial Times,* 4 September 2010; David Johnson, "The London Blitz: *The City Ablaze,"* 1981; Ian Jack "Motley Notes," *Granta* 91, 2005.
21. Abella on Gershman.
22. Srebrnik found that Jewish Communists believed the pact and the subsequent partition of Poland would be a blessing for Poland's Jews.

five thousand Polish civilians were killed in the final four months of 1939, seven thousand of them Jews.

In *Bloodlands*, author Timothy Snyder, a professor of history at Yale University, tells us that on 17 September 1939 a half million Red Army troops crossed into Poland. But this was not to rescue Jews from the Nazis. By 1940 the Nazis unhappily found that there were now roughly two million Jews on their side of the Molotov-Ribbentrop Line. How to cleanse the Reich of their presence? Adolf Eichmann, Nazi deportation specialist, recommended to his Soviet colleagues that these Jews be transported to Birobidzhan, Stalin's Siberian zone of Jewish settlement. The scheme, however cruelly conceived, did have the unintended element of a rescue operation. Stalin would not agree; rescuing Jews from the Nazis was not among his priorities.[23]

In 1940 and 1941 millions of Jews dispossessed and displaced by the pact would be herded into ghettos, set up as temporary transit areas, and improvised labor camps in Lodz and Warsaw as a stage in a Final Solution, which the Nazis initially conceived as a deportation scheme, dispatching the Jews to the island of Madagascar. When it was evident that this was an impractical solution, that only murder could solve the problem, the USSR did not interfere.

Might the fate of the Jews of Eastern Europe have taken a different turn if the Communist parties in the United States and Canada and elsewhere had opposed the pact? It is difficult to imagine a Communist Party not obeying Comintern orders. In any event, it is unlikely that it would have made much difference to the Jews and Poles and others most directly concerned.

In June 1940 the Canadian government acted. Under the Defense of Canada Regulations and the provisions of the War Measures Act, the CPC and its affiliates were declared illegal for their opposition to the war against Germany.[24] The powers the government possessed under the act provided for internment without trial, the outlawing of political organizations, the seizure of property, and the restriction of freedom of the press.

---

23. Timothy Snyder, "Molotov-Ribbentrop Europe," *Bloodlands: Europe Between Hitler and Stalin*, Basic Books, 2010.
24. "Defense of Canada Regulations," I. O. Patenaude, Printer to the King, Ottawa, 1940.

Over 100 party members were interned. The Minister of Justice, Louis St. Laurent, issued an order that Freddy be detained. On 11 June 1940 he apparently left the country to hide out in the United States with Sam Carr.[25]

The pact ought not to have come as a surprise. The previous spring, Walter Krivitsky, a high-ranking Soviet defector, told anybody who would listen that it was right around the corner, that Stalin was a great admirer of Hitler and had been after a pact with the Führer for some time.

The Krivitsky story is set out in great detail in Gary Kern's *A Death in Washington: Walter G. Krivitsky and the Stalin Terror*. Born Samuel Ginzberg in 1899 at the edge of the Hapsburg Empire, when he defected in 1937 Krivitsky was a top GRU operative, coordinator of Soviet military espionage in Western Europe. The most important Soviet defector up to that time, Krivitsky had joined the party in 1917. A long-time socialist colleague, Ignace Poretsky, unable to bear the Soviet purges of the 1930s, wrote to the Central Committee of the Communist Party denouncing Stalin's abuse. Poretsky, who also went by the name Ignace Reiss, was soon after assassinated in Switzerland. Krivitsky was instructed to organize the murder of Poretsky's wife. On 19 November 1937 Krivitsky appealed to the French Minister of the Interior for political asylum: "I have decided not to deliver myself with sealed lips to the ordeals of the Stalinist terror which has nothing in common with the cause I call my own." Believing he had risen to number two on the Soviet hit list after Leon Trotsky and fearing assassination, Krivitsky left France for the United States, arriving in America with wife Antonia and son Alexander on 10 November 1938—*Kristallnacht*.

In a piece published in *The Saturday Evening Post* the following April, Krivitsky warned the civilized world that Hitler and Stalin would soon make a deal, that Stalin had been in pursuit of one since 1934, the Nazi destruction of Czechoslovakia a month earlier an unheeded warning. The immediate response was a vicious smear from Soviet sympathizers in America. Joining the attack on Krivitsky by Nathanael West, Irwin

---

25. Srebrnik. I have been unable to confirm that Freddy in fact left the country with Sam Carr on that date.

Shaw, and Malcolm Cowley, among a number of others, were Henry Luce's *Time* and tabloid king Walter Winchell.[26]

A Moscow friend who'd never heard of Walter Krivitsky told me that one source of Stalin's romance with Hitler was his mistrust of the British *and* the French. The terms of the Treaty of Versailles had marginalized both Germany and revolutionary Russia. After 1919, they found they had interests in common. In the late 1920s, Junkers, the German bomber works, had opened a plant in Moscow. In the 1930s, Hermann Goering ran a flying school in Smolensk that trained German and Russian pilots.

Stalin's admiration for the Führer was heightened by Hitler's 1934 purge of Nazi Party brownshirts. With that action Stalin recognized the Führer as a master dictator, a man after his own heart. If Stalin's determination to reach an agreement with Hitler had a beginning, that, Krivitsky believed, was it. Despite reports that Hitler was unshakably opposed to a deal, Stalin persisted, going so far as to attempt to woo an indifferent Adolf by establishing himself as a fighter of fascism, allied with the democracies. To reinforce that maneuver, even as the Nazis and the Japanese were working on a pact to encircle the USSR, Stalin leapt into the Spanish Civil War. Apparently, his basic aim remained an alliance with the Nazis. Krivitsky believed that the arrest and execution of Bolshevik heroes in 1938—men that Hitler loathed—was part of that increasingly desperate scheme. In February 1939, Stalin ordered a new petroleum policy, selling only to Germany and Italy, assuring Hitler of the supplies he needed for his war in Western Europe.

Warned by a Krivitsky associate that the Soviets had two agents inside the British government, the British requested a debriefing. Krivitsky agreed to travel to Great Britain via Canada. Accompanied by a member of British security, Krivitsky arrived in Montreal with his family on a Delaware-Hudson train in December 1939, registering at the Windsor Hotel as Walter Thomas. He left for England in mid-January 1940 wife and son remaining in Montreal. In a series of MI5 debriefing sessions, Krivitsky named one hundred Soviet agents worldwide, over half of them involved in delivering British secrets to the Russians.

---

26. Gary Kern (ed.) *Walter G. Krivitsky: MI5 Debriefing and Other Documents on Soviet Intelligence*, trans. and introduction by Gary Kern, Xenos Books, 2004; Gary Kern *A Death in Washington*, 2003; Walter G. Krivitsky, *In Stalin's Secret Service*, Harper Bros., 1939; Enigma Books, 2002.

Returning to Montreal at the end of February for an RCMP de-briefing, Krivitsky exposed a number of CPC members working against the allied war effort. There was a newspaper report of "scores" of arrests of men and women guilty of "acts disruptive of the progress of the war." Krivitsky probably knew something of GRU operations in Canada but not anything about Freddy, who at the time was in the employ of the NKVD.

The Krivitskys registered son Alexander at a private school, St. Georges, moved into a Westmount residence on Grosvenor Avenue and were thinking about settling in the city. Until 21 August 1940, the day Spaniard Ramón Mercader dealt Trotsky that fatal blow in Mexico. The news seemed to have unnerved Krivitsky who became convinced that he was now at the top of Stalin's hit list, that he was next, that he needed to leave Montreal without delay.

In the early morning of 10 February 1941 Krivitsky was found dead of a gunshot wound to the head in Room 532 of the Bellevue Hotel in Washington, D.C. The original suspicion was that it was a NKVD hit. The more likely explanation, biographer Kern concluded, was suicide.

By chance Krivitsky had one day run into a Soviet thug named Sergei Basov in the Horn & Hardart Automat in Times Square. Basov had somehow managed to become a naturalized American citizen. "You wouldn't dare," Krivitsky challenged, "try to kill me here." To which Basov replied that in fact he could murder Krivitsky with impunity. After tormenting Krivitsky about the horrible fate suffered by his wife's brothers, he delivered an unnerving prediction. "You will not," said Basov, "be able to live by yourself in a world in which you have never belonged."

While the pact held, Freddy, marching arm in arm with local fascist goons, was an outspoken advocate of isolationism, opposed to support from the citizens of Quebec for Canada's British and American allies. Nazi supporters and the party now shared a slogan—Keep Quebec Out of the War! It was an isolationism not so different from the one advocated by the Bloc. As Freddy put it in the pamphlet *1917–1940*: "In spite of ourselves our people of Quebec are engaged in a war which has nothing to do with us.... Many (French-Canadians) are being deceived by the web of lies that this war is for the defense of justice, liberty, democracy and Christianity." It was, Freddy insisted, a fable that "thousands of Nazi war planes will soon come to bombard our sea shores unless they are stopped in Europe." The true purpose of the war was the "domination of Britain and profits resulting from this domination for the Canadian and English financiers and industrialists." The agreement between Canada and the U.S. for joint defense was not to defend "our shores but to wage war for the control of the orient by the American and Canadian imperialists." Freddy further predicted an increase in taxes and the suppression of democratic rights: "Many will be shot in cold blood by the wealthy business people who have organized the committees of civic protection who have armed themselves in order to suppress by violence the growing resentment of the people against the war.... Our people must decide once and for all that our war must be waged here in our country against those who are responsible for our misery."[27]

The RCMP were definitely looking to put their hands on Fred Rose. Here is a partial December 1940 transcript of a who's-on-first conversation between RCMP Superintendent Bavin and Inspector Harvison

H: While Leopold was down here the other day we were talking about this [deleted] case, and he was very eager that we try to tie the activities of these O.G.P.U. agents in with the Canadian Communist Party. We have done that.

B: That is very satisfactory.

H: The man who started the whole business here was Fred Rose.

B: That's what he suspected, a contact there. Now, where is that gentleman?

H: Right here.

B: No, Fred Rose.

H: That's what we wish we knew.

B: There's no chance of getting after him?

H: Well, we're trying....Rose—we keep hearing of him around the province but we haven't been lucky enough to pick him up.

B: It would be great if we could find him wouldn't it.

H: Yes, but this ties the connection right away.[28]

---

27. Fred Rose, *1917–1940*, 1940. Originally published in French for distribution in Quebec.
28. "Conversation between Supt. Bavin and Insp. Harvison," RCMP, 17 December 1940.

While Freddy's outspoken support for the pact no doubt pleased his Moscow *aufpassers* at the same time it allowed him to return to the cause of promoting revolutionary crisis by pumping up bad feeling between Quebec and the rest of the country.[29]

At the time Freddy was backing the pact, Stalin's thugs had seized the great Russian theatre director Vsevolod Myerhold, apparently for no other reason than his opposition to socialist realism. Myerhold's letter to Molotov is well known but let me cite of few sentences from it: "The investigators began to use force on me, a sick 65-year-old man. I was made to lie face down and beaten on the soles of my feet and my spine with a rubber strap... For the next few days, when those parts of my legs were covered with extensive internal hemorrhaging, they again beat the red-blue-and-yellow bruises with the strap and the pain was so intense that it felt as if boiling water was being poured on these sensitive areas. I howled and wept from the pain. When I lay down on the cot and fell asleep, after 18 hours of interrogation, in order to go back in an hour's time for more, I was woken up by my own groaning and because I was jerking about like a patient in the last stages of typhoid fever."[30] Myerhold was sentenced to death by firing squad on 1 February 1940, the sentence likely carried out the next day.

In the last days of May 1941 the end of the pact loomed. A couple of months earlier, in March, a Nazi government directive ordered the elimination of the Bolshevik-Jewish intelligentsia. On the eve of the Nazi attack on the USSR, 21 June 1941, one last long freight train loaded with grain chugged along the track to Germany.

Operation Barbarossa began at a time when Stalin, who had taken Hitler at his word, was apparently more suspicious of Churchill than of Hitler. Stalin dismissed dozens of alerts informing him that Operation Barbarossa had begun, convinced the attack was a plot on the part of the Führer's generals he ordered his military to hold back. A week earlier, he dismissed the warning from spymaster Richard Sorge. Posing as a German journalist in Japan, Sorge had acquired access to Nazi war plans. Said Stalin: "There's this bastard who's set up factories and

29. Rose, "1940: A Review."
30. Simon Sebag Montefiore, *Stalin: The Court of the Red Czar*, Alfred A. Knopf, 2003.

brothels in Japan and even deigned to report the date of the German attack as 22 June. Are you suggesting I should believe him too?"[31]

In the early morning of 23 June General Zhukov telephoned. The Germans, said the general, are bombing our towns. The only thing the general could hear from the other end of the line was the sound of Stalin's breathing.[32]

Old line party sympathizers will say, as Jacob Golos did, that the pact with Hitler amounted to a shrewd move on Stalin's part to better prepare for the struggle against the Nazis, that the agreement prevented Hitler, cheered on by the capitalist nations, from attacking the USSR, that the motherland of Communism needed to be preserved at all costs, that the alliance was just a stalling tactic. One may find in our own time the claim that the pact was a "brilliant strategic coup" on Stalin's part.[33]

Soon after Hitler moved east, Freddy and the party shamelessly reversed direction. It was now, Freddy argued, the duty of all Canadians to oppose isolationism. In May 1942, Norman Robertson, Under-Secretary of State, Department of External Affairs, forwarded to RCMP Commissioner S. T. Wood copies of letters he'd received from Freddy. In a March letter, Freddy pointed out the apparent hostility to Canada's wartime ally, the USSR, coming from the RCMP and the Montreal Police Department's *Red Squad,* in league with local and visiting fascists, something the government ought not to tolerate. In April Freddy advised Robertson that action was needed to deal with the obstructive role Canadian fascists were playing. Interned conscription foe and one-time provincial Conservative Party head Camillien Houde might be induced to back that effort:

"I have it from good authority that Houde would like to get out of the internment camp. He has quite an ego and may not make an approach to the Liberals. Why not approach him. He'd be willing to

---

31. Montefiore. See also Dr. Dennis B. Casey, "Richard Sorge: Spy of All Spies," *Air Intelligence Agency,* Lackland AFB, Texas, October 2004. By the fall of 1940 both sides appeared to understand that the pact was living on borrowed time. To prevent if possible a Nazi attack from the west and a Japanese assault from the east, Beria put into play *Operation Snow,* a scheme to accelerate friction between the United States and Japan to lessen the chances of a Japanese attack. See Jerrold L. Schecter and Leona Schecter, *Sacred Secrets: How Soviet Intelligence Changed American History,* Brassey's 2002.
32. Anthony Reid and David Fisher.
33. George Hallam, "German-Soviet Pact was Brilliant Strategic Coup," *Financial Times,* 5/6 September 2009. See too Jan Cienski, "Polish War Wounds Still Haunt Foreign Ties," *Financial Times,* 1 September 2009; Stefan Wagstyl, "Stalin Still Looms Large Over Eastern Europe," *Financial Times,* 30 August 2009.

issue a statement in support of the war and may even be convinced to urge a YES vote. He still has a whole lot of influence in the province, especially in the cities. I'm confident that some deal could be made with Houde, and it would bring good results. The tens of thousands of unemployed that he had influence over are now employed. In contact with the workers in the factories they would become an important factor for a YES vote. Houde may even be in a position to sway some of the people who are active in the NO campaign."[34]

Freddy, who had that same month switched his espionage activity from NKVD to GRU, claimed that if he were "out in the open" he might be able to "do something to swing the YES vote, given the fact that the sentiment in the factories amongst the French-Canadian workers has not changed." The national plebiscite held in the spring of 1940 showed the country terribly divided over the question of invoking conscription, mandatory military service, Quebec and the rest of the country on opposite sides. Mackenzie King held off for three years.

Freddy's offer to help with the war effort underwent serious review. In August RCMP Commissioner Wood wrote to the justice minister Louis St. Laurent pointing out that Freddy was one of twenty Communists ordered detained under the provisions of Regulation 21 of the Defense of Canada Regulations who had remained undetained. The cases of those detained were now under review. For Freddy's conditional release to be considered, he first needed to be taken into custody. On 18 September Louis St. Laurent issued the order.[35]

On 25 September 1942 Freddy and "other important Communists" came out of hiding and gave themselves up to the RCMP in Toronto. The justice minister signed an order for Freddy to be held in the "Toronto Gaol in Toronto." Release required him to complete a questionnaire in which he conceded that: he'd been a member of the Communist Party of Canada; that he'd occupied an official position with the party; that as an official of the party he'd participated in and supported the party's subversive policies; that in the pamphlet "1940—

---

34. Correspondence, Norman Robertson to S. T. Wood, 1 May 1942; Correspondence Fred Rose to Norman Robertson, 23 March 1942; 15 April 1942.
35. Correspondence, S. T. Wood to Louis St. Laurent, 15 August 1942; Louis St. Laurent, Order for the detention of Fred Rose made under the authority of regulation 21 of the Defense of Canada Regulations, 18 September 1942.

A Review" he disloyally opposed the Canadian-U.S.A. Defense alliance; that in the pamphlet *1917–1940* he attacked Canada's war effort and expressed disloyal statements; and that his disloyal activities, being designed to weaken Canada's war effort, were of assistance and benefit to the enemy.[36]

The RCMP then forwarded to the justice minister a "Brief covering our knowledge of the activities of Fred ROSENBERG—ROSE." The brief, detailing Freddy's personal and political history, was a formality containing little that was new. A member of the Force would attend Freddy's appeal hearing and would present evidence of Freddy's activities as recorded in the files of the *Red Squad,* including the claim that during the March 1940 Dole Strike, Freddy had instructed the union leader that "the time had arrived not to 'pull punches' to keep strike breakers from going to work, meaning that strong-arm methods had to be used in connection with the strike."[37]

During a hearing at the Don Gaol on 2 October 1942, Freddy claimed that "many misunderstandings" had been cleared up, that he now realized the war was a "just war" that was being undermined by fascist elements in Quebec, that there was now a "political pot boiling" in Quebec of fascists stirring up anti-British sentiments, and he thought that "if he were free to circulate amongst the workers of that Province he might be able to minimize its effect and thereby contribute to the National Unity." The judge believed Freddy was exaggerating his influence, but decided that freeing him would get the party behind the war.[38]

On 6 October 1942 the justice minister relayed to RCMP Commissioner Wood the recommendation of an Advisory Committee that Freddy be released with certain conditions: he was to report to the RCMP in Montreal twice a week, he was not to participate in any activities of the Communist Party of Canada, and that prior to his release he sign an undertaking to abide by these conditions. Which he did that same day.[39]

---

36. Fred Rose, Interrogation forms duly completed, 28 September 1942.
37. F. J. Mead, Asst. Commr. for Commissioner to the Deputy Minister, Department of Justice, "Brief covering our knowledge of the activities of Fred ROSENBERG ROSE," 24 September 1942.
38. "In the matter of Fred Rosenberg alias Rose," Don Jail, 2 October 1942.
39. Correspondence, Louis St. Laurent, Minister of Justice to S. T. Wood, The Commissioner, Royal Canadian Mounted Police, Ottawa, 6 October 1942.

As it turned out, Camillien Houde was not prepared to go as far as Freddy was and wasn't released from internment, altogether unrepentant, until 1944.

In the course of the 1943 election campaign in Cartier, Freddy had unapologetically publicized the endorsement he'd received from Fina Nelson, a woman whose son Willie had been killed in action serving with the RAF at a time when the party may have opposed Canadian participation in the war. She provided the campaign with a strong letter of support, addressed to "the mothers and fathers of Cartier.... Fred Rose fought the crime of Munich that made Hitler strong. Where were the others then? Where was the voice of Mr. Phillips and Mr. Lewis then?.... On August 9th—this coming Monday—you have a chance to strike a blow for everything my Willie loved." In 1944, the LPP paid tribute to a "fallen comrade" one Muni Erlick who gave his life "in the battle against the Nazi beast." Freddy's 1945 campaign literature spoke of a boy's body picked up "on the battlefield deep inside Germany. His dog-tags and his identification papers had been ripped from his body by the shell which killed him." A boy "who died for Canada, to keep the murderous Nazis out of the land he loved."[40]

Expressions of dissatisfaction over the inconsistent line the party had taken were dismissed as the work of Trotskyites and the CCF. The Russians were now allies in the war against Hitler and it was the duty, Freddy argued, of all Canadians to oppose the "false and dangerous isolationist doctrines of *Le Devoir* and Bourassa." The war, he said, "is at a historic turning point. Hitler thought that he would be sailing up our St. Lawrence River to plant his crooked Swastika of fascist slavery on Mount Royal, to make our Canada a Nazi colony... Quebec today engages in a righteous, just war for national existence. Even after the USSR joined the struggle against Hitler, the Kremlin above all feared the overthrow of the Nazi regime by anti-Soviet, pro-Western forces inside Germany."[41]

In 1944, the MP Fred Rose demanded a royal commission to in-

---

40. Fina Nelson, "To the mothers and fathers of Cartier." "The LPP Pays Tribute to a Fallen Comrade," *The Canadian Tribune,* 9 September 1944; RCMP report, 22 May 1945.
41. Fred Rose, *Make 1942 a Happy and Victorious New Year,* a translation of "Anne Heureuse et Victorieuse" January 1942, a pamphlet designed to explain the party's policy switch to French Canada. See too, Fred Rose, "Hitler's Fifth Column in Quebec," Progress Publishing Company, 1942.

vestigate the origins in Canada of pro-fascist and Nazi propaganda. A year later he protested the proposed release of local Nazi Adrien Arcand, arguing in a telegram to the acting justice minister that Arcand and his party had been directly linked with Hitler. Freddy attacked the British Minister of Home Security, Herbert Morrison, for the unconditional release from confinement of Captain Archibald Henry Maule Ramsay, a British Army officer who in the late 1930s had expressed strident anti-Semitic views. Ramsay ought, said Freddy, to be delivered to "the bar of justice where he deserves to stand alongside Hitler, Himmler, Goering, Goebbels, Hess, Mussolini…and all the other war criminals who sought to crush freedom throughout the world."[42]

When the war ended, Canadians surveyed rated Stalin among the most admired of world figures, a mere two points below President Harry Truman, only one point below the king and queen of England.[43]

---

42. "A Royal Commission Needed," editorial, *The Ottawa Citizen*, 5 July 1944; "Return Ramsay to Cell, Calls Fred Rose, MP," *The Canadian Tribune,* 7 October 1944.
43. Robert Teigrob, *Warming up to the Cold War*, University of Toronto Press, 2009.

VI.

Igor Flees

"History is punctuated by spies, defectors and others who revealed the most inflammatory secrets of their age."

John Burns
The New York Times

It remained for Freddy to be done in not by his political chameleon act but by Igor Sergeievich Gouzenko, a Soviet citizen desperate to escape the sort of regime Freddy was striving to establish in Canada. The unraveling of Freddy began on 5 September 1945, a month less a day after the bombing of Hiroshima, three days after the formal Japanese surrender on the battleship USS *Missouri* in Tokyo Bay. On this pleasant, late summer Ottawa evening, the temperature about 70 degrees Fahrenheit, the twenty-six year old Soviet encryption specialist working under diplomatic cover left the Soviet embassy at 285 Charlotte Street for the last time with a shirtful of documents. A few years later he remembered the evening as "unseasonably hot and sultry." Aware of the dangerous course he was embarking on, he'd armed himself with a Lebel revolver, a French Foreign Legion issue weapon.[1]

The documents under his shirt, all in Cyrillic script, all authentic, were intended to buy him and his wife Svetlana and infant son Andrei safe haven in Canada by revealing that the embassy was a front for an elaborate espionage scheme to acquire atomic bomb secrets for the USSR. The Soviets had after all spied on their wartime allies right through the war, allies they regarded as future enemies.

Igor now looking west, Freddy gazing ever eastward...

On a July afternoon in 1944 Igor had been called in to see his superior, Col. Nikolai Zabotin. A GRU lieutenant, Igor, code name *Klark*, had absent-mindedly left some drafts of dispatches sitting on the desk of his work area, a small office, number 12, in an area on the embassy's second floor, cut off from rest of the premises by double steel doors. The papers were discovered by an embassy charlady who turned them over to the ambassador. Igor had in the past been spoken to by Zabotin about tardiness. There was also a question about his having chosen to live in an apartment building apart from his Soviet colleagues. For reasons, said Zabotin, unstated, the immediate recall of you and your family has been ordered by the Director. The recall order had been initiated by GRU Deputy Director Mikhail Milshtein following a visit to the Ottawa embassy.[2]

For Igor it was the worst kind of bad news. Recall to Stalinland could amount to a death sentence. Seeing the writing on the wall, Igor collected the drafts of cables sent to Moscow, cables received from Moscow, and sheets from Col. Zabotin's notebook to trade for asylum.

In one account, Igor claimed he left the embassy the evening of 5 September with 109 documents hidden in his shirt, some more than one page. In a subsequent RCMP debriefing, he said he'd begun stashing some of the documents in his Somerset Street apartment while the escape plan was in progress. In a later account the some became a smaller number, two. Igor's documents, the total number perhaps in fact exceeding 200, revealed that Freddy, referred to in 14 of the documents,

---

1. Amy Knight, "The Defection," in *How the Cold War Began: The Gouzenko Affair and the Hunt for Soviet Spies*, McClelland & Stewart Ltd., 2005; "Miscellaneous Historical Items: Igor Gouzenko's Gun," *CSIS*, 26 September 2005.
2. Schecter & Schecter, *Sacred Secrets*. Jerrold Schecter told me in an email that his source was the late Anatoli Sudoplatov.

ran a network of Canadian agents that included scientists, professors, military people, and government employees.[3]

With Col. Zabotin away at a National Film Board screening, Igor's next move was to board a city tram for the offices of *The Ottawa Journal*. In one version of Igor's visits to the paper—there was more than one— the *Journal*'s night editor did not see that a great scoop had landed on his desk. People at the paper that evening recalled the episode differently. The Russian, they said, spread no documents across a reporter's desk, appeared petrified with fright, spoke broken English with a thick Russian accent, and was virtually incoherent.[4]

Did Igor attempt to cover up the embarrassment of his poor initial showing? Was *Journal* staff looking to deflect ridicule for blowing a big story?

Whatever really happened at the *Journal* that evening matters less than how Igor Gouzenko ended up in RCMP custody the morning of 7 September 1945, less than 48 hours later, when neither the Russians *nor* the Canadian prime minister wanted him there and so became a key witness in the trial of Fred Rose for conspiracy to violate the Official Secrets Act of Canada.

When on the morning of 6 September 1945 Norman Robertson, Under-Secretary of State in the Department of External Affairs, learned that Igor Gouzenko, his wife Svetlana, infant son Andrei, and a collection of Soviet documents were sitting in the outer office of the Minister of Justice, Louis St. Laurent, he hurried off in the company of an assistant to inform the prime minister.

Robertson, who appears to have been notified as soon as Igor showed up in the justice minister's office, may have been onto the case the previous evening.

The prime minister didn't care for trouble and this Gouzenko business looked like a considerable amount. A dedicated diarist, Mackenzie King began keeping a secret record of the details of the Gouzenko defection. The first entry is dated 6 September 1945, the last one

---

3. Fred Rose cover names DEBOISE, DeBOUZ in *Corby Case* documents 1, 11, 18, 26, 35, 37, 49, 50, 53, 55, 60, 61, 62, 64. The RCMP determined that the Ottawa-Moscow cable traffic was being handled by C. N. Telegraphs and C. P. Telegraphs, the latter having received the lion's share of the business. "Re Corby Case," TOP SECRET, RCMP, Ottawa, 1 May 1946.

4. John Sawatsky, *Gouzenko: The Untold Story*, Macmillan, 1984.

9 November 1945. The entries from 10 November to 31 December 1945 are for the time being missing or at any rate inaccessible.[5]

Said the prime minister to his diary on Thursday, 6 September 1945:

> To my surprise, I was met by Robertson and Wrong, both looking very serious. Robertson said that a most terrible thing had happened. It was like a bomb on top of everything and one could not say how serious it might be or to what it might lead. He then told me that this morning, just after an hour or so earlier, a man had turned up with his wife at the office of the Minister of Justice. He asked to see the Minister. He said he was from the Russian Embassy. That he was threatened with deportation and that once deported that would mean certain death. That the Russian democracy was different from ours..... He went on to say that he had in his possession documents that he had taken from the Embassy and was prepared to give to the Government. They would be seen to disclose that Russia had her spies and secret service people in Canada and in the U.S. and was practicing a species of espionage. That some of these men were around Stettinius in the States, and that one was in our own Research Laboratories here assumedly seeking to get secret information with regard to the atomic bomb.... Robertson and Wrong were asking my advice, whether they should not have the mounted police take him in hand and secure the documents which he had. The man when told that the Minister of Justice would not see him, then said he would have to commit suicide right there.... I said to both Robertson and Wrong that I thought we should be extremely careful in becoming a party to any course of action which would link the govt of Canada with this matter in a manner which might cause Russia to feel that we had performed an unfriendly act.

Humphrey Hume Wrong was Robertson's assistant, Edward Reilly Stettinius the American secretary of state. Apparently King had always liked Robertson though the feeling was not mutual.

Robertson had been told that Igor was threatening suicide; it is not clear whether he knew Igor was carrying a piece. Mackenzie King's first instruction to Robertson was to do nothing, that Igor might be a "crank trying to preserve his own life, that the man had in some way incurred the displeasure of the Embassy and [was] really seeking to shield himself. I do not believe his story about...treachery." Intrigued by the possibility

---

5. Mackenzie King's *Separate Diary of the Gouzenko Affair.* The pages of this secret and confidential diary are reproduced as an appendix at the end of the last volume we have of the 1945 Diary as SECRET AND CONFIDENTIAL DIARY RELATING TO RUSSIAN ESPIONAGE ACTIVITIES – SEPTEMBER 6 TO OCTOBER 31, 1945. J. W. Pickersgill and D. F. Forster, *The Mackenzie King Record,* vol. 3, 1945–1946, University of Toronto Press, 1970.

that the cipher clerk had absconded with the Russian codes, Robertson read the situation differently. For Robertson, the prize was the Soviet code book or, if that was not among the documents, Igor's knowledge of the codes. He told the prime minister he had no idea if the code book was among the material Igor was offering to turn over. Said Mackenzie King: "For us to come into possession of a secret code book—of a Russian secret code book—would be a source of major complications."

Robertson thought of getting the police to seize the papers. Later in the day, hearing that a desperate Igor had returned to his apartment, Mackenzie King told Robertson to keep an eye on things "to instruct a Secret Service man in plain clothes to watch the premises. Should a suicide occur the city police were to follow in and secure what there was in the way of documents." At one point Mackenzie King, to cover his bases, contemplated requesting a private audience with Stalin to beg his patience and understanding.

Igor provided the RCMP with a detailed account of the events of 5, 6, and 7 September 1945. At the time he was probably unfamiliar with all the people he'd dealt with in the period that began the evening of 5 September and with some of the related details, and perhaps understandably a little confused. On the other hand, his initial account seems otherwise remarkably coherent. The allegation that he arrived at RCMP headquarters the morning of 7 September in a crazed state doesn't appear to be justified.[6]

> 5 September: After turning over in my mind a hundred times the question of where I should go with my statement, I came to the conclusion that this must be made to a newspaper, in order that the whole matter become known to the Canadian people and that public opinion in Canada should demand action from the Canadian Government.... I considered that it was dangerous for the whole undertaking to turn to the R.C.M. Police at first as...if there were a Soviet agent there and all this subject were turned over to him, he would be able to direct it into a channel favorable to Soviet Intelligence....when I came out of the Soviet Embassy building at 8.30 p.m. ... I boarded a street car and arrived at the building of the newspaper —Ottawa Journal..... The chief Editor of the paper... was on the sixth floor. On arriving at the sixth floor, however, I was undecided about submitting my statement and went down in the elevator and walked home..... After drinking a cup of tea I returned to the building of the "Ottawa Journal"...the Chief Editor was not there then... I turned to an elderly

6. Amy Knight, *The Gouzenko Affair.*

man...who was pointed out to me as the senior among those present at the time. I told him the gist of the matter....he said he had no authority to print my statement and that it would be best to go to the Justice building to the Royal Canadian Mounted Police or to wait until morning when the Chief Editor would come.... I decided to go to the Justice building.... I asked the man on duty...where I could see the Minister of Justice.... I left the Justice Building that evening without seeing the Minister....

6 September: The following morning I came to the Justice Building with my wife and child. On learning from the man on duty where the office of the Minister of Justice was located we went there. Only a secretary...was there. He said that the Minister of Justice was probably in the Parliament Buildings. He conducted us to the office of the Minister of Justice in the Parliament Buildings where he introduced us to the personal secretary of the Minister of Justice...to whom I outlined briefly the gist of the matter, pointing out that I wished to make a statement to the Minister of Justice personally....he told me the Minister of Justice would be in the Justice Building. Placing us in an automobile, he drove us to the Justice building and conducted us to the previously mentioned office of the secretary of the Department of Justice and, after telling us to wait, went out somewhere. We waited about two hours. Eventually the secretary of the Department of Justice returned and said that the Minister of Justice could not receive us.....my wife and I decided to go again to the editorial office of the newspaper the "Ottawa Journal"....the Chief Editor was not there. We were met by a lady reporter whom I informed that I wished to break away from the Soviet regime.... She turned for advice to one of the employees who, evidently, was the senior there. He advised me to apply to the bureau of naturalization of the R.C.M. Police. On arriving at the bureau of naturalization I again repeated the gist of the matter to the head of this bureau. The head of the bureau advised me to go to a Magistrate's office on Nicholas Street. I asked him to give me protection. He did not give any.... As it was already mid-day and our child had not been fed yet and was very tired and sleepy, we went home. We did not go into our apartment, as we considered it dangerous to do so, but to the apartment of an English acquaintance, Mrs. Bourke, who lives in a neighboring house.... We did not tell her anything except that we said we had decided to go to the city together to shop and asked that our child might sleep with her and if she would look after him during that time. Arriving by street car on Nicholas Street we entered the Magistrate's building. The man to whom we had been sent was not there. His office was locked as it was lunch hour. A little later his secretary came.... She listened to us and then said she would consult with someone.... For a long time she tried to come to some arrangement with acquainted editors, correspondents of newspapers (Citizen, Ottawa Journal, and a French newspaper) and with a Catholic

priest. Not one of them decided to print my statement. However, one correspondent (from the Ottawa Journal) came himself and listened to me. He asked me to show him the documents. I showed him the dossier of SAM CARR. He advised me to go to Inspector Leopold and gave me his address. The secretary asked me if I had good acquaintances in Canada with whom I could hide while she obtained for me a landing card. I replied that such acquaintances could hardly be found. She explained to me the whole procedure of naturalization, supplied me with an application and told me to complete it and submit two photographs. When we left the building of the magistrate it was already 5 o'clock p.m. of September 6th.... When we came to our neighbor we found that the child had awakened.... After a little while my wife entered our apartment through the back door on the balcony. On her return she told me that she found nothing suspicious there and that I could go in with the child.... In the apartment I lay down on the bed, extremely tired..... On a bench in the park I saw two people who once in a while glanced at the windows of my apartment. Sometime later (about 6 to 6.30) someone knocked on the door of my apartment. I did not answer. The knocking continued for about 10 to 15 minutes. As the child ran across our living room, whoever was knocking was convinced we were at home. In the end he called me by name—just once. I did not reply. From the voice I recognized LAVRENTIEV, a young man who arrived to work in Canada in the apparatus of the Military Attaché as the second chauffeur..... On receiving no reply he went away. My wife and I decided it was dangerous to leave the child in our apartment. She suggested leaving the child for the night with our neighbor in the same house. Leaving our apartment by the back door on the balcony I climbed over the balcony of our neighbor, who was at the time on the balcony with his wife and child. My neighbor was a military man..... I told him briefly what was the matter and asked him if we could leave the child with him for the night.... I climbed back over the balcony to my apartment and my neighbor came out on his balcony. At that moment a tall man in a dark suit approached my balcony....on seeing there was another door there, went away. When he saw this, my neighbor said: I shall go and call the police. He mounted his bicycle and went for the police. The other neighbor, a lady in the apartment opposite mine in the same house, invited us to spend the night in her apartment. Together with the child we went into her apartment. By that time the police had arrived. After listening to what was involved he said that a police car would be on duty in the park all night. If anything should happen, we must give a signal—snap the light out in the bathroom. We went to bed. At approximately 12 o'clock the noise of an arriving car was heard.... The lady of the house snapped off the light in the bathroom, this giving the police the signal.... I looked out of the window and saw that the police car had not arrived.... (As it was explained later, the policemen had gone for lunch.) My wife, who was looking through the keyhole saw how PAVLOV, ROGOV, ANGELOV, and FARA-FONTOV broke the lock of our apartment....they entered my apartment, switched on the light and a little later put it out. The police car arrived at that moment. The police opened the door of my apartment, switched on the light and saw how PAVLOV, ROGOV, ANGELOV and FARA-FONTOV crawled out from behind the furniture.... The policeman asked them for their names and after looking at their documents remained in doubt. We heard how he repeated several times: I don't know what to do with you, to which PAVLOV replied: Let us go and that is all. Finally the policeman allowed them to go. The policeman remained on duty with us.... Soon after this an Inspector of the City Police arrived. He listened to me and on learning that I wished to make a statement to the R. C. M. Police, said that he would drive me himself to the building...at 11 o'clock next morning. At 4 o'clock in the morning someone knocked at the door.... The policeman came out to see.... This time it was GORSHKOV, the chauffer of the Military Attaché. The policeman looked at his certificate and allowed him to go.

7 September: In the morning of September 7th the Inspector of the City Police escorted by two policemen drove me to R .C. M. Police where I finally was able to make my statement.[7]

This account was composed on 7 September with, it is fair to assume, some language help, for members of the RCMP identified as Inspector John Leopold, Inspector William Williams and Superintendent Charles Edward Rivett-Carnac. When on 6 September Igor and Svetlana walked into the office of Crown Attorney Raoul Mercier, Svetlana Gouzenko was in tears and Igor was on the verge of a nervous collapse. At a royal commission hearing, Mercier's secretary testified that the Gouzenkos produced a bulky packet they claimed contained atomic bomb data taken from the embassy. When Mercier arrived at the office he telephoned a government official. I advise you, said the official, to get rid of those people immediately. Finally, after making any number of phone calls, late that afternoon, Mercier's secretary was able to arrange a meeting between the Gouzenkos and the RCMP for the following morning.[8]

---

7. "Gouzenko Statement; Account of Steps Taken by Corby in Ottawa on September 5th, 6th, and 7th, *1945,*" *W. L. M. King Papers, Memoranda and Notes, 1940–1950*, Volume 390, pages C274151–C274154.
8. Joe Finn, "Atomic Bomb Data Given to Attorney," *The Ottawa Citizen*, 18 February 1946.

Igor's version was otherwise fully supported by witnesses directly involved in the events of 5, 6, and 7 September.[9]

Apparently KGB security chief Vitalii Pavlov was unaware of the
actions Igor had taken, that he'd been to government offices and discussed his plight with a neighbor, a Canadian Air Force officer named
Harold Main, only a few hours earlier, that both local and federal police
had apparently been alerted to the fact that Igor felt himself to be in
enormous danger, that Igor had taken refuge in the apartment of
another resident, and above all that Norman Robertson had asked the
RCMP to keep Igor under close surveillance and was throughout the day
receiving detailed updates.

Igor had told the Mains he feared for his life, that the Russians were
going to try to kill him and his wife, that they were trying to steal the
secrets of the atom bomb and start WWIII, that he had a list of the
names of the people involved, a list that included Canadian government
personnel.

Hearing about Igor's predicament a Mrs. Elliott, who lived at no. 6
on the same floor, assured the Gouzenkos that they could stay with her,
that she had more room than the Mains; her husband was away at work,
and wouldn't return till morning. Mrs. Elliott's apartment was directly
across the hall from theirs.

Main remembered that at around 8 p.m. when he was out on the
back veranda talking to Igor, Igor said he saw a man approaching the
building by the back laneway. In fact, the man was an RCMP sergeant,
Cecil Bayfield, sent by Robertson to keep an eye on the human traffic
moving in and out of the building.

Once Igor and his family were settled in Mrs. Elliott's apartment
Main, who didn't have a phone, went by bicycle to report the matter to
the Ottawa police. It was about 9 p.m. At the station, Main spoke to
Inspector of Detectives, Duncan MacDonnell. He told MacDonnell that
Igor, a neighbor and a member of the Russian legation, feared for his
life. MacDonnell got in touch with Inspector William Williams of the
RCMP, in charge of the criminal investigation branch. It was apparently

---

9. The account that follows of how Igor Gouzenko was taken into protective custody by the RCMP is based
on statements by the individuals here named to the *Royal Commission to Investigate the facts Relating to the
Circumstances Surrounding the Communication by Public Officials and Other Persons in Positions of Trust of Secret and
Confidential Information to Agents of a Foreign Power, 1946.*

the first contact Ottawa city police had with the RCMP. MacDonnell then instructed Sergeant Major Lee of the city police to drive over to 511 Somerset with two officers, John McCullough and Thomas Walsh.

The three local cops arrived at 511 at roughly 9:25 p.m. A distraught Igor told McCullough and Walsh that people were following him, that he thought they were in the area of the apartment building. McCullough went down to the car and got Lee to come up to talk to the frightened man. Lee worked out a signal with Mrs. Elliott: if anything happened she was to turn off the bathroom light. The sergeant then sent one of the constables for a handgun, thinking that the presence of a cop with a gun might calm Igor down. Igor said nothing about the piece in his possession.

Ten minutes or so later Williams showed up at MacDonnell's office. Williams asked MacDonnell if a Russian had come to see him with a complaint. No, said MacDonnell, not a Russian, but a Canadian soldier with a story about a Russian. Williams said he knew about Igor, that Igor had been to the RCMP earlier in the day. Perhaps he'd heard about the phone call and confused it with a visit. Williams revealed he'd received instructions to keep tabs on the Russian, that at roughly 4:45 p.m. he'd observed Igor emerging from the Court House on Nicholas Street.

It was about 11:40 p.m. Main said when he heard the sound of knocking on Igor's apartment door. Thinking it was the police, Main opened his own door to find three Russians standing there, one in uniform. A fellow of about thirty in plain clothes, later identified as Pavlov, asked Main if he knew where Igor was. Main said he didn't and shut his door. Igor was not in his apartment at the time but in Mrs. Elliot's windowless dinette area. Svetlana was observing the action through the Elliott apartment door keyhole. Main said he heard another knock at Igor's door, then sounds of the Russians going down the stairs, as if leaving the building.

It might have been five minutes, maybe less, before the Russians returned. Now there were four, later identified as Pavlov, Pavel Angelov, a member of the Military Attaché's staff, Alexander Faranfontov, a KGB cipher clerk, and Lt. Col. Rogov. Main heard someone jimmying open the door to Igor's apartment.

Looking through the keyhole Svetlana recognized Pavlov. That man, she said, is the chief of the Russian Gestapo in Canada. I never dreamed he would come himself.

Mrs. Elliott turned off the bathroom light, the agreed upon signal in the event of trouble. When no one showed up Mrs. Elliott phoned the police.

Arriving on the scene, Walsh and McCullough found the four Russians ransacking Igor's apartment. Pavlov demanded to know who'd put in the call to the police. Igor was in Toronto he said, and they were there to get some important papers that belonged to them, that the apartment was Soviet property and they had a right to be there, that they had the key. Pavlov insisted the city cops leave the apartment immediately. When McCullough asked Pavlov why, if he and his colleagues had permission to be there and had a key, they had broken in. Pavlov exploded, claiming a diplomatic insult.

Mrs. Elliott said she had to hold on to Svetlana because once the police arrived, Svetlana wanted to go out and confront the Russians. Igor had left the dinette area and taken up a position at the Elliott apartment keyhole.

One of the constables phoned the station from Mrs. Elliott's apartment to notify Inspector MacDonnell who arrived at 511 with Lee and met the two constables and the four Russians in apartment no. 4. It was now roughly a quarter past midnight. MacDonnell, who didn't think they could hold the Russians, decided he would contact the RCMP. MacDonnell asked the Russians to remain, left Walsh and McCullough with them and went to phone Williams whose line was busy. MacDonnell said it took him a considerable time before he reached Williams. Who was Williams on the phone with? MacDonnell didn't say, perhaps he didn't know. Neither did he say what he and Williams talked about, only that by the time he returned to apt. 4, the Russians had left. Seeing them leave upset Igor. The scene in the apartment had gone on for about a half-hour.

MacDonnell, after making the phone call to Williams, went back to 511 to talk to Igor and Svetlana, both now in a highly agitated state. Igor explained he had some documents he wanted to turn over to the government. Walsh and McCullough on orders from MacDonnell remained with Igor the rest of the night.

After the break-in Svetlana went back into their apartment with one of the officers. Everything, she said, was all right, the Russians hadn't found the documents, which in their confusion the Gouzenkos had left in the apartment. MacDonnell then went to consult with Williams at his home. Together they drove back to 511. Williams remained in the car. MacDonnell went up to speak to Igor who said he wanted to see the RCMP. Williams had apparently been instructed to take no action that would make it appear that Igor had been seized by the Canadian government.

MacDonnell went back to tell Williams what had happened. Williams asked MacDonnell if he would go with him to see an RCMP intelligence officer. Which they did. MacDonnell explained the evening's events to the unidentified officer. Bayfield? MacDonnell and Williams then returned to 511. It was now near one a.m. MacDonnell said that as he was getting out of the car he saw Walsh following two men. MacDonnell asked them who they were. It turned out they were from External Affairs. Williams said he recognized one of them. The man, unidentified, told Williams that Norman Robertson wanted to see him at his home.

MacDonnell and Williams then drove to Robertson's home. After MacDonnell told Robertson what had happened, Robertson asked him if Igor wanted to see the RCMP. MacDonnell said he did, also that the Ottawa cops were giving him protection that night. Robertson said that if Igor wanted to see the RCMP not to bring him in until ten the next morning or shortly after. The instruction about the overnight delay was not explained. Did Robertson believe he needed to confer with the prime minister? MacDonnell returned to 511, and went up and spoke to Igor again. MacDonnell asked Igor about the documents, if they were copies or originals. Originals, said Igor. Igor then offered to show them to MacDonnell. MacDonnell said to leave that until he saw the RCMP in the morning.

Igor recalled that at 4 o'clock in the morning there was another knock at the apartment door.

One of the cops came out to see what was happening. It was Gorshkov, the first chauffeur of the Military Attaché. The policeman examined his papers and allowed him to leave.

Evy Wilson, a Gouzenko daughter, told me that Soviet embassy chauffeurs were in fact senior Russian officials, dangerous men disguised as lowly functionaries.

About 7 a.m. Mr. Elliott returned home. The Gouzenkos left the Elliott's apartment for their own apartment with the two Ottawa cops. At 10 a.m. MacDonnell and the two police officers drove Igor to Williams' office in the Justice Building. Svetlana and Andrei remained at 511. At the Justice Building, MacDonnell escorted Igor to the office of Acting Director of Criminal Investigations, Superintendent C. E. Rivett-Carnac. Present was John Leopold, who spoke Russian. Leopold asked Igor what he wanted. Igor told his story and asked that the family be taken into protective custody as he feared for his safety and that of his wife and child. He had, Igor said, information he wanted to give the police and produced the documents. Rivett-Carnac suggested the assistance of a translator was required to help with the contents of the documents.

Igor may have been a little confused, certainly anxious. He'd been sent back out into the streets of Ottawa the previous day. Could it happen again? To give Igor the opportunity to calm down, an interview with John Leopold was arranged for the afternoon. Williams did not attend the interview. Williams recalled that when Igor arrived at his office the Russian had in his possession, concealed in his overcoat, a bundle of papers, the nature of which would he said support his allegations concerning the espionage being conducted by the Soviet Union.

John Leopold said he met Igor for the first time the morning of 7 September 1945 at 10:45 a.m. at the Justice Building. Igor produced the documents, the documents were examined and photostatted. Leopold kept the photostats, the originals were turned over to Robertson for safe keeping and stashed in a Corby's whiskey box in his office. Thus did the Igor affair acquire the *nom de défection* Corby.

Igor was at some point on 6 September supposed to have had a telephone conversation with the RCMP's John Leopold who'd agreed to meet him at 9:30 the next morning at RCMP headquarters in the Justice Building. Perhaps it was a conversation that had taken place in Raoul Mercier's office.

Igor believed the KGB chief Vitalii Pavlov, responsible for embassy security, to be a fellow capable of anything, including depositing his body in an embassy incinerator. It was with Pavlov in mind that Igor said of the KGB: They prefer to murder ten innocent people if they can catch one who might be guilty. Igor asked his wife Svetlana to keep the documents in her handbag in the event that they might run into Pavlov somewhere.

Vitalii Pavlov was well-known in Ottawa circles. Charles Ritchie writing in *The Siren Years*, a memoir about his life in government, recalled a February 1945 dinner party for External Affairs people and foreign diplomats at which Pavlov was present. Ritchie described the Russian as resembling Harpo Marx—but with fanatical eyes. Pavlov, he recalled, launched into an attack on his External Affairs hosts and Canada. The country, he said, was stifled by the church and owned by Americans, and why didn't the head of the department's European Division speak Russian.[10]

A favorite version of how Igor, his wife and infant son were welcomed in from the cold has Norman Robertson seeking the advice of a high-ranking British intelligence official that evening.

Robertson, whose view of the defection seemed from the beginning to differ substantially from that of the prime minister, had instructed the RCMP to keep a close eye on the Russian's movements. A former RCMP staff sergeant, Cecil Bayfield, told journalist John Sawatsky that in the late evening of 5 September 1945 information had been received about the Gouzenko defection, i.e., before Gouzenko found his way to the outer office of the Minister of Justice.[11]

On 6 September 1945, Mackenzie King informed his diary that: "… the head of the British Secret Service arrived at the Seignory [*sic*] Club today. Robertson was going down to see him tonight. I told him he should stay and make this individual come to Ottawa to talk with him. This was finally arranged." The following day, he noted that the meeting had taken place: "Someone at the head of British Secret Intelligence had come to the Seignory [*sic*] Club yesterday. He came up and saw R. last night. R. will a little later tell me of his talks with him on the whole situation. This man returned to the Seignory [*sic*] Club at night."

10. Charles Ritchie, *The Siren Years: A Canadian Diplomat Abroad, 1937–1945*, Macmillan of Canada, 1974.
11. Sawatsky, *Gouzenko: The Untold Story*.

In neither entry was the individual named. The generally accepted version of events is that this person was William Stephenson, *aka Intrepid,* head of British Security Coordination based in New York City, that at that meeting Stephenson convinced Robertson to rescind the Canadian prime minister's order to send the Russian back to the embassy.[12]

An alternate view, based on a close reading of the Mackenzie King diary entries for 6 and 7 September 1945 and related research, is that if Norman Robertson met a representative of British intelligence the evening of 6 September, that person was MI6 chief Stewart Menzies.[13]

On 10 September Mackenzie King told his diary he'd instructed Robertson "to write out all that he knew of the matter," meaning the Gouzenko defection. Robertson apparently composed such an account, a dossier Mackenzie King took with him to Washington, D.C. on 29 September in a green binder and read out to American president Harry S. Truman. The document, which might confirm Robertson's meeting with a British intelligence official, the identity of the official and what he'd advised, does not appear to be among Robertson's papers, neither is it in the files of the current Department of Foreign Affairs, then External Affairs. The department, when I enquired, referred me to the Privy Council Office (PCO). In response to a written request, the PCO said they had no idea what I was talking about.[14]

All of which to conclude that if there had been a meeting that evening, we know next to nothing about it. Could it have been something Robertson invented to get round the prime minister's reluctance to hold onto Igor?

---

12. Montgomery Hyde, "The Defector" in *The Atom Bomb Spies,* Hamish Hamilton Ltd., 1980; also John Sawatsky, "The Russians Are Here" in *Gouzenko: The Untold Story.* Biographical accounts of *Intrepid's* later exploits lean to the inventive. See Nigel West's "Introduction" to *The Secret History of British Intelligence in the Americas, 1940–1945,* Fromm International, 1999; also Timothy J. Naftali, "Intrepid's Last Deception: Documenting the Career of Sir William Stephenson," in Wesley K. Wark (ed.), *Espionage: Past, Present, Future?,* Frank Cass and Co., 1994.

13. John Bryden, "The New Enemy (September–December 1945)" in *Best-Kept Secret: Canadian Intelligence in the Second World War,* Lester Publishing, 1993.

14. Correspondence, Herb Barrett, PCO, 17 May 2004. Professor Jack Granatstein has suggested to me that the Robertson document might very well be sitting in a closed Department of External Affairs file or hidden away in a Mackenzie King file somewhere. Norman Robertson passed on in 1968, a decade a half before the Sawatsky interviews. Professor Keith Jeffery, an authority on the history of MI6, told me in a 2 October 2010 email that there is no record of Menzies travelling to North America much before 1949, a claim John Bryden disputes.

It is clear that Robertson didn't seem to have required much if any arm-twisting. Taking Gouzenko and his documents into custody was clearly a course of action he'd favored from the start. What in fact appeared decisive in delivering Gouzenko into the hands of the RCMP, whether Mackenzie King wanted him there or not, was not the wise counsel of a British intelligence specialist but the Pavlov break-in.

The prime minister, who didn't always distinguish Ottawa cops from the RCMP, was told later in the day that Igor's documents had been photostatted, that they revealed a large-scale espionage scheme. There remained at that point some idea among Canadian officialdom that the embassy documents be returned to the embassy.

After a five-hour grilling, Leopold judged Igor to be completely genuine. If there had been a phone conversation with Igor the previous afternoon, the Russian-speaking Leopold didn't mention it. In time, relations between the men deteriorated.

Robertson seems to have handled the operation in a way calculated to keep the government's hands on Igor while allaying Mackenzie King's fear of being accused of a diplomat snatch and document grab.

Williams organized the nervous Gouzenko family's departure from the city. In the late afternoon, at a little before six p.m. 7 September Igor and Svetlana and Andrei were taken to a tourist camp on the outskirts of Ottawa. The Gouzenkos were terribly uneasy, suspicious, greatly fearing for their safety. They remained at the camp in Williams' protective custody until 7 October when they were turned over to the RCMP's G. B. McClellan, and taken to Camp X, a top-secret WWII espionage training and radio communications facility operated by British security 10 miles east of Belleville, Ontario.[15]

The Russians for all their cleverness had no idea Mackenzie King would react to news of the defection by wanting to deliver the defector back to the embassy. The prime minister probably never suspected that the Russians would waste little time breaking into Igor's apartment, creating an incident that helped dump Igor into his hands.

Might events have taken a different turn if Pavlov had waited a day or two?

Fully absorbed in fashioning gaseous self-aggrandizing statements

---

15. Sue Ferguson with Hazel Willis, "Forgotten Truths About Camp X," *Macleans,* 14 April 2003

for his diary, Mackenzie King seemed hardly to notice how it was that Igor wound up in RCMP protection. When all was said and done, Igor himself believed he owed his salvation to Pavlov not Norman Robertson, someone he might never have known about, or to the RCMP, perhaps a source of the tension that endured between them in the years to come.

Igor would not have had a clue about the lingering distrust between Robertson and the RCMP or the role of a key Robertson lieutenant, RCMP staff sergeant, Cecil Bayfield. In Bayfield's recollection of the affair there is no reference to Robertson. All he would say when asked about Igor decades later by John Sawatsky was that on the evening of 5 September "we received information about a man from the Russian embassy in Ottawa who was possibly going to defect." Who the *we* were and how precisely the information was obtained Bayfield did not explain, saying only that it came to us in a roundabout way. What is clear is that the RCMP were on the case from the start. The next day, 6 September, Bayfield said he took up surveillance of a man who later turned out to be Igor Gouzenko.... His wife was with him.... They went from the Crown Attorney's office and then up to the Justice Building.... I then went over and saw them go home to apartment four at 511 Somerset Street West. There is a park right across from his home and I then took up a position there on a park bench and waited ... [Igor] looked out the window and saw two men watching the apartment. One of those men was myself, but he didn't know that.

In RCMP hands Igor, said Bayfield, told him he was initially afraid to go to the police, afraid they were gestapo in league with the KGB. He rejected the *Journal* staff's suggestion that he and Svetlana go to the police, which was why they went to the Crown Attorney's office the next day, the afternoon of 6 September, to complete an application for naturalization. It is unclear when the conversation between Bayfield and Igor occurred. What Bayfield was prepared to tell Sawatsky was that he'd remained at his post on the evening of 6 September. At about eight o'clock, while he was watching the building at 511 Somerset from the park bench, the two Ottawa City Police constables, Walsh and McCullough, arrived. They noticed Bayfield in plainclothes sitting on the bench. Not knowing who he was Walsh asked him to move on. Bayfield said nothing about what he was doing there, didn't argue, got up and circled the area. A couple of hours later, Pavlov and the three Russian embassy heavies showed. After midnight, after the Russians had left, Bayfield entered the building. He let himself into the Gouzenko apartment with a skeleton key and found the place in a shambles.[16]

Mackenzie King soon informed his diary that Igor's documents were evidence of a Russian intrigue against the Christian world. There is no record in the diary of conversations with Robertson or phone calls in the hours leading up to or following the apartment break-in. The diary seems to be saying that the prime minister didn't learn about the break-in or about Igor having been taken into RCMP custody until the next morning.

The 7 September 1945 diary entry, dictated at 11 a.m., in other words after Igor had arrived at the Justice Building, gets some of the timing wrong and seems intended to make the point that the prime minister in fact possessed no knowledge of what had transpired the previous evening and perhaps he didn't:

> This morning I phoned Robertson to get further word from him. I said to him I was phoning to find out if he [Igor] was still alive. He told me that he was but that the night's events had not given him much rest... At 12 midnight four men from the Embassy...came to the apartment...forced the door open and got in. They made a search but were unable to discover anything. It was at this stage that the local police asked the assistance of the RCMP—of this I am not certain...it was between 2 and 3 a.m. that word was sent to Robertson that the man wanted to make some statement to the RCMP. I asked about the documents. Robertson said they were still in the man's possession. They might be turned in by him to the police. If they were they would be given back to the Embassy... meanwhile we might photostat copies.

On 8 September the Department of External Affairs received formal notification from the Soviet embassy that "Igor Gouzenko was a thief who had stolen money from the embassy and called for urgent measures to seek and arrest I Gusenko [*sic*] and to hand him over for deportation as a capital criminal."

---

16. Sawatsky, *Gouzenko, the Untold Story*.

Robertson turned the matter over to Laurent Beaudry, the Assistant Under Secretary, chief of the diplomatic division, who knew absolutely nothing about the Igor matter. Knowing nothing, Beaudry drafted what turned out to be inane notes for Robertson's signature. In the initial reply the department innocently asked the Russians for a description of the man. One was received on 11 September. On that day, a note with Robertson's signature was sent to the Soviet ambassador to say that Canadian police had no authority to arrest Igor and turn him over to the embassy and if they did they might be open to civil action. A file was set up in the department to hold the correspondence between the parties— the Russians, the RCMP and the department.[17]

In an 8 September diary entry Mackenzie King noted that the FBI were on their way to Ottawa to review the documents. On 12 September FBI director J. Edgar Hoover wrote to Matthew Connelly, Secretary to the President, Harry Truman. Hoover's major concern, one he seemed to believe would be shared by the president, was the fingering of Alan Nunn May: "With regard to the atomic bomb project, Dr. Allen May [*sic*] a British scientist assigned to the McGill University Laboratory in Canada has been identified as a paid Soviet spy of long standing." This suggests the information he received was not in written form. On 24 September Hoover sent a detailed memo, marked TOP SECRET, BY SPECIAL MESSENGER, to Fredrick B. Lyon, Chief, Division of Foreign Activity Correlation, State Department outlining the major Gouzenko revelations.[18]

In the days that followed, two members of British security, Peter Dwyer and John-Paul Evans, received daily RCMP briefings relayed to London via William Stephenson's super secure feed from Rockefeller Plaza in New York City—right to the desk to Kim Philby, head of MI6 and Stalin's man at the agency. Philby, who was secretly keeping Moscow in the loop, sought to limit British curiosity about Igor and his

---

17. "The Testimony of Laurent Beaudry," 21 February 1946, Robert Bothwell and J. L. Granatstein, *The Gouzenko Transcripts: The Evidence Presented to the Kellock-Taschereau Royal Commission of 1946*; J. L. Granatstein, *A Man of Influence: Norman A. Robertson and Canadian Statecraft 1929–1968*, Deneau, 1981.

18. Correspondence, J. Edgar Hoover to Matthew Connelly, Secretary to the President, The White House, Washington, D.C. 12 September 1945; John Edgar Hoover to Frederick B. Lyon, United States Department of Justice, 24 September 1945.

documents, claiming in a note that Igor's information was genuine though not necessarily accurate in all details.[19]

Mackenzie King came in time to see Igor's defection as an event that placed him in the midst of a struggle between the NKVD and the spirit world. On 11 September, the day that the notes about arresting Igor were exchanged between the Soviet embassy and Norman Robertson, the prime minister, *sotto voce*, shared this confidence with the diary: "I cannot believe this information has come to me as a matter of chance. I can only pray for guidance that I may be able to be an instrument in the control of powers beyond to help save a desperate situation, to maintain peace now that it has been nominally established." And subsequently: "The best course would be to have the British and U.S. governments and ourselves work together on the highest level, and let the Russians know what we know with a view to disclosing from them whether they intended to really try to be friends and work for a peaceful world..." It was, he mumbled to his diary, "...impossible not to see the working of forces from beyond in what has come into the possession of our government in this matter."

On 24 September the prime minister said he knew what was in the documents: "The names of those who are agents of the Russian service for espionage purposes, copies of documents that have passed to and fro...lead right into the Research Bldgs. here in Ottawa, the Laboratories in Montreal, to British scientists working there who have even more knowledge of the atomic bomb developments than almost anyone; to persons in our own E. A. Dept. [External Affairs] and in the Registry Office in Earnscliffe where all documents of a most secret sort have passed through the hands of one person in particular who has been supplying information to Rose, a member of parliament." Said a 12 July 1945 Russian document: "To the Director, reference No. 8393. 1. Debouz received the data from a conversation with officers who had taken part on the Western Front. The data were received from conversations with the latter." Debouz, we know, was Freddy's cover name; the discovery of Freddy's involvement elicited no diary comment.

Perhaps to fully clear the prime minister of any suspicion that his

---

19. Randy Boswell, "Notorious Turncoat Philby Ran Interference in Gouzenko Spy Sensation, Author Finds," *Postmedia*. 30 September 2010. Based on a conversation with Prof. Keith Jeffery.

officials had acted inappropriately, Igor was encouraged to produce a statement to the RCMP dated 10 October 1945 describing how glad he was to have found the strength within himself "to have taken this step and to warn Canada and the other democratic countries of the danger which hangs over them."

After Igor had been hidden away, Mackenzie King consulted with President Harry Truman and Prime Minister Clement Atlee. The parties were unable to agree on what ought to happen next. Among the spyfish hooked by Igor's revelations, the big one was Alan Nunn May. Also named was Kathleen Willsher, a secretary at the British High Commission in Ottawa. The British were urging arrests. The allegations seemed to reach high up in the American administration, to Alger Hiss, assistant to Secretary of State Edward Stettinius, as well as to a Soviet mole in the upper ranks of British counter-intelligence. Based on advice he'd received that the information was insufficient to secure criminal convictions, Mackenzie King wanted to hold off, in agreement with the American president that nothing should be done until all the facts were in. Soviet agent Kim Philby, who as MI6 chief was receiving regular briefings on the Igor business, reported to Moscow in November 1945 that the Canadian head of state was resisting British pressure to order arrests until the FBI had completed its interrogation of Elizabeth Bentley.[20]

In October 1945 Mackenzie King met ex-British Prime Minister Winston Churchill in London and told him about the Gouzenko business. Mackenzie King recorded details of the meeting in his diary. Churchill did not appear surprised. He referred to the Bolsheviks as Jesuits without Jesus, realists in the extreme who would go to any length to achieve a purpose.

Freddy's pals at the embassy did tip him off about the defection but not about the purloined documents or their contents. Perhaps they themselves were unaware of the particular documents Igor had taken. One of the Ruskies, as Freddy put it to fellow spook Gordon Lunan, has flown the coop. Badly shaken but convinced that Mackenzie King did not want an international incident on Canadian soil, he advised Lunan to

---

20. Weinstein and Vassiliev, *The Haunted Wood*.

do nothing. Lie low, was Freddy's advice to party associates and fellow spooks. Nothing will happen. For a few months nothing did.[21]

Among the tales Igor's documents told was that all was not well inside the embassy. Jealousy and animosity had reached such a level that Moscow was forced to intervene. There was a poisonous GRU-KGB rivalry in securing secret information and prized recruits. When Pavlov wanted to approach Sam Carr who was then working for Zabotin, Moscow told him to back off. Members of the spy entities carried poisonous aspersions about each other back to Moscow.

There were also disputes over living quarters. As in any organization, players were seeking to rise in the ranks. The larger the number of agents Pavlov or Zabotin had in the field the better they looked in the faraway Soviet capital. We recall Elizabeth Bentley's observation about the virtual uselessness of the information she and Golos were getting from Hazen Sise, and how little really vital information the entire Canadian operation had produced.[22]

For the RCMP, the major impact of the Gouzenko defection was an unmistakable shift in priorities. It was now understood that the Russians were much less interested in fomenting revolution by inciting disgruntled Canadian workers to bring down the government than in acquiring military, scientific, and technological information.[23]

---

21. Gordon Lunan, *The Making of a Spy,* Robert Davies, 1995; Wiesbord, *The Strangest Dream.*
22. "Spies Were Jealous," *The Windsor Daily Star,* 16 July 1946.
23. "The RCMP Takes Over," *CSIS,* 26 September 2005. There were earlier clues as to Soviet motives, among them the RCMP debriefing of Walter Krivitsky prior to both the Bentley *and* the Gouzenko defections. Krivitsky was in Canada 26 December 1939 to 31 October 1940 and for a period in 1941. See Gary Kern's *A Death in Washington.* The record of RCMP Inspector H. R. Gagnon's debriefing sessions with Krivitsky is apparently nowhere to be found. There was at the time a business office but no Soviet diplomatic mission in Canada.

VII.

To Investigate

On Sunday, 3 February 1946, Mackenzie King told his diary that he'd received "two very sad but remarkably fine and brave letters by Leo and Mrs. Amery."[1]

Leo, at one time first lord of the British Admiralty, never told his son John about his own Hungarian Jewish mother and his conversion to Protestantism. Father and son were in agreement about the terrible danger posed by the Bolsheviks. It was a view held by most members of their class. Amery the younger chose to act. His anti-Bolshevik activities included pro-Nazi radio broadcasts at a time when England and Germany were at war, and the formation of *The Legion of St. George,* a scheme for sending British prisoners of war held by the Germans east into battle with the USSR. The war over, John Amery's social position could not save him. Brought to trial for treason near the end of November 1945, he readily admitted his guilt, was convicted and hanged.[2]

A short time after the hanging the king and queen invited the family for lunch and commiseration at Buckingham Palace. The prime minister did not disclose to his diary the contents of the letters.

Later that same evening, the hope he'd clung to that the Gouzenko business would fade away was shattered. The American radio person-

---

1. Mackenzie King Diary, Sunday 3 February 1946.
2. Rebecca West, *The New Meaning of Treason*, The Viking Press, 1964.

ality, Drew Pearson, alerted by someone, fingers point to FBI chief Edgar Hoover, broadcast news of Igor's revelations of an elaborate Soviet espionage network involving Canadian, American and British citizens. The prime minister did not learn about the broadcast until the following afternoon when Robertson phoned to tell him that the Gouzenko story "had leaked out."[3]

There would now need to be arrests and trials and for those things to transpire an investigation was needed to produce some hard evidence.

With the cat was out of the bag, the prime minister sought the advice of E. K. Williams, president of the Canadian Bar Association. On the one hand, the diplomatic status of the Russians, key players in the scheme, meant that they could not be taken into custody or put on trial or even questioned. On the other, the material Igor had turned over to the RCMP, backed up only by his recollections, offered intriguing leads but would not otherwise do well in a Canadian courtroom. To make it stick some coercion was needed. Williams recommended the government establish a royal commission less to enquire into the actual veracity of Igor's allegations than to pressure the men and women named in the documents to talk, to make statements that might be used in successful prosecutions.

The official purpose of the inquiry, under Order in Council P.C. 411 of 5 February 1946, was: "To investigate the facts relating to and the circumstances surrounding the communication, by public officials and other persons in positions of trust of secret and confidential information to agents of a foreign power. The work of the commission would be guided by the War Measures Act: That all the privileges, immunities and powers given by Order in Council P.C. 1639 passed on the 2nd March 1942, shall apply." The commission would sit in secret, witnesses would not be advised of their rights, access to counsel would be denied.[4]

---

3. Mackenzie King Diary, Monday, 4 February 1946.
4. The Royal Commission appointed under Order in Council P.C. 411 of February 5 1946 to "investigate the facts relating to and the circumstances surrounding the communication, by public officials and other persons in positions of trust, of secret and confidential information to agents of a foreign power." There is a voluminous literature on various aspects of the commission's work, much of it highly critical. See, for example, Dominique Clement, "The Royal Commission on Espionage and the Spy Trials of 1946–49: A Case Study," *Left History,* 7:2. 2000; Gary Marcuse and Reg Whitaker, *Cold War Canada: The Making of a National Insecurity State: 1945–1957,* University of Toronto Press, 1994; "Justice and Justice Only? a draft memorandum on the 4th Report of the Kellock- Taschereau Commission," prepared by the Emergency Committee for Civil Rights.

The method would have the advantage of circumventing the judicial process. E. K. Williams would act as the commission's senior legal advisor.

The commission's first interim report appeared on 2 March 1946, the second on 14 March 1946, the third on 28 March 1946, the final report dated 27 June 1946 was tabled in the House, which is to say made public, on 15 July 1946.

Unlike Elizabeth Bentley, Igor Gouzenko had more than one story to tell. The embassy documents named Canadian university professors, military personnel and government employees. Among those uncovered was the British physicist Alan Nunn May, the first identified atomic bomb spy, who worked at the Montreal Laboratory established by the National Research Council (NRC) for Manhattan Project related research, Sam Carr, a national Communist Party organizer, and the MP Fred Rose.

Freddy, the documents revealed, was responsible for organizing a group of agents at the NRC. There was no identification in the documents of Bruno Pontecorvo, the Italian physicist who worked at the lab with Nunn May and on the Chalk River heavy water project. Pontecorvo moved to England in 1948 before defecting to the USSR in 1950. In Canada, he was controlled by the KGB *rezident* in Mexico City, which explains why he was not identified in Igor's GRU materials. Pontecorvo always insisted his work had no military application. Igor did alert the RCMP to a parallel KGB spy operation, a warning that was ignored. Pontecorvo was never charged with espionage. Many years later the Russians admitted he had been one of their agents.[5]

The groundwork for the commission had been laid in the Privy Council Office on 6 October 1945 in P.C. 6444: "AND WHEREAS it is deemed necessary for the security, defense, peace, order and welfare of Canada that the Acting Prime Minister or the Minister of Justice should be authorized to order the detention of such persons in such places and under such conditions as the Acting Prime Minister or the Minister of Justice may from time to time determine.... Any person shall, while detained by virtue of an order made under the Order, be deemed to be

---

5. "Italian Fiasco," in Harry Chapman Pincher, *Treachery: Betrayals, Blunders, and Cover-ups: Six Decades of Espionage Against America and Great Britain*, Random House, 2009.

in legal custody.

The following day, 7 October 1945, an order was sent to the Commissioner of the RCMP from the office of the acting prime minister "to interrogate and/or detain Fred ROSE in such place and under such circumstances as may from time to time be determined. And I hereby authorize you to enter any premises occupied or used by said Fred ROSE at any time and to search said premises and every person found thereon and to seize any article found on the said premises or any such person which you have reasonable grounds for believing to be evidence that secret and confidential information has been communicated to a Foreign Power."[6]

There does not appear to be any record of the order having been in any way acted upon. On the other hand, it seemed to be business as usual for both the party and the RCMP. The party held meetings and members delivered speeches, the Force diligently reported on party activities. It would seem that information about Igor's flight was withheld from both the party and the RCMP rank and file.

Two Canadian Supreme Court justices were put in charge of the commission, Roy Kellock and Robert Taschereau. Not exactly a Soviet-style enquiry, the commission was to function with wartime powers that allowed the government to hold people without trial or explanation, out of touch from family and counsel, which is to say the enquiry as conceived by Williams could do what a criminal proceeding would not have been able to. It had a double purpose: first, as much as possible, to coerce the suspects Igor identified into incriminating themselves and others so that successful trials could take place; second, to make clear by questions asked and questions avoided that Igor had not been abducted by Canadian authorities but had voluntarily delivered himself and his documents into the hands of the RCMP.

Had Canadian citizens violated the Official Secrets Act of Canada? Under the Act, provisions for establishing guilt were murky; once hauled into court the onus was on the accused to establish his or her innocence.

It is the unofficial RCMP view that Robertson ran the commission, persuaded that the method was justified by the circumstances, that the

---

6. The Mackenzie King Records, vol. 2, 1944–1945. I have been advised by the PCO that the document was issued over the signature of James Lorimer Ilsley, Acting Prime Minister, because Mackenzie King was at the time in Washington, D.C. on government business related to the Gouzenko matter.

prospects for obtaining incriminating statements increased when the suspects were held in isolation from wives and lawyers who might encourage the talk to cease.

Igor, the commission's first witness, appeared a number of times between 13 February and 17 May 1946 to respond to questions raised by the pilfered cables. References to Fred Rose soon emerged. In response to a question from Williams, Igor explained that *Debouz*, a name found in messages Zabotin sent on to Moscow, was a cover name for the MP from Cartier, changed from the cover name *Fred*. The Gouzenko testimony left little doubt that Freddy had been deeply involved in the embassy's espionage activity.

On the basis of Igor's statements before the commission on 13 and 14 February, orders were issued for the interrogation and, for that purpose, detention of nine people. On the morning of 15 February 1946, the prime minister reviewed the press release of a statement, issued on the letterhead of Robertson's department, with Robertson. It began: "Information of undoubted authenticity has reached the Canadian Government which establishes that there have been disclosures of secret and confidential information to unauthorized persons, including some members of the staff of a foreign mission in Ottawa." At 4 p.m. that afternoon the prime minister called in the Soviet Chargé d'Affaires Nikolai Belokhvostikov and Vitalii Pavlov, the mission's designated Second Secretary, and handed them pre-release copies of the statement in which the heads of the commission and counsel were named. The Russian diplomats were informed that though not formally identified as such the USSR was considered the offending party. The statement would be made public at 5 p.m.

Arrests followed. To minimize public criticism, Robertson ordered that they not be made as originally scheduled at three in the morning.[7]

The arrested included McGill University professor Raymond Boyer, National Research Council engineers S. W. Mazerall and Durnford Smith, J. S. Benning, with the Department of Munitions and Supply, Emma Woikin, an External Affairs code clerk, David Shugar, who worked on anti-submarine technology, Capt. David Gordon Lunan, an army officer with the Wartime Information Board, Matt Nightingale, an

7. Jack Batten, *In Court*, Macmillan of Canada, 1982.

RCAF officer, and Kathleen Willsher who worked in the office of the High Commissioner United Kingdom. They were escorted by RCMP officers to the Rockcliffe barracks for some softening up before being brought before commission interrogators.

What, Lunan was asked, did he know about Fred Rose? I want to see my wife and my lawyer, said Lunan. His Rockcliffe interrogator was RCMP Inspector Clifford "Slim" Harvison. At the moment, said Harvison, you have no rights. You are obliged by law to answer my questions. Pressed to speak, though they had every right to remain silent, to say nothing, the statements of the Rockcliffe detainees, obtained under duress, were intended to be used against them in their appearances before the commission, and then in the courts. Harvison's questioning of Lunan made it clear that the Force regarded the espionage affair as part of a Jewish plot. "Are you," Harvison prodded Lunan, "going to stand by and let people with names like Rosenberg, Kogan, Mazerall, Rabinovich and Halperin sell Canada down the river?" A military man, Lunan believed he could be executed. Confused and fearful, he talked. In a memoir, *The Making of a Spy,* Lunan described beefy escorts and backstairs routes to the commission hearings. The RCMP facility was located on the floor below the commission hearing room, proceedings were discussed with commissioners and commission counsel in the elevators and over lunch.[8]

The wife of Matt Nightingale, an RCAF officer whose name came up in Igor's commission testimony and who had been in contact with members of the Soviet embassy, sent a letter of protest to the publication *PM* describing how on 15 February 1946 four beefy men in plain clothes, claiming to be members of the RCMP, had knocked on the couple's apartment door, barged in, conducted a search of the apartment without showing a warrant and escorted her husband to the Rockcliffe barracks. I am not, Nightingale told his wife in a handwritten note, "even allowed to see the Privy Council order under which I was arrested. As far as I know, no charge has been placed against me but I don't know. I have been given vague hints that serious allegations have been made about me but I have not been told who made them or how."

An RCMP Inspector M. F. Anthony appeared, as Harvison did in

---

8. Gordon Lunan, *The Making of a Spy*, Robert Davies Publishing, 1995.

his questioning of Lunan, to give the game away. At a trial that acquitted him of espionage, Nightingale said that while he was being held in detention there were several interviews with Anthony who showed him a photo of Sam Carr and told him it was his duty to help "send these damn Jews back where they came from." The ever timid Canadian Jewish Congress sought the approval from RCMP Commissioner Wood to issue a statement: "The Jewish community of Canada was pleased to have the official denial by the Royal Canadian Mounted Police of a charge of anti-Semitism leveled against one of its officers."[9]

David Shugar wrote MP John Diefenbaker that he was being held in a nine by eight foot cell, a light bulb shining 24 hours, and threatened with punishment if he refused to testify before the commission. Following a failed hunger strike, he wrote to the justice minister to complain that all his rights had been stripped away. Shugar did not understand that the Order-in-Council had made the proceedings completely legal. Summoned and sworn 8 March 1946, commission official Kellock told him he was obliged to name names, "because that is the law.... You must not waste our time."[10]

The MP Fred Rose could not be subject to that kind of treatment. In two meetings on 26 February 1946, the first in Robertson's office, Robertson and Williams reviewed another option. As recorded in an RCMP report, Robertson put this question to RCMP Superintendent C. E. Rivett-Carnac: "I suppose the best thing that could happen would be for Fred Rose and Sam Carr to disappear?" Said Rivett-Carnac: "As far as I am personally concerned I feel that Fred Rose, who is one of the chief instigators of this affair together with his friends in the Russian embassy, should be brought before the Commission and should be punished to the full extent of the law." A second meeting took place that evening in the Justice Building. The report of these meetings, both authored by Rivett-Carnac, continues: "As this question of the possible disappearance of Fred Rose placed a different complexion on the whole question as to whether he would be interrogated by the Royal

9. "Canada's Spy Hunters Raided Officer's Home," *PM*, 27 February 1946; "Bare Jew-Baiting in RCMP Spy-Probe Third Man Freed," *The Canadian Tribune*, 16 November 1946; press release undated, *Press Office of the Canadian Jewish Congress*.

10. David Shugar, "Interrogation at Rockcliffe," 22 February 1946; transcript of commission testimony 8 March 1946, Letter from David Shugar to John Diefenbaker, 9 March 1946, *John Diefenbaker Papers*, Vol. 82.

Commission I purposely asked Mr. E. K. Williams, K.C. what was proposed in respect to Rose. I considered it important that Mr. Williams should express an opinion in connection with this matter as otherwise it might be quite possible that Fred Rose would disappear and the Order for his detention be subsequently issued, in which event it would look as though the Police had failed in their responsibilities from the standpoint of securing his apprehension. I explained to Mr. Williams that at the present juncture we did not know whether to place a 24-hour surveillance on Rose which might lead to his becoming aware of the fact that he was being shadowed, with subsequent complications, or to continue with the general surveillance of this individual which is in force at present." The response from Williams: "...it would be a very good thing if Rose was to disappear. Asked why, Williams replied: "It would relieve a very embarrassing situation."

Rivett-Carnac didn't much object to the proposal about Freddy disappearing, only that it might cast the Force in a poor light, making it look as though the Police had failed in their responsibilities.[11]

Freddy had appeared briefly before the commission on 18 April 1946. His lead lawyer, Joseph Cohen, argued for an adjournment of his appearance until the trial, scheduled to begin in May, was over. The commission's interrogation of Freddy before the trial began, he said, would be prejudicial. When the commission overruled the plea, Freddy refused on 26 April 1946 to take the Bible in his right hand and be sworn because, he said, the commission's procedures coerced self-incrimination.[12]

Freddy was a, if not *the,* prime commission target. In the handling of his case, a bully show was not only out of the question but unnecessary. The Crown had two highly cooperative witnesses: Igor for one, Professor Raymond Boyer for another. At one point Boyer insisted that not to talk amounted to an act of dishonor.

Some of the point of the commission's tough guy operation may have been to cover up RCMP incompetence and obsession with allegedly subversive Jewish labor organizers. Then as currently, the ineptitude of agencies entrusted with national security leads, on the one

11. Charles E. Rivett-Carnac, "Re: Corby, Secret Memorandum," Ottawa, 27 February 1946.
12. "The Evidence of Fred Rose," 18, 26 April 1946, Bothwell and Granatstein (eds.) *The Gouzenko Transcripts*, 1982.

hand, to the false option—security vs. freedom—and on the other to legitimate targets hiding behind civil rights claims.

Among Igor's documents was one claiming that Zabotin had instructed Freddy to help recruit an American scientist, Dr. Arthur Steinberg. Steinberg had been a doctoral student in genetics at Columbia University who taught at McGill University from 1940–1944. In Montreal, Steinberg joined a Canadian-Soviet support group where he met Fred Rose. At McGill he became good friends with Raymond Boyer, who he assisted with RDX research data, which may have been what persuaded Freddy he possessed knowledge about the bomb. Freddy had told Zabotin that Steinberg was a good friend of his and had done work on atomic energy. Steinberg was given the code name BERGER. Steinberg did agree to meet the head of the Bureau of Technical Information of the Purchasing Commission, someone named Sorvin. Sorvin reported that Steinberg claimed he was but an ordinary draughtsman and would soon leave for Java, that he'd said it is not good to engage in this sort of thing—for we are allies.[13]

Not long after NFB head John Grierson's royal commission testimony Mackenzie King told his diary that the NFB was a commie nest, perhaps a reaction to Grierson's claim of a friendly acquaintance with Pavlov.

Apart from Igor, the commission's key witness against Freddy was Raymond Boyer. Code name *the Professor,* his testimony was heard on 7 and 8 March 1946. As the record shows, the purpose of the Boyer interrogation was threefold: to get him to cough up the names and duties of individuals the RCMP might not have known much or anything about, to connect Freddy and himself to a conspiracy to violate the Official Secrets Act of Canada, and to see if the information supplied to the Russians had anything to do with atomic bomb research.

Independently wealthy, Prof. Boyer was described by the Russians as: "Frenchman. Noted chemist, about 40 years of age. Works in McGill University, Montreal. Is the best of the specialists on BB on the American Continent. Gives full information on explosives and chemical plants. Very rich. He is afraid to work. (Gave the formula of RDX, up to the present there was no evaluation from the boss/Master.) "BB" meaning

13. Amy Knight, "The Right Wing Unleashed," in *How the Cold War Began.*

explosives, "boss/Master" an unidentified personality in Moscow, "afraid to work" meaning he would not join the party or become more involved.

The commission transcript makes two things evident: on the one hand Boyer had been prepared for his testimony by conversations with Inspector Harvison, and on the other he was unaware that he was being set up.

The questioning began harmlessly enough with biography. Boyer told the commission he was not and never had been a member of the party. In 1939, he'd joined a study group on Marxism. He said he possessed a quite limited knowledge of the Russian language and had made modest financial contributions to Freddy's election campaigns in 1943 and 1945. With little of the pressure of a HUAC hearing bearing down on him, Boyer didn't need to be pressed to divulge what he knew of the politics of colleagues. David Shugar's political ideology was, Boyer volunteered, Labour-Progressive, Communist; Dr. P. R. Wallace, president of the Canadian Association of Scientific Workers, of which Boyer himself was Dominion president, was not a Communist but did know a good deal about Marxism; the Association's one-time Secretary, Frank Chubb leaned Labour-Progressive, Communist, one-time university colleague Arthur Steinberg was sympathetic to communism, and so on. Boyer correctly identified the photo of Alan Nunn May as a member of the association, someone he said he suspected was a Communist.

Boyer told the commission he'd known Freddy since 1938, that in 1943 Freddy phoned and asked him to come over to his apartment and tell him about the explosive RDX. We know from Elizabeth Bentley's recollections that this was a topic of much interest to the Russians who, Freddy told Boyer, were anxious to know about it. C. D. Howe, head of the Department of Munitions and Supply, had been approached for the formula by the Russians. Canada was willing to supply it but the Americans were opposed. I was, Boyer testified, "very anxious that the Russians should continue asking, because I knew...they could not start to produce RDX with the information I gave."

A clear aim of the commission's sessions with Boyer, whether or not Boyer understood this and he seemed not to, was to use his own words to implicate him in an espionage conspiracy with Freddy.

You were willing, Williams asked, to give the information you did give to Mr. Rose knowing that it would be transmitted by him to the Russians? Yes, said Boyer, he made that quite clear. Kellock: So far as these combinations and methods of use that you have been mentioning and that you told Rose, so far as you knew at that time you were telling him something that was new to the Russians? Boyer: That is correct. Williams: You were handing over to somebody, who was obviously an emissary of the Russians, information which your oath of secrecy forbade you to give? Boyer: That is correct.

Points were raised about the components, about the stages of RDX production involving a laboratory phase, Boyer's area, a pilot plant stage, and a mass production stage. Do you not think, asked Williams, that if they had that formula they could design a plant, eventually, at least? Oh, yes, Boyer replied.

Boyer said that when he told Freddy about the four key RDX ingredients, he saw Freddy taking notes he was certain would be passed on to the Soviets. As for the RDX information, hadn't much of it been made public in the early 1940s? There had indeed been stories in the papers about the new manufacturing process but not, Boyer said, about the components. As for the claim that the Russians had been invited to visit an RDX plant in Grand' Mère in the company of a Canadian government official, Boyer said the pilot plant was in Shawinigan not Grand' Mère. Apparently, the Russians had been given the impression that the RDX plant had something to do with uranium production. "Was that ever discussed between you and Fred Rose?" Boyer: "No."[14]

At his own trial in March 1947, Boyer told the court that all the information he'd passed on to Fred Rose was already known and not contrary to his oath of secrecy.

Freddy, atomic spy manqué, in fact possessed little technical understanding of these matters. He had apparently confused the RDX plant in Shawinigan, he believed was in Grand' Mère, with the nuclear research being conducted at Chalk River, Ontario. Like many others he was probably unaware of the deadly effects of atomic radiation. He seemed to have assumed Boyer's RDX research involved nuclear weaponry, that the bomb simply represented a more powerful type of explosive. By

---

14. The Testimony of Dr. Raymond Boyer, 7, 8 March 1946, Bothwell and J. L. Granatstein.

mid-September 1945 the horror of the bomb was evident. In Hiroshima and Nagasaki reporters had observed people dying in agony of radiation burns, knowledge the press was pressured to keep under wraps.

In August 1943 a Soviet technical mission to the United States had inquired about RDX. A year later two Soviet experts, B. Fomin and P. Solodov visited the Shawinigan plant.[15] They or others involved in the technical mission contacted Freddy, *Lesovian* parliament member and known GRU agent, for help. Freddy might have seen this as an opportunity to pump up his espionage street cred. He soon persuaded Boyer to come over to his place and tell him all about RDX.

In the commission's interrogation of Boyer the term conspiracy never arose nor did the likelihood that Boyer would be charged and found guilty of such an act for which he would be sentenced to a prison term. Having performed the required dirty work, Kellock ended the session with a Pilate-like washing of the hands: "On the evidence and in view of your own evidence it will be difficult for us to come to any other conclusion than that we are of the opinion that we must report that you have communicated secret information to the agents of a foreign power, the disclosure of which might be or may have been inimical to the interests of Canada.... Whether or not a charge should be laid against you in the courts, or may be laid against you in the courts, is something with which we have nothing to do."

The Russians eventually admitted they were given information but that it didn't amount to anything they didn't already know.[16]

The Canadian Communist Party denied any knowledge of or involvement in a Soviet espionage network in Canada. Freddy's comrades were throwing him to the wolves.

Ever on the lookout for signs and omens on 4 March 1946 while dictating a diary entry, the prime minister happened to glance at the clock on his table and saw that the hands were exactly together at twelve, which seemed to indicate, as he put it, that: "Nothing could be more significant than what is happening at this moment. The statement from the interim report of the commissioners on Russian espionage is

---

15. John T. Edward, "Wartime Research on RDX," *Journal of Chemical Education*, Vol. 64, No. 7, July 1987.

16. "Soviet Embassy in U.S. Does Not Deny Spy Charges," *The Ottawa Citizen*, 19 February 1946. That same day the *Citizen* reported that Joseph E. Davies, a former American ambassador to the USSR, claimed that Russia had every moral right to seek atomic bomb secrets through military espionage.

now being given to the press, a copy having been given to the Russian Embassy."

Following the 14 March 1946 release of the second interim commission report, the prime minister sent the Soviet foreign minister Vyacheslav Mikhailovich Molotov a note imploring him to explain to Generalissimo Stalin the importance he placed on Soviet-Canada friendship and his certainty that the espionage operation being investigated was undertaken without the authority of the Soviet ambassador. As Russians understood but the prime minister would not have, Ambassador Zarubin was excluded from involvement in GRU's spying activities. There was no reply from Comrade Stalin.

As commission testimony was being heard, Mackenzie King grew concerned over Jewish influence in Canada and suspicious that his own valet was a *red*. In a 20 February 1946 entry the prime minister confided to his diary his uneasiness over Jewish influence and tendencies, and a connection between Jews and the Russians. Referring to the Democratic Party in America: "I am coming to feel that the democratic [*sic*] party have allowed themselves to be too greatly controlled by the Jews and Jewish influence and that Russia has sympathizers in high and influential places to a much greater number than has been believed.... I must say that the evidence is very strong, not against all Jews, which is quite wrong, as one cannot indict race any more than one can a nation, but that in a large percentage of the race there are tendencies and trends which are dangerous indeed." He seemed to believe or want to believe the false claim that most of those apprehended were Jews or had Jewish wives or were of Jewish descent.

The final commission report was vague on the part played by the RCMP and silent on the role of Norman Robertson. It contained a reference to Pavlov and the break-in but nothing on the elaborate interaction between city cops and the RCMP overseen by Robertson the evening of 6 September. The report noted the existence of a team that procured false Canadian passports and related travel documents for agents in Canada and elsewhere. If the commission had been informed by the FBI about Freddy's link to the Ovakimyan-Golos-Bentley network the report said nothing about it.

The MP from Cartier Fred Rose would be put on trial and the

Professor would be the key witness against him. The chief villains, the Russians, protected by diplomatic privilege, offered no assistance to their Canadian accomplices, the fate of illegals.

On the other hand, the documents Igor collected represented a limited sample of a much larger volume of Soviet cables. The material that ended up in the hands of Canadian officials, including fourteen documents naming Fred Rose, had not been, as Igor explained, gathered at random but with great care to make a point. The point was reinforced in Igor's autobiography. Igor left little doubt that as far as he was concerned Freddy was the absolute number one bad guy, a fellow of even lower character than his Communist masters: I selected the documents, Igor wrote, which made a strong case against the key agents.[17]

Of all the persons, said the commission's final report, "mentioned in the Russian documents as well as by the witnesses throughout this Inquiry, none, Soviet officials excepted, have been more repeatedly and prominently mentioned, either under their names or cover-names, than Fred Rose and his fellow spy and conspirator, Sam Carr."

On 24 May 1946, Victoria Day, a few days before the start of Freddy's trial, Mackenzie King on a visit to London had been invited to Buckingham Palace for lunch with George VI, the Queen, and the Princesses, Elizabeth and Margaret: "We went into the small private dining room and had luncheon at a round table. I was seated to the King's right and to the left of the Queen.... The King was especially interested in getting particulars of the Russian espionage matter. He had followed it pretty closely and seemed to be remarkably familiar with details. He told me that he thought what we had done might be a very helpful exposé in regard to similar situations in different countries. He spoke of feeling very greatly concerned about Russian attitude and behavior. Their establishment of the 5th column and the like. Later in the afternoon, I sent H.M. a copy of Gouzenko's confession." Was the prime minister referring to Igor's royal commission testimony? Had he, anticipating the occasion, traveled to England with a bound copy? There was no mention in the diary entry of Freddy or the lunch menu.

In 1957 Robert Taschereau cast the single dissenting vote in the 8-1 Supreme Court ruling declaring the padlock law illegal.

---

17. Igor Gouzenko, *This Was My Choice*, J. M. Dent & Sons (Canada) Ltd., 1948.

Fred Rose in 1929 as National Secretary of the Young Communist League.

Nazi Foreign Minister von Ribbentrop and Joseph Stalin look pleased at the signing of the German-Soviet Non-Aggression pact of August 1939.

Fred Rose campaign poster in 1943.

Tim Buck leader of the CPC,
Communist Party of Canada.

Fred Rose Yiddish language
campaign literature.

Denise Nielsen first communist elected
to the Canadian parliament.

Communist publication objecting
to the Padlock law.

Rose Labor-Progressive Party campaign flyer, 1943.

Dinner to honor Fred Rose M.P. at the Mount Royal Hotel 1943.

Walter Krivitsky using an assumed
identity in 1939.

Gaik Ovakimian North American
NKVD rezident.

Jacob Golos NKVD agent in New York
until 1943.

Elizabeth Bentley NKVD courier until
she confessed to the FBI in 1945.

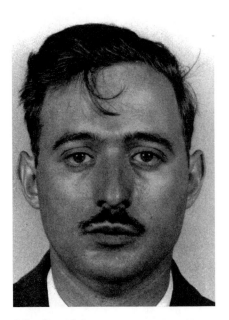

Julius Rosenberg

Igor Gouzenko, cipher clerk at the Soviet embassy in Ottawa until he defected in 1945.

Gouzenko wearing a hood interviewed by Hearst reporter Bob Considine.

Colonel Nikolai Zabotin of the GRU.

Vitalii Pavlov NKVD rezident in Ottawa.

Alan Nunn May

Bruno Pontecorvo

Gordon Lunan

Edward Mazerall

Prime Minister William Lyon Mackenzie King

Kathleen Willsher   Emma Woikin

Prime Minister Clement Attlee, President Harry Truman and Prime Minister Mackenzie King.

Norman Robertson with Mackenzie King at a conference in London.

Alger Hiss

Whittaker Chambers

J. Edgar Hoover

Kim Philby

Sir Roger Hollis

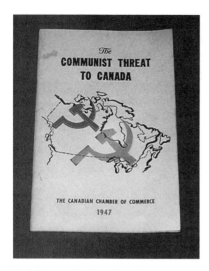

Anti-Communist brochure issued by
the Chamber of Commerce in 1947.

Communist party leader Sam Carr escorted
by plainclothes policemen.

Professor Raymond Boyer whose testimony led to Fred Rose's guilty verdict.

Hazen Sise and his wife in 1973.

Fred Rose on trial in 1946.

Fred Rose on his way
to court with his lawyer
Joseph Cohen.

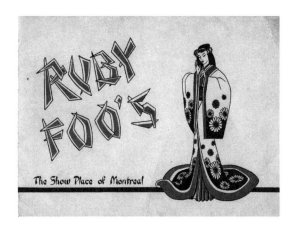

Ruby Foo's Chinese restaurant, where one time impoverished Cartier litvaks now dined.

The Ruby Foo's establishment in Montreal in the 1970s.

VIII.

Arrest and Trial

"...one black, thundering day there was an article about our street in *Time* magazine. For several years we had been electing communists to represent us at Ottawa and in the provincial legislature. Our M.P. was arrested. An atomic spy."

Mordecai Richler, *The Street.*

"Witch hunt," declared party leaders in early March 1946. An RCMP report noted that Freddy had been absent from an LPP meeting in Montreal. Suspicion circulated that he had once again gone underground.[1] He was in fact out of the country on some business but soon returned.

On 6 March Freddy was a featured speaker at a mass meeting at Toronto's Massey Hall, along with Dorise Nielsen and Tim Buck, in support of the party's campaign for 250,000 low-rental homes. The Communists, said the RCMP report, were using "the shortage of

---

1. *The Canadian Tribune,* 2 March 1946; "The Labour Progressive Party," RCMP, "C" Division, Montreal, P.Q., March 1946.

housing as one of their strong points of agitation." The previous day 1,000 persons attended a rally at the High School of Montreal in Montreal at which Rose and Mrs. Nielsen spoke to an audience "made up for the most part of Jewish persons recognized as members or sympathizers to the Party in this locality."[2]

Following the 14 March 1946 release of the commission's second interim report, an unduly concerned and excited Louis St. Laurent telephoned Mackenzie King to tell him that the advice he'd had from three lawyers was that Raymond Boyer's testimony linking Fred Rose to RDX espionage now necessitated the man's immediate arrest. That same day charges were preferred against both men.[3]

There was some concern that Freddy might choose to remain in the parliament building, defying arrest and creating a scene. The prime minister rejected the suggestion that the case be dealt with by a Bill of Attainder, involving the nullification of the MP's civil rights.

Freddy was, as Mackenzie King said he would be, in his Commons seat on 14 March. He was arrested at his Ottawa apartment that evening.

On 15 March 1946 a search warrant was issued for Freddy's Montreal residence and office and his Ottawa apartment. Four typewriters and correspondence were seized. Among the documents was a long letter an accused party "stool pigeon" *Doug* had written to Harry Binder. In a groveling tract the apparently blameless Doug Johnstone struggled to defend himself from the Binder accusation. I want to state, he wrote, "that from a political point of view your suspicions are quite justifiable because no true socialist movement can afford to have stool pigeons in its membership."[4] Given the detailed reports on party meetings and discussions the Mounties were receiving, there clearly was, as Harry Binder suspected, a ringer in party ranks. It wasn't Doug, a fellow entirely unknown to the Force.

Freddy was escorted to Montreal by RCMP Inspector Clifford Harvison. Present at the arraignment the following day were his lawyers, Joseph Cohen, Albert Marcus and Abe Feiner.

---

2. "Re: Labour Progressive Party, Montreal, P.Q.," RCMP, "C" Division reports, 5, 6 March 1946.
3. William Lyon Mackenzie King, Diary, 14 March 1946.
4. "Exhibit Report" RCMP, "C" Division, Montreal, P.Q., 15 March 1946, also a reference to material seized in Ottawa, by RCMP "A" Division.

It was more or less a week earlier that Winston Churchill, British prime minister no longer, arrived at Westminster College in Fulton, Missouri in the company of President Harry Truman to receive an honorary degree. The degree conferred Churchill rose to inform America and the world that an *iron curtain* had descended across Europe, that it would be wrong for America and Great Britain to share A-bomb knowledge with their erstwhile Moscow ally. Churchill was looking for American help in restoring the battered empire, an entreaty Truman ignored.

On 16 March Freddy and Boyer appeared before a judge, the preliminary hearing set to open 22 March.

In Montreal, authorities claimed they feared trouble from Freddy's supporters. There were several demonstrations, one or two public meetings, some arrests and fines for three young men caught distributing the single-sheet flyer "Why was Fred Rose Arrested?" A crowd that had gathered for a meeting was dispersed by police there to arrest anyone observed distributing the flyers.[5]

The RCMP and the city police department's anti-Communist squad waited for four hours at downtown Philips Square for a scheduled demonstration that never happened. As reported by the RCMP, Harry Binder told a meeting of party functionaries on 19 March 1946 that "much fear existed amongst members of the English section and especially the professionals in view of Dr. Boyer having turned 'stool pigeon'," and that canceling the Philips Square demo was a smart move. Party honchos Tim Buck, Sam Carr, and Freddy thought the demonstrations would be used by the government as a pretext for launching an increasingly violent attack on the party.[6]

Out on $10,000 bail, Freddy was back in his Commons seat 18 March. On that day, Mackenzie King asked the House to consider the possibility that perhaps the Soviet leader knew nothing of the Soviet espionage operation. He was, he said, giving some thought to a visit to Moscow to get Stalin's explanation. It was a proposition the RCMP

---

5. "Rose Backers Fined $10 for Distributing Papers," *The Montreal Standard,* 16 March 1946; "Rose Backers Expected to Make Trouble," *The Montreal Daily Star,* 16 March 1946; "New Rose Circulars Lead to Arrests," *The Montreal Gazette,* 20 March 1946.
6. Re Harry Binder, "Labour Progressive Party, Montreal, P.Q.," RCMP, "C" Division, Montreal, P.Q.," 26, 29 March 1946.

heard as the sound of a finger nail running the width of a long black-board. The Force persuaded the prime minister to put the idea out of his head.

Igor, scheduled to testify at the pre-trial hearing, was said to be much apprehensive about making a public appearance. Police, it was reported, walked up and down each long row of seats, peered under the benches, and locked all the doors except the main door through which Igor and his bodyguards would enter.[7]

Philippe Brais, the Crown Prosecutor, referred to Freddy as "a betrayer of his country" and, raising his voice, called Freddy "a traitor to His Majesty."[8] Igor testified at the hearing for three days, 22, 23, and 25 March. In response to questions about himself and the documents, he repeated the account he'd given the RCMP and the royal commission.

Boyer, described as looking "impeccable in his dark blue suit" appeared on 26 March. He told the court what he'd told the commission that he'd given Freddy details of the RDX explosive in late 1943 and 1944, that he had been "anxious to do what (he) could to give the Soviet Union the process."[9] On 28 March Freddy was committed to trial by Judge Rene Theberge. His bail was revoked and he was ordered back to jail, to "be kept until delivered, according to law" which obliged Freddy to spend a night in a cell. The next day Freddy's lead lawyer Joseph Cohen made an application for bail, which was opposed by the prosecution team, Federal Crown Prosecutor F. Philippe Brais KC and Chief Crown Prosecutor for the Montreal District Oscar Gagnon KC. The trial judge Wilfred Lazure agreed to bail of $25,000 with a proviso. Rose, said the judge "...I have come to the conclusion to let you go free on bail because I want you to feel sure that before this court at your trial you will get justice." While at liberty Freddy was to refrain from holding public meetings, to tell his friends to keep quiet, and not undertake the distribution of pamphlets. Freddy promised the judge he would be good.[10]

7. *The Montreal Daily Star,* 22 March 1946. Also, "The Examination of Igor Gouzenko," 22, 23, 25 March 1946; "The Examination of Raymond Boyer," 26 March 1946.
8. "Gave Top War Secrets to Help Communists," *The Montreal Daily Star,* 26 March 1946.
9. "Gave Top Secrets," *The Montreal Daily Star,* 26 March 1946.
10. "Rose Free on Bail—Warned to Keep Quiet," *The Montreal Daily Star,* 29 March 1946.

In the course of the proceedings Joseph Cohen pointed out legal oddities in the Official Secrets Act, provisions that "depart radically from the well-known principles of British Justice....we find in this Official Secrets Act...the strange provision that an accused may be convicted and it shall not be necessary to show that the accused person is guilty of any particular act tending to show purposes prejudicial to the interests of the State. Notwithstanding that no such act is proved against him he may be convicted if, from the circumstances of the cases, or his conduct, or his known bad character, it appears that his purpose was prejudicial to the interests of the State."

A couple of radio stations in Montreal had begun repeating the Russian embassy claim that Igor was a thief and a liar.[11]

At a 16 April 1946 meeting of the party's Provincial Committee leading Quebec party member Evariste Dubé wondered whether, with the opening of the trial near, the National Executive believed Freddy would be sent to the penitentiary. The party, Harry Binder said, expected a conviction. There had been talk of ousting Sam Carr. Someone asked if Carr had gone into hiding in Montreal. He would, said Binder, "be foolish not to hide." The party contributed several thousand dollars to Freddy's defense.[12]

The Fred Rose trial opened 27 May 1946.[13] The following day, Cohen assisted by Valmore Bienvenue K C, Abe Feiner and Albert Marcus was able to persuade the court to sever the charges, which meant two separate trials, one for conspiracy, the other for Official Secrets Act violations.[14]

The prosecution strategy, constructed out of Igor's documents, his testimony and that of Raymond Boyer, was to demonstrate to the jury that: i) an elaborate Soviet espionage scheme had operated out of the USSR's Ottawa embassy; ii) that Freddy had been deeply involved in it; and iii) that he had *conspired* with Raymond Boyer to turn over the improved RDX formula to Col. Zabotin in violation of the Official Secrets

11. "Memorandum re trial—no. 3," 5 April 1946.
12. Re Harry Binder, "Labour Progressive Party, Montreal, P.Q.," RCMP, "C" Division, 20, 25 April 1946.
13. Selected Fred Rose trial transcripts and related documents obtained through the kind cooperation of the Hon. Michel Robert, Chief Justice of Quebec, Quebec Court of Appeal, series en appeal 2154, 500-01-1946, Palais de Justice, Montreal, Quebec.
14. "Cogent Argument of Rose's Defense Wins One Motion, Delays Decision," *The Montreal Gazette*, 28 May 1946.

Act. There was in the trial as there was in the course of the royal commission inquiry an attempt to link Freddy to Soviet atomic bomb espionage.

Brais presented the Crown's case to the jury: "…the evidence which the Crown intends to place before you bears on the charge, the charge of conspiracy." The essential point in the information sworn by René J. Noel of the RCMP on 14 March 1946 ordering Freddy's arrest was that between the "1st day of January 1943 and the 31st day of December 1944, FRED ROSE, electrician did commit indictable offenses in that he did unlawfully …conspire with DOCTOR RAYMOND BOYER, together and with one another… contrary to the Official Secrets Act, 3 George VI, Chapter 49," that Freddy had acted in a manner "prejudicial to the safety and interest of Canada by communicating information calculated to be directly and indirectly useful to a foreign power, to wit, the Union of Soviet Socialist Republics."[15]

By law, two elements are required to prove conspiracy: a common plan and a concrete step taken, the criminal deed itself not needing to be carried out as planned.

For Cohen, the case against Freddy rested on the initial plank of the prosecution strategy: to persuade the jury that there was a major Soviet espionage operation at the embassy, which, as Cohen put it, made Igor "the main witness against us."

The code name *DeBouz*, also referred to in the translated documents as *Debouz*, was coined from Freddy's opening request upon arriving at the embassy: Where's da booze? Perhaps it was during the trial that Freddy first learned the Russians referred to him by that term.

Cohen sought with no success to have Igor's documents excluded from the proceedings, arguing that according to the 1708 Diplomatic Privileges Act of the British Parliament in the reign of Queen Anne they were protected by the rules of diplomatic immunity. Prosecution lawyers, in a pre-trial review, were aware Cohen would raise the issue, but were confident the claim needed to come from the "interested country." The judge rejected the defense request on the grounds that "the privilege of diplomatic immunity can be invoked, and invoked only

---

15. The Hon. F. Philippe Brais for the Prosecution, 28 May 1946; "The Information and Complaint of René J. Noel," 14 March 1946.

by the foreign government interested in this matter, through its ambassador or duly appointed representative; this privilege is personal to
the ambassador, his assistants and servants, and it affects also his
belongings, his papers and documents....it can be claimed...only when
the ambassador or some members of his retinue are on trial themselves
or when a charge is being laid against them, or a legal process is issued
against their properties."[16]

Judge Lazure further ruled that the testimony given to the royal
commission would be inadmissible, meaning Igor and Boyer and the
others would have to repeat that testimony with Freddy looking on.

Cohen, albeit an experienced criminal lawyer, sought to bolster
Freddy's defense by enlisting on the defense team the crusading left-
wing British barrister, Denis Nowell Pritt. Tim Buck would claim that
this was done at his suggestion. Pritt later said he'd taken on the case for
a nominal fee, out of a sense of duty.[17] The Quebec bar refused to admit
him which limited his role to advising on cross examination. Pritt found
the evidence against Freddy thin and unrelated to the conspiracy charge,
a finding that, as it turned out, was irrelevant. Pritt, recalled Buck, had
said that Freddy "would be acquitted or he will be declared guilty on the
basis of politics."

To prove to the jury that there had been an intricate Russian espionage operation Freddy was enmeshed in, the Crown called various witnesses, the key ones being Igor Gouzenko and Raymond Boyer. The
people who possessed the most informed knowledge of the matter, the
Russians Zabotin, Sokolov, Rogov, and the others, could not and would
not be heard from. The evidence crucial to Fred Rose's conviction for
conspiracy could only come from the mouth of Raymond Boyer and
did.

Trial day no. 3, 29 May 1946, Igor was called to the witness stand.
Wearing a brown suit and matching tie he was described as looking
weak. Igor spoke in a low voice, with a pronounced Russian accent at
times experiencing language difficulties. He had, the prosecution pointed
out, left a sick bed. Next day, Igor in a gray suit and dark spotted tie,

16. Correspondence, Bram and Campbell, Barristers-Solicitors to Gerald Fauteux, 29 April 1946; Judge
Lazure, *Rex v. Rose*, Quebec Court of King's Bench, 28 May 1946.
17. "Noted British Lawyer Here to Help M.P.," *The Montreal Daily Star*, 10 June 1946; D. N. Pritt, "Fred
Rose," in *The Autobiography of D. H. Pritt, Brasshats and Bureaucrats, part 2,* Lawrence and Wishart, 1966.

seemed better, fresher. Brais explained to the court that he had been under observation for acute appendicitis. The court was cleared of all spectators except for the press and others connected with the case.[18]

Igor, who testified for five days, explained that he'd gone to *The Journal* not the RCMP because he believed "there might be agents of the NKVD in the Royal Mounted Police" that he believed he needed to make a public statement and the newspaper seemed to him the best way to do that. In a pre-trial attempt to persuade prospective jury members that Igor was an erratic character, Cohen asked him about his suspicions that the RCMP had been penetrated by the Soviets. Igor, who in the USSR had been given the third degree by experts, pointed to Freddy. If, he said, the Soviets got to an MP they could get to anybody. Igor wasn't entirely wrong. As John Sawatsky pointed out in *For Services Rendered: Leslie James Bennett and the RCMP Security Service* (1982), there were indeed Soviets agents in the RCMP.

While Igor was in the witness box a half dozen RCMP men in civilian dress stationed themselves in various parts of the courtroom keeping an eye on the audience, never on the proceedings behind their backs. For effect, throughout the trial, that six-man Mountie bodyguard always accompanied Igor during his appearances, posing that they were on the alert for danger emanating from both inside and outside the courtroom: "The Mountie whose job it was to stand directly behind the former Russian cipher clerk kept his eyes almost constantly on the two large windows on either side of the courtroom to guard the room's interior. Through these windows there was always the possibility of a bullet coming, fired by a hidden sniper placed in a higher location in an adjoining building....there was always at least one Mountie whose eyes kept sweeping these vantage points for the flash of a rifle or other fire-arm intended to take the life of the espionage ring's tipoff man."[19]

The documents Igor had absconded with described an espionage scheme based at the embassy that pointed to Freddy as a key figure, responsible for organizing a group of agents at the NRC, where research related to the development of the A-bomb was in progress.

18. *The Montreal Daily Star*, 29, 30 May 1946; "Deposition of Igor Gouzenko."
19. "Hidden Snipers Watched for Rose Trial," *The Montreal Daily Star,* 7 June 1946.

The questioning of Igor by Brais, apparently to clarify the content of documents and confirm Igor's competence to do that, was also intended to reveal details of the relationship of embassy officials, Col. Zabotin, Rogov, Motinov, and others, to Gordon Lunan, Israel Halperin, David Shugar, Sam Carr, Edward Mazerall, Alan Nunn May, and others.

There was a reference in the questioning of Igor to a key piece of evidence in the form of a document that said that "a list of the material received from agents and sent to Moscow in one parcel in January 1945" by Zabotin included "material furnished by Fred Rose" relating to a "conversation with Professor [Boyer]....a specialist on explosives... He gave material...on the formula for RDX in November 1944."

Igor testified that following the victory over Japan Zabotin told embassy staff yesterday's allies were "today's neighbors and tomorrow's enemies."

In his testimony to the commission, Igor had explained the references in the documents to Freddy's contacts and to meetings and related activities involving Canadian agents he'd recruited, among them Israel Halperin, a professor of mathematics who worked on classified artillery research for the Canadian army.

On one occasion, there might have been others, the Russians were unable to confirm the accuracy of the information received from their Canadian assets. A cable drafted but not sent to Moscow, from Motinov, signed by Zabotin: "To the Director: The Professor has advised that the Director of the National Chemical Research Committee...told me about a new plant in Grand Mere [*sic*] in the Province of Quebec. This plant will produce uranium. The engineering personnel is being obtained from McGill University and is already moving into the district of the new plant."

Perhaps unable to understand what Boyer had told him about RDX, Freddy was the likely source of the confusion. The prosecutor did not ask Igor why the cable was not forwarded. Perhaps the reference to uranium was sufficient to serve the purpose of including it among the other trial exhibits, thereby suggesting that the Boyer-Rose conspiracy in fact had a larger, more lethal purpose. Then too, Motinov and Zabotin and company may not in fact have known much more about atomic bomb research than Freddy did.

While Igor testified Stalin, citing health reasons, apparently sent word that he was putting off a scheduled visit to the United States.

In Cohen's cross examination, Igor confirmed that he first thought about defecting in August 1944 after he'd learned than he was to be sent back to the USSR. In July 1945 he began to remove documents from the embassy, at first just one. In August he took a telegram that referred to Freddy, the one that said "Debouz, had obtained particulars from conversations with officers who took part on the Western Front, particulars obtained from conversations with the latter" and mentioned Freddy's re-election, also that Tim Buck and Sam Carr both failed in their 1945 election bids. The conversation with the military people concerned heavy artillery.

Igor then seemed to recall that between August and September 1945 he took other documents. Cohen: "So in July you took one document and in August you took another document and on September 5th you took the balance of the documents?" Igor: "That's right."

Why, Cohen asked Igor, did he decide to defect on 5 September 1945? Igor said he'd been assigned the task of training his replacement named Kulakov, who "was working in the room everyday with me." On 5 September Kulakov was "on duty in the house of the Military Attaché; the Military attaché himself, his whole staff, Zabotin, Rogov and others, were in [*sic*] the National Film Board: they were seeing a picture and it was the only day I got to do this."

Igor testified that he'd never met Freddy or seen him at the embassy, that he'd only seen documents that referred to him, both as *Fred* and as *Debouz*, that all the information he'd provided about Freddy came from those documents.

On 6 June, the last day of the cross examination, Igor said there was no file on Freddy at the embassy, though there were files on others, Gordon Lunan, Sam Carr, Durnford Smith. Cohen attempted to persuade the jury that the documents referring to Freddy were no more to be taken seriously than the ones that referred to David Shugar who had been acquitted. Judge Lazure would not allow the point.

Raymond Boyer, the key witness against Freddy, followed Igor to the witness stand. Identified as Freddy's key co-conspirator, he repeated what he'd told the commission, that he assumed the RDX information he gave Freddy would be passed on to a Russian technical mission in Canada. Boyer, following his arrest, had spoken freely to the RCMP and insisted that what he'd done he'd done to help a Canadian wartime ally, though he knew it was against the law to do so. At issue was the improved formula the professor had worked on for manufacturing the explosive RDX.

Boyer said the RDX plant was built on a side road a mile and a half or two miles off the Shawinigan-Grand Mere highway. He knew, he said, that the Russian Technical Mission had requested the RDX process from Canada officially, and that the Americans had opposed the request. Freddy, he said, learned about that situation from him, which does not refute the claim that Freddy got in touch with Boyer after receiving a request for assistance from members of the Soviet technical mission. At some point Freddy phoned and invited Boyer over to his apartment.

There were three discussions with Freddy about RDX, one in late 1943, another in the spring or summer of 1944, about the fact that there was a new RDX process. It turned out there were five elements in the new process not four, but Boyer said he only gave Freddy four. A third RDX discussion at Freddy's apartment took place in November 1944. In response to a question from Brais, Boyer said the newspaper stories about a new RDX process did not reveal certain aspects of the process he had shared with Freddy.

Boyer said he'd met Zabotin once. The Russian had visited his home in Montreal in connection with a clothing drive.

Freddy refused to testify. The trial, he said, was intended, "to smear honest and patriotic Canadians."

Many years later, commenting on Boyer's claim that he'd been taking notes to hand over to Col. Zabotin when Boyer was describing the RDX formula, Freddy told an acquaintance that Boyer could have had no idea what he was scribbling.[20]

The time to make that statement had long passed. In the course of the trial, Cohen had attempted to point out the complexity of the RDX process, that it was not something Boyer might have successfully explained to Freddy, a person with almost zero scientific training in a few minutes.

---

20. Weisbord, *The Strangest Dream*.

Cohen: "...you told us that when you were discussing, on this occasion, RDX with Rose that he once took notes on the back of an envelope on an armchair?

Boyer: As I remember it, yes.

Cohen: Lengthy notes? Did it take long to write these notes?

Boyer: What do you mean?

Cohen: Was he writing for a long time?

Boyer: No, I wouldn't say a long time.

Cohen: How long?

Boyer: Well, perhaps ten minutes, perhaps five minutes.

Cohen: Could you tell Rose more in five or ten minutes about RDX than you could tell me along the lines of the question that I asked you yesterday, where you undertook to instruct me in RDX?

Boyer: No.

Boyer said he told Freddy about four of the compounds—hexametromythalen, ammonium nitrate, acetic acid, and anhydride. Not the fifth, nitric acid used in the RDX facility at the Woolwich Arsenal, because he did not know about it.[21]

During the Boyer trial in December 1947, the Assistant Director of the Explosives Research Division, Department of Munitions and Supply, Kenneth H. Cheetham, testified that he had been instructed to accompany two Soviet explosive experts, B. E. Fomin and P. Solodov, through the RDX plant in Shawinigan. This took place on 8 August 1944. The Russians, he said, saw everything, discussed various aspects of the manufacturing process, and spoke to plant employees. There was no question of withholding any information from them; the process was discussed without reservation.[22]

In February 1943 the British government had received a request from their WW2 Soviet allies for information about the production of the explosive based on the Anglo-Soviet Technical Agreement. The British were willing to help Stalin fight the Nazis. The American Joint Chiefs of Staff opposed the sharing of this weapons information.[23]

---

21. Deposition of Raymond Boyer.
22. Donald H. Avery, *The Science of War: Canadian Scientists and Allied Military Technology During the Second World War*, University of Toronto Press, 1998.
23. Donald Avery, "Allied Scientific Cooperation and Soviet Espionage in Canada," Intelligence and National Security, Vol. 8, No. 3, July 1993.

Important work on RDX was being done in Canada by *the Professor* and his colleagues. Mackenzie King was the official patron of the National Council for Canadian Soviet Friendship founded in June 1943, the Professor a member. Boyer's unhappiness with the American decision may have prodded him into whispering in Zabotin's ear. Perhaps Sokolov, understanding Boyer's reluctance to become directly involved, put Freddy on the case. Boyer received the first RDX phone call from Rose in late 1943. In the course of the Boyer trial it was revealed that in August 1944, Fred Rose was approached by the Soviet technical mission in Canada for RDX information.[24]

The information Freddy turned over to the Russians, following the first conversation with Boyer in 1943, may have been, given his near complete lack of familiarity with the topic, of limited value. Thus the second meeting with Boyer encouraged by the August 1944 Russian request. A third meeting might have been necessary due to additional problems in the information Freddy was passing on. Boyer was not asked to explain why there were three meetings each one months apart.

Apparently Fomin and Solodov on their tour of the RDX plant were told whatever they wanted to know about the manufacture of the explosive. Unlike Freddy, these were individuals who would have had no difficulty understanding what was being said to them.

But that information too may have been inadequate. "We may note," concluded Prof. Edward, a one-time Boyer graduate student, "that after May 1945 the Russians probably knew everything of practical importance about the German processes for making RDX through their occupation of eastern Germany, and hence any information transmitted to them in August 1944 had only fleeting importance."

Cohen pointed out that there had been a story about RDX in *Life* magazine and that Russians had been invited to visit an RDX plant, so how secret could the secret have been? He informed the court that two of his key witnesses had become unavailable: Ronald Herbert, who might have provided details of the visit of the Russian specialists to the RDX plant, and an official in the federal Department of Munitions and Supply who had accompanied the Russians on the tour.

---

24. John T. Edward, "Wartime Research on RDX," Journal of Chemical Education, Vol. 64, No. 7, July 1987.

What the lawyer did not know was that a Shawinigan plant staffer claimed that during 1943 he'd shipped hundreds of thousands of pounds of RDX to Russia under the Mutual Aid plan. Or so he told a *Montreal Gazette* reporter in December, 1947.

To reinforce the connection between the conspiracy and the Party, the prosecution team called RCMP constable Leonard Gendron to the stand. He testified that on 16 April 1943 he'd observed Freddy hanging around Montreal's Windsor Station. Off the train that arrived at 9:50 a.m. stepped party head Tim Buck. The two walked north and entered a building at 2048 Union Avenue, the home of Gordon Lunan. The following evening, Freddy, Tim Buck, and Sam Carr gathered at the same address.

Gordon Lunan, Matt Nightingale, Eric Adams, Emma Woikin, and Harold Gerson all refused to testify at Freddy's trial and were charged with contempt of court.

The Canadian espionage operation did provide the Soviets with atomic bomb information but that was not anything Freddy had anything to do with. The 162 micrograms of Uranium 233 and 235 the Russians received from Alan Nunn May, who worked on the bomb project at Chalk River, Ontario, as well as at the NRC in Montreal, and for which he received two bottles of whiskey and $200, were delivered directly to Col. Zabotin. RDX research had no connection to the bomb though Freddy himself might have thought it did. The data the Russians acquired from the spy work of Bruno Pontecorvo remains an unknown.

What was the crime for which Freddy would be convicted and go to prison? Apart from the single purloined document stating that Col. Zabotin had received RDX information from Prof. Boyer via Freddy, there was no evidence, other than Boyer's testimony, that Freddy had delivered the RDX formula or any other technical secret to the USSR. Prof. Boyer's testimony about the alleged plan to do that was, Cohen argued, the only possible source of a proven conspiracy implicating his client. All considered, the Crown succeeded in nailing Freddy on a bare technicality which, however meager, was more than a match for the formidable Joseph Cohen. Freddy would do time, less for anything he'd done than for what he'd imagined he'd done.

With the trial in progress *L'Action Catholique,* in a 7 June 1946 editorial "It is High Time to Block Their Way," said of party leader Tim Buck that "….had it not been for certain Jews from Central Europe, and a minority of blind French-Canadians, he would never have managed to elect a member of parliament…his protégé Fred Rose is now before a court of justice."[25]

The Fred Rose trial took place in a Quebec courtroom while the padlock law remained the law of the province. The veneer of impartiality conveyed by a Jewish judge and a Jewish prosecution team in the 1951 trial of Julius and Ethel Rosenberg was not here required. The padlock law target was less Communists than *Jewish* Communists, no more beloved by the Jewish establishment than by the Duplessis regime.

A former Cohen law partner told me Cohen believed it was the Mounties in the courtroom that turned the jury against his client. We never, he said recounting the Mountie maneuver, had a chance. Perhaps it was the case that once the Russians would not claim diplomatic immunity for Igor's documents—it remains unclear whether this would have been a viable legal option—and Raymond Boyer resolved to tell all, the case was pretty much lost. As for Joseph Cohen's courtroom battle to get a not-guilty verdict, it was pointed out to me by another of Cohen's law partners that there were from the start two strikes against him: the political atmosphere and the facts were both against him.[26]

Front page newspaper headlines on the last day of the trial told of a meteor that exploded over Rhode Island and of the decision of the Canadian government not to build an atomic bomb. Among the fabled accounts of what transpired on that day is that on the morning of Saturday, 15 June 1946, with the weather in the mid-seventies, the jury was promised a picnic if they got done before lunch, and so came up with a verdict of guilty after a fast fifteen-minute deliberation. In fact, no picnic was promised. Lengthy addresses to the jury by the defense and the prosecution, consumed most of the day.

Rose, said Cohen, was charged with conspiring with twenty-two people and others, likening the indictment to a recipe: "Take a section of the Criminal Code which has terrible latitude in regard to evidence…add

---

25. "It Is High Time to Block Their Way," *L'Action Catholique,* 7 June 1946. Trans. by AMB at RCMP Headquarters.
26. Private communications.

holus bolus articles of the Official Secrets Act, add Russian sauce with the other names in the indictment, add a number of others, without naming them, mix until confused, heat to a boiling point and give it to Rose." There was, said Cohen referring to the testimony of Prof. Boyer, no evidence of conspiracy.

Before the members of the jury were sent off to deliberate Mr. Justice Wilfred Lazure disingenuously reminded them of the *de facto* political character of the alleged crime by pointing out that the trial was not about the politics of the accused. The question to be answered, he said, was whether Freddy was guilty of conspiracy, which was to say, whether he had been involved in an agreement to accomplish an unlawful purpose. Was there an understanding between Freddy and others to violate the Official Secrets Act? You may, he said of the testimony of Raymond Boyer, view that evidence as the evidence of an accomplice who admitted communicating certain secret war information to the accused. In other words, what was critical was not whether Freddy had obtained information from Boyer he knew to be unlawfully received and communicated that information to the representative of a foreign power, but merely whether he and Boyer had been involved in a scheme to do that, and had taken step two. If that was the case, then Freddy was guilty as charged, i.e., of conspiracy to violate the Official Secrets Act.

The evidence, said the judge, "shows a general conspiracy or a general plot of espionage in Canada between certain Russian people and a certain number of Canadians…" The judge further pointed out to the jury that "the discovery of the four ingredients for a new way to produce RDX was very important, and that Russia was after it, and that it was exactly what the accused got from Boyer; and in the documents it is shown clearly that the RDX formula was obtained from the Professor by Rose, and went to Moscow through Sokolov."

It was 11 p.m. when the jury went off to deliberate. Judge Lazure had concluded his address to the jury with the uncertainty about whether he could expect a verdict that evening. Juryman no.2 assured the judge that arriving at a verdict would not take long: "…I would suggest to your lordship, with the concurrence of the rest of the jury, that perhaps you might wait for a little longer." It took a mere 31 minutes.[27]

Waiting to hear the verdict Freddy was described as standing between two burly policemen, appearing more diminutive than ever, attempting to put on a jaunty expression while nervously wetting his lips.

An appeal against the conviction was entered on 17 June 1946.[28]

On June 20 Judge Lazure sentenced Freddy to a six-year term in St. Vincent de Paul Penitentiary, one day longer than was required to deprive him of his elected seat in the House of Commons.[29]

Freddy was convicted under *3 George VI, Chapter 49, An Act respecting Official Secrets* which said in part that: "Any person who attempts to commit any offense under this Act, or solicits or incites or endeavors to persuade another person to commit an offense, or aids or abets or does any act preparatory to the commission of an offense under this Act, shall be guilty of an offense under this Act.... Where no specific penalty is provided in this Act, any person who is guilty of an offense under this Act shall be deemed to be guilty of an indictable offense, and shall on conviction be punishable by a fine not exceeding two thousand dollars, or by imprisonment for a term not exceeding seven years with or without hard labor, or by both fine and imprisonment; but such person may, at the election of the Attorney General, be prosecuted summarily...and if so prosecuted, shall be punishable by fine not exceeding five hundred dollars, or by imprisonment not exceeding twelve months, with or without hard labor, or by both fine and imprisonment."

All considered, Judge Lazure, whom the Act presented with sentencing options, imposed a harsher punishment than he was absolutely required to.

Freddy was tried, convicted and would serve a prison term for *conspiring* to violate the Official Secrets Act, i.e., for *plotting t*o turn over to the Soviet technical mission via Col. Zabotin information about RDX he'd gotten from explosives expert Raymond Boyer, *not* for actually having done so.

---

27. Judge Lazure, "Address to the Jury," 15 June 1946.
28. "Rose to File Appeal In Spying Conviction," *The Montreal Daily Star,* 17 June 1946.
29. The King v. Fred Rose, in the Court of King's Bench, Montreal, 20 June 1946.

In the motion to appeal, Cohen cited a range of legal errors and the 18th century statute from the reign of Queen Anne, claiming the Soviet documents presented in evidence had "diplomatic privilege."

The conviction barred Freddy from occupying his seat in the House of Commons. According to House rules, no member may occupy a seat while serving a sentence following conviction for a criminal offense.[30]

Awaiting the results of the appeal, Freddy was denied bail on an offer of $25,000 and held in solitary confinement in Bordeaux Jail. A Court of Appeal judge, Mr. Justice Gregor Barclay, ruled that the grounds of appeal "are almost entirely pure questions of law, not requiring frequent consultation with the prisoner. In view of this, of the Crown's representations, the applicant's record and the special circumstances of this case, I have come to the conclusion that the ends of justice will be best served by refusing this application." Referring to Freddy's 1931 conviction for "seditious utterances" and his 1942 internment, the judge added that "In addition to supplying this record based upon official documents and statements which are not contradicted by counsel of the applicant…counsel for the Crown has stated that he was instructed to inform me that there is grave reason to believe that the accused will not surrender himself if released on bail." Instructed by whom the court was not told.[31]

The Fred Rose Defense Committee asked why it was that "murderers, gangsters, and peddlers of narcotics are granted bail pending their appeals" but a working-class member of Parliament for Cartier was considered "too dangerous."[32]

In early July Fanny Rose travelled to Ottawa to discuss her husband's case with members of Parliament. She was seeking to arrange bail. The refusal to grant bail while the appeal was pending, she said, was unjust and bordered on persecution. In Bordeaux, Freddy was being held in solitary confinement, not permitted out of his cell for fresh air, not allowed visitors other than his wife and his lawyer. Freddy said that he was unable to obtain newspapers, not allowed to use the jail writing

---

30. "Rose Barred From Commons," *Sydney Post-Record* (Nova Scotia), 24 June 1946.
31. Fred Rose, "C" Division, RCMP, Montreal, 26 June 1946. A report on the decision by appeal court judge Gregor Barclay not to grant bail.
32. *The Fred Rose Defense Committee*, 27 July 1946.

room, could not receive food or cigarettes, and was not taken out for exercise.[33]

The prison governor, Dr. D. Z. Lesage, denied that Freddy was being isolated and persecuted. He was, Lesage said, receiving regular inmate treatment, was given the usual amount of exercise and had a window in his cell he could open and close at will.[34]

A Progressive Conservative Member of Parliament received a round of applause from fellow MPs when he rose to ask the prime minister when he would declare the Cartier seat vacant. Nothing, said Mackenzie King, would happen until the appeal against his conviction has been heard.[35]

To help pass the time and get out of his cell, Freddy put in a request to work in Bordeaux Jail's large garden.[36]

Still an MP, Freddy in a letter dated 9 July 1946, wrote to the Minister of Justice, Louis St. Laurent, pointing out the unfairness and prejudice of his treatment by the prosecutor Philippe Brais, and the RCMP, and asking that he be allowed out on bail while his appeal was pending. All of the dozen or so Jews among the one hundred persons called for jury duty were dismissed: "Hardly was a Jewish name called when Mr. Brais said: 'Stand aside.'"[37]

Attempting to point out that by his behavior it ought to be clear that he had no intention of skipping bail, that the regulations in Bordeaux were such that he "was practically in solitary confinement," that the time in Bordeaux would be not counted as part of the sentence if the appeal failed, Freddy asked that if bail was out of the question, he be transferred to the penitentiary while the appeal was pending. The letter was tabled in the House at the request of a CCF member. There is no record of a reply.

Fanny Rose said the request did not mean they had given up hope of a successful appeal.

33. "Mrs. Rose Visits M.P.s in Ottawa," *The Montreal Gazette,* 4 July 1946.

34. "Jail Governor Denies Charge," *The Montreal Daily Star,* 4 July 1946.

35. "Rose Seat Not Vacant Till Appeal—Mr. King," *The Toronto Daily Star,* 5 July 1946.

36. "Rose Working in City Jail at Own Request," *The Montreal Daily Star,* 9 July 1946.

37. Correspondence, Fred Rose to the Hon. Louis St. Laurent, Minister of Justice, Ottawa, 9 July 1946. The 16 May 1946 Fred Rose jury list has this entry: "3412—Hyman S. Finenerg. This man is a foreman in a clothing factory. Naturalized on 13-12-40. He is a Russian Jew, 57 yrs, landed in Canada in 1891." The list contained the names of individuals who "committed certain offenses." In one case, selling liquor to Indians, in another a subscriber to *The Canadian Tribune,* the party paper. The offense of Mr. Fineberg is unstated.

A second bail application in September by another of Freddy's lawyer's, Albert Marcus, did little beyond delaying the decision of the Court of Appeal by a month.[38]

In October Mrs. Rose claimed that her husband was, despite assertions to the contrary, being subjected on orders from Maurice Duplessis, "to continued persecution and discrimination," that Freddy was still being held "in complete solitary confinement. Letters are being withheld without explanation" that he was "not even allowed to read magazines like *The Nation* and *The New Republic*."[39]

The Fred Rose Defense Committee argued that in the previous decade of 157 persons whose cases were on appeal only three had been denied bail. Near 4,000 signatures were collected by the defense committee on a petition requesting the Minister of Justice arrange for Fred Rose to be released on bail. But that too did not change the judge's mind, nor did Fanny's request to plead the case in person with the prime minister.[40]

Freddy, said party head Tim Buck, would be expelled from the party if his pending appeal was dismissed.[41]

In mid-November Harry Binder wrote LPP comrades about the circumstances of the incarcerated Fred Rose: "Up in Bordeaux Jail there is a 'treatment' known as 'Deadlock.' Between 'Deadlock' and the condition known as 'solitary confinement' there is very little difference…. Fred Rose has been kept for over four months in 'deadlock.' He is given no suitable work; he is allowed to read only moronic literature; he is not given the means of writing; his letters are subject to the strictest political censorship; and he gets only 30 minutes of exercise in a bleak jail-yard day…. That's the way Duplessis is treating the elected member of parliament for Cartier…. I know that recently there were only two other prisoners in 'deadlock' at Bordeaux. One was a desperado who had shot his way out of a couple of jails; the other was a notorious swindler…. And Fred Rose denied bail in spite of a nationwide outcry by organized labor and the people's organizations—awaiting the outcome of an

---

38. "Rose to Make New Bail Bid," *The Montreal Standard*, 21 September 1946; "Bail Try Again Fails for Rose," *The Montreal Daily Star*, 23 September 1946.
39. "Rose 'Persecuted in Jail' Wife Charges," *The Montreal Standard*, 19 October 1946.
40. *The Fred Rose Defense Committee*, 11 November 1946.
41. "Fred Rose Faces LPP Expulsion," *The Sault Daily Star*, 18 November 1946.

appeal which may not be decided for months—is being given this treatment." Letter recipients were pressed to attend a public meeting later that month at which the conditions in which Freddy was being held would be aired. The RCMP man who "discreetly attended" reported that there were "800 persons present composed mostly of Jews and other European persons of the Cartier constituency." Fanny Rose was one of the speakers.[42]

In early December Fanny said that Freddy had apparently been assigned work under the jail electrician. When she went to visit him she was denied admission and learned he was no longer working but in solitary confinement. What were described as "flying squads composed of municipal, provincial and Royal Canadian Police" were sent out to block distribution of a Defense of Fred Rose committee leaflet. A McGill University student, Simon Malamed, was arrested for distributing the leaflets.[43]

All five appeal court judges ruled to dismiss the appeal, the ruling made public 20 December 1946.

On the question of diplomatic immunity for Igor's documents, the judges Galipeault, St. Jacques, Barclay, Bisonnette, and Gagné ruled that: "The privilege of diplomatic immunity given to an Ambassador by international law extends to himself, his personnel, dwelling, documents, archives and correspondence, and can be renounced only by his own State.... Where, therefore, the Executive has submitted documents stolen from the Russian Embassy, which might otherwise be held privileged, for use in a prosecution of one of its own citizens, and Russia has made no claim to immunity in respect of the documents, the Courts have no jurisdiction to determine whether the documents are privileged, and whether the Executive has committed a breach of international law. The Executive having become seized of the documents and having determined to use them, the documents were the property of the Executive, and free from any privilege." A related point made by one of the judges was that according to the evidence, "the Ambassador himself had not, and it was not his duty to have, access to the room in which these documents were prepared and kept."

---

42. Harry Binder, "Letter to LPP Comrades," 15 November 1946.
43. "Quebec Police Hunt Leaflets Defending Rose," *The (Toronto) Evening Telegram*, 10 December 1946.

Judge Lazure's instruction to the jury on the charge of conspiracy was cited in detail by Judge Gagné who concluded that: "…the jurors were not led astray. They knew perfectly well that the accused could not be convicted unless the evidence established that he had plotted with other persons to commit one of the offenses enumerated."

It was a finding of the Crown that Boyer testified with "very considerable reluctance when called," that his deposition contained "extraordinary equivocations and tenuous explanations." Nevertheless testify he did.

In the course of the appeal proceedings Cohen had pointed out that at the heart of "the alleged conspiracy" the prosecution sought to establish that the appellant—Freddy—"took casual notes on a scrap of paper" of Boyer's account of the RDX formula: "We invite this honorable court to read the stenographic report as transcribed by the official court stenographer. This man, trained and experienced in taking short hand notes of witnesses could not get the names of the ingredients accurately, and the ingredients as they appear in the transcribed deposition are misspelled to such an extent that they are entirely misleading and are actually not the ingredients used in the process. We are asked to believe that the appellant, an electrician by trade, and without scientific training, could do better than the official court stenographer, bearing in mind that the appellant made no attempt to obtain more accurate information or to have the names of the ingredients spelled out."

Further, Freddy's lawyer drew the appeal court's attention to the Boyer statement that the RDX process was quite complicated, that he Boyer would not attempt to explain it to a person without scientific training. I do not, said Boyer, think I could explain it to you. The witness, observed Cohen, could not explain it to counsel because counsel was without scientific training and would not be able to repeat it, "there was no question of casual notes on the back of an envelope. The witness would have had all the time he desired to attempt to explain this process to counsel in simple language which could be understood by him and repeated. This could not be done."

As well, Cohen raised an objection to the prosecution's strategy for bolstering what appeared to be the less than solid Boyer testimony: "Here again we must take strong exception to the fact that the witness was called by the Crown on the twelfth day of the trial after a formidable mass of depositions had been made and documents filed, when such evidence and documents legally did not make evidence against the appellant unless the link with the alleged conspiracy had been established. In examining the evidence of witness Boyer, we must bear in mind the rule that unless the evidence of this witness links the appellant with the alleged conspiracy, there is no case against the appellant.... We conclude that the evidence of Boyer is such that no group of intelligent men, considering this evidence dispassionately and without prejudice, could find in this evidence a link to connect the appellant with the alleged conspiracy."

However impeccable the logic, the argument cut no ice with the appeal court. In the view of the court, a flawed conspiracy was no less a conspiracy than one better organized for success. The prosecution rejected what it took to be Cohen's attempt to characterize Freddy as an altogether inept emissary of secret intelligence data and thus an inadequate conspiracy partner: "The defense would have us believe that Rose—himself an electrician by trade—was an ignoramus, utterly unable to make anything out of what Boyer was explaining to him. But, if Rose could not understand what was said to him, why send him as an envoy? Why should Boyer break his oath of secrecy? Why should he confer with Rose on *four* separate occasions, over a period of many months? Why, if as he says, he so ardently desired the advancement of the Russian cause, did he not himself go to the Russians or have them come to him.... [Boyer's] extraordinary explanation...is that Rose was to be his emissary—Rose too ignorant to understand what it was all about! .... The motive of both men would appear all too clear."

The appeal court in a unanimous judgment ruled that the charge against Freddy of conspiracy to violate the Official Secrets Act had been proven. As for the claim of diplomatic immunity for the Gouzenko documents, the accused, "was a Canadian citizen and not a person attached to any Embassy and the documents put in by the Crown were in the possession of the State. Where documents are delivered to a court of justice for the prosecution of a crime committed by one of the citizens of the country, the courts cannot give effect to immunity by reason of diplomatic privilege."

The evidence, said Judge Gagné, was "overwhelmingly conclusive." Further, the court was not prepared to reduce the sentence: "Condemned to 6 years in the penitentiary, the appellant appeals also against the sentence. At the hearing, he first asked that the term be reduced but he stresses above all that, in case the appeal on the merits would be dismissed, the Court decide that the penalty should run not from the judgment on appeal but from the date of the sentence, since the accused has been in prison since that date.

"I must say that upon the petition for leave to appeal, he complains that the sentence is excessive in view of special circumstances not mentioned. He adds that the trial Judge applied erroneous principles, was influenced by illegal considerations and did not consider all the pertinent circumstances in fixing the quantum. The appellant thus invokes the only ground which would permit this court to interfere since sentence is left to the discretion of the trial Judge, but nothing in his petition justifies these grounds. The law provides a maximum of 7 years imprisonment. The Judge condemned him to 6 years. The crime of which the appellant is found guilty is one of the most serious there is and I do not believe there is any reason for this Court to interfere." The request that "the Court count the duration of the sentence from its date and not from the judgment on appeal" was also dismissed.[44]

There is no record of an application by Freddy's lawyers for leave to appeal the case to the Supreme Court of Canada.[45]

A week later, the press reported that Freddy did not intend to resign his seat.[46]

With the news that the appeal had been dismissed, on the morning of 27 December 1946 the party's Provincial Executive Committee met in a room at 254 St. Catherine Street East in Montreal to consider their next move. The party's constitution, Harry Binder explained, required that Freddy be expelled from the party, that this would be the

---

44. "Rose vs the King," 88 CCC 114, Quebec Court of King's Bench, Appeal Side; "Fred Rose, Appellant vs His Majesty, the King, Respondent, Appellant's Factum"; "Fred Rose, Appellant vs His Majesty, the King, Respondent, Respondent's Factum on Questions of Fact."

45. The claim in Weisbord: that "The Supreme Court of Canada, whose justices included R. L. Kellock and Robert Tasschereau, two of the commissioners on the Royal Commission refused to hear the appeal "would appear to be false. I have been advised by the Records Centre, Supreme Court of Canada that they are unable to find any record "that this case applied for leave to appeal to the Supreme Court of Canada." By email 12 November 2010.

46. "I Do Not Intend to Resign Seat, Says Fred Rose," *The Toronto Globe and Mail*, 27 December 1946.

recommendation of National Executive Committee comrades. There were those at the meeting who were opposed. Gui Caron, a prominent party figure in Quebec, said he was not in favor. Henri Gagnon, another high profile Quebec party member, argued that the party should continue its activities in defense of Fred Rose and expose the motivation behind the espionage trials, that a campaign to denounce the Kellock-Tashereau inquiry would liberate Freddy within a year.

Others expressed similar views. Only Harry Binder was opposed to keeping Freddy in the party, claiming that if Freddy were not expelled the comrades in the province of Quebec might otherwise be accused of contempt of court and the party declared illegal, which would do damage to a planned major trade union action. Some agreed, citing the well-known anti-communist element in the trade unions. The Provincial Committee decided to put the discussion on hold till the Montreal visit of Tim Buck the following month. The RCMP had, through a plant, been able to obtain a detailed account of the proceedings, who was there, who said what. It was their view that the National Committee, though in agreement with Harry Binder, would nevertheless rule against Freddy's expulsion, an action that might create serious dissension among the party's leaders in Quebec. A few weeks later, at a meeting of the LPP's Quebec Executive Committee, Gui Caron relayed the thinking of the Executive Committee on Freddy's unsuccessful appeal: there now needed to be a national campaign for another trial. Caron thought that the Fred Rose Defense Committee ought to be the key organizing body of the campaign, to be kicked off by Tim Buck during his forthcoming stay in Montreal.[47]

In November 1946 an American named Joe McCarthy contacted the RCMP claiming an interest in Freddy's trial documents. There is a note from RCMP Superintendent Rivett-Carnac to the Toronto division explaining that the documents would be forwarded to Toronto to be made available to this person. He was not in the note in any other way identified, only that he was an American: "…would you please hand them over to McCarthy and impress on him that we want them back when they have served their purpose." Rivett-Carnac said he was as well

---

47. Labour Progressive Party, Provincial Executive Committee meeting, 27 December 1946, RCMP "C" Division report.

providing photographs and information on the status of "the various espionage cases" and asked that McCarthy be informed that he Rivett-Carnac would be in Toronto and was interested in having lunch with him.

Why did the RCMP get so busy with this guy? Could he have been *that* Joe McCarthy? The FBI told me they were not, then or now, convinced that that McCarthy was the infamous senator from Wisconsin. Too early they thought for Senator Joe, who'd only just won his senate seat. Besides, Joe seemed at the time of his election not to have had any big interest in anything apart from the election, certainly no interest in hunting down Communists in the US government, apparently a pursuit that came later. The senator's papers archived at Marquette University in Wisconsin appear to contain, a university archivist told me, no record of any correspondence between the senator and the RCMP. Joe McCarthy, I was informed by the FBI, was not an uncommon American name, that it could have been anybody.[48]

On 9 April 1949 Sam Carr was sentenced to a six-year prison term for passport forgery. I wasn't, he said, "charged with espionage, they had no evidence on that. I was National Organizer of the Party and it was obvious they were going after the Party." Carr, moreover, denied that he had anything to do with obtaining a passport for anyone connected with the Soviet embassy. Which was true. The argument of his defense lawyer that he was a tragic child of the Russian revolution who had seen his father killed and whose crime could not be ranked with that of Freddy was dismissed.[49]

On 22 July 1946 a warrant was issued for the arrest of Freda Linton. Named as a member of the spy ring, Freda, a Fred Rose girlfriend, had disappeared before she could be brought before the royal commission. For many years she lived like Igor under a false name, fearful of discovery. According to a family member, she was helped by the party to

---

48. Correspondence between RCMP Superintendent C. E. Rivett-Carnac, Headquarters, Ottawa, Ontario, and D/Sgt H. J. Spanton, "O" Division, Toronto, Ontario, 18, 19, November 1946. "Your remarks regarding placing (the Fred Rose trial depositions) in the possession of "Joe" have been noted"; email communication with John Fox, FBI historian, 17 June 2005; email communication with Phil Runkel, Department of Special Collections and University Archives, Raynor Memorial Libraries, Marquette University, 11 August 2005 and 3, 5, and 13 October 2005. So who was "Joe"?

49. Erna Paris, "The World of the Jewish Communists," in *Jews: An Account of Their Experience in Canada,* Macmillan of Canada, 1980; "Carr Denies Ever Helping Soviet to Get Passport," *The Toronto Daily Star,* 7 April 1949; "Jail Sam Carr for Six Years Over Passport," *The Toronto Globe and Mail,* 9 April 1949.

hide out, meeting party people in a darkened Montreal movie theatre where she was handed small sums of money. The party was supposed to have relocated Freda somewhere in the American northwest, perhaps Seattle. She got work there, married a merchant seaman. The FBI found her living under her husband's name. Unable to arrest her, they told her husband the story. Do you, they asked him, know you are living with a Communist spy? The husband abandoned her. Seven months later, pregnant, alone, and with nowhere to go, Freda decided to return to Montreal.

A newspaper report about the Carr conviction said that Freda was now the only person in the spy probe unaccounted for. Two days later, the thirty-three year old Ms. Linton sat in the Montreal office of lawyer Joseph Cohen, who'd arranged her surrender to the RCMP. Ms. Linton would not reveal her married name to the press. Described by a reporter as a dark-haired, good-looking woman, she was arraigned the following day. The special prosecutor in the case was Guy Favreau, Jean Drapeau's lawyer in his libel action against Freddy. Freda was initially charged with assisting Freddy obtain "secrets of RDX" for the Russians from Prof. Boyer. The charges were dropped, the Crown claiming a lack of evidence.

Years later, Freda conceded her error in confusing the interests of the USSR with those of Canada's working class. Freda lived out her days in Toronto with a daughter, born the year she returned to Canada. As an adult the daughter would not ever talk to anybody about any of this. She sent a relative in Montreal a newspaper photo of her mother and herself as an infant. Still terrified of being identified, her infant face as well as her mother's were blacked out with a marker.[50]

Emma Woikin, Kathleen Willsher, Gordon Lunan, Edward Mazerall, Harold Gerson, Scott Benning and Durnford Smith could not be linked directly to the Fred Rose-Raymond Boyer conspiracy prosecution. They were in separate cases tried of the same offense, violating the OSA.

---

50. "Police Seek Ex-Secretary for Espionage," *The Vancouver Sun*, 22 July 1946; "Freda Linton Gives Self Up," *The Gazette*, Tuesday, 12 April 1949. Private communication, Kirwan Cox.

Eric Adams, Matt Nightingale, and Agatha Chapman were acquitted, as was Halperin who kept his mouth shut and walked. Scott Benning was acquitted on appeal.

Alan Nunn May, tried in England, got ten years, served six, Gordon Lunan five, Durnford Smith five, Edward Wilfred Mazerall four, Kathleen Willsher three, Emma Woikin two and a half, Prof. Raymond Boyer two.[51]

As for the question of diplomatic immunity for the Gouzenko documents, there doesn't appear sixty-four years later to be a commonly held view. Says an authority on international relations: "...there is no such thing as 'diplomatic immunity' for documents that are handed over to local authorities by a person enjoying diplomatic status. Igor Gouzenko had diplomatic status when he handed over documents to the Canadian authorities. The Soviets had no 'legal' case to reclaim those documents. Had the Soviets been able to exclude those documents from the evidentiary process this may have made judicial proceedings against individuals named as espionage agents in those documents all the more problematic. Certainly the documentary evidence was key to the prosecution. If there was other evidence of complicity in espionage, e.g., arising from police surveillance, that may have helped, but no doubt the documentary evidence from the Soviet embassy was all the more compelling."

The response from a government lawyer: "There are many ways to prevent the use of certain documents or evidence in trials (several dozen exemptions may apply whether it is "solicitor-client privilege" or one of the long list). What you refer to as "diplomatic immunity" I understood as being an attempt to prevent the use and disclosure of any damning evidence through one technique or another, based on historic precedents in law that could be claimed (whether or not the expression "diplomatic immunity" was appropriate or applicable in this situation—I always understood the term to apply to diplomats not documents).

Did the Soviets in fact have any sort of "legal" case to reclaim the Gouzenko documents? Were those documents Soviet property? The owner of stolen property has a legal case to reclaim that property. However, for the Russians to have done that would have amounted to an implicit acknowledgment that the documents were authentic and evi-

---

51. "1946 Espionage Trials," CSIS records, RCMP, June, 1960.

dence of espionage. A complicating factor was that some of the material Gouzenko turned over was in fact Canadian government property that agents stole on the Soviets' behalf. The original thief could not make a claim to reclaim property that was stolen by him in the first place and never legally belonged to him.

Was Igor responsible for sending Freddy to prison and unleashing the forces of reaction in Canada and elsewhere? The legalities aside, things could have turned out differently had Soviet authorities requested immunity for the documents. The request might have been granted, perhaps on some extra-legal basis by the Government of Canada, gotten Freddy off, and killed dead Igor's career as an anti-Soviet whistle blower. For reasons that remain moot, Stalin did not make such a request. Why he didn't and the consequence if he had remain matters of speculation. The finding in the Rose appeal of one of the five appeal court judges, Judge Bissonnette, was cited in at least one other known case: "If the acts committed by the diplomatic corps have contravened the legislation of the country to which it is accredited, and if, *a fortiori*, their immediate aim has been to imperil the safety of the State, there is no longer any immunity for the residence or the documents, things, effects, armaments that may be found therein."[52]

Among the oddities of the battle between the party and the RCMP was that they both seemed to be on the same wave length, both taking it as an item of faith that at the heart of the party was an alchemical melting pot that linked men and women of different ethnic groups and races in a larger subversive working class consciousness. John Leopold noted that at the party's September 1943 banquet "many speeches were given in French and …numerous references were made to French-Canadians joining the Labour Progressive Party. It was estimated that half the crowd were Jewish; a group of Negroes attended." An LPP social evening in November 1944 "consisted of dancing and refreshments with no political discussions. Some 350 persons were present with

---

52. The claim of diplomatic immunity for the Gouzenko documents remains a grey area. These are the views of Martin Rudner, Distinguished Research Professor Emeritus, Norman Paterson School of International Affairs, Carleton University and a government lawyer who wished to remain anonymous. See Grant V. McClanahan, *Diplomatic Immunity: Principles, Practices, Problems*, St. Martin's Press, 1989. McClanahan, citing C. E. Wilson, *Diplomatic Privileges and Immunities,* University of Arizona Press, 1967, refers directly to the Fred Rose appeal ruling even if he seems to get the date wrong: "In a 1947 opinion involving Soviet spies in Canada Canadian Justice Bissonnette ruled that "the diplomatic agent must do or attempt nothing against the safety of the State that has consented to receive him."

approximately 80% Jews and the remainder Christians and some Negroes." It wouldn't last. Only a few days later *The Canadian Tribune* reported that at the party's Quebec convention English and French sections met separately: "The newly organized French Section of the L.P.P. also warmly endorsed Cardinal Villeneuve's recent speech made on his return from France." The Cardinal was apparently now supporting the war effort.[53]

At the party's Second National Convention in Toronto in early June 1946, while the trial of Fred Rose was in progress, dissatisfaction was reported coming from French-Canadian party leaders, some maintaining that "the Jewish faction of the L.P.P. controlled the entire proceedings 'behind the scenes,' Buck receiving his guidance from (Joe) Salsberg and (Joshua) Gershman."[54]

---

53. RCMP memorandum, "Labour Progressive Party, Second National Convention, Toronto, 1–5 June 1946." *The Canadian Tribune*, 10 July 1946: Jews, it was apparently said, cast too much influence in the party within the Province of Quebec.
54. J. Leopold, 30 September 1943; RCMP "C" Division Montreal, 21 November 1944; Reg Wilson "Back McNaughton in Recruiting Drive," *The Canadian Tribune*, 25 November 1944.

IX.

In Stir

Said the RCMP's G. L. Sauvant in a 16 July 1946 letter to the Deputy Minister of Justice: "Fred ROSE is a Montreal man and no doubt will meet many of his constituents in St. Vincent de Paul Penitentiary should he be incarcerated there. Fred ROSE being known as a communist, I am led to believe that should he be transferred elsewhere his influence on other convicts would not be so noxious." Fred Rose, said Sauvant, certain the appeal would be dismissed, would best be transferred to Dorchester Penitentiary in New Brunswick.[1]

Upon learning that Fred Rose was sentenced to serve time in St. Vincent de Paul, Col. G. Lebel, the prison warden, advised the Superintendent of Prisons that it would "be in the best interest of both local and central administration, if ROSE, when released by the authorities of the Bordeaux Jail, was transferred to a smaller institution where the mentality of the convicts would not be as readily responsive to communistic ideology as the population of this Institution." Said the Superintendent in a handwritten note added to the letter: "St. Vincent de

---

1. Unless otherwise specified, the source of the information relating to the incarceration of Fred Rose in the St. Vincent de Paul Penitentiary is inmate file RG73 (Correctional Service), Series C, Penitentiary Branch, Inmate Case Files, Volume 179, File 4857, parts. 1 & 2, Fred Rose, 31 December 1946 to 9 August 1951.

Paul overcrowded (1100 covts). We should, I think, avoid every possible course which might bring unrest, if not more serious trouble. Transferring him elsewhere would limit the pernicious influence he may have on others."

The Commissioner wrote to the Deputy Minister of Justice, acknowledging that St. Vincent de Paul was filled almost to capacity. Because, he said, "of experience in the past with convicted persons of known communistic activities, the Warden has recommended that the transfer of Rose to a smaller penitentiary be considered."

On 31 December 1946 Freddy, described by *The Montreal Gazette* as the "Labor Progressive Communist Party member for the teeming garment trade area" began serving his six-year sentence in St. Vincent de Paul as convict 4857.

The Gazette reported that a guard talking about Freddy to an inmate said that he would "fix this guy when he gets here."[2]

A couple of weeks after his transfer to St. Vincent de Paul, Freddy wrote to J. L. Ilsley the Minister of Justice requesting permission to discuss legal matters relating to an anticipated termination of his status as an MP with his lawyer Albert Marcus. I need, said Freddy, legal advice. He also requested in the letter that the typewriters and other materials seized the previous March be returned to his wife at the couple's Montreal address. There does not appear to be a record of a ministerial reply.[3]

On 24 January 1947 Freddy wrote to the Speaker of the House, Gaspard Fauteux: "Mr. Speaker: If the will of the people is to prevail, if justice is to be done, there can be no question of my expulsion from the house. To the contrary, I should be in my seat in the House of Commons and not in the penitentiary. Parliament is the highest of Courts. Through its actions in my case it will decide whether hysteria is to continue or whether reason and justice are to prevail. Respectfully, Fred Rose, M.P."[4]

The letter was returned to him, never reaching his fellow MPs. It did not, Freddy learned, comply with the regulation form for petitions.

---

2. "Exposes Pen's Brutal Regime Tells of Plan to 'Fix' Jailed MP," *The Canadian Tribune*, 26 July 1947.
3. Correspondence, Fred Rose to the Rt. Honorable J. L. Ilsley, 16 January 1947.
4. Correspondence, Fred Rose to Speaker of the House, Gaspard Fauteux, 24 January 1947.

Prison authorities had made every effort to prevent Freddy from acquiring knowledge of the appropriate form.

On 30 January 1947 Freddy was expelled from Parliament. In a 31 March 1947 by election, the Cartier seat was won by the Liberal Maurice Hartt. The LPP candidate Michael Buhay, Freddy's LPP replacement, finished in third place behind Paul Massé.

Earlier that month, the conspiracy trial of "millionaire scientist" Raymond Boyer got underway. Freddy was brought from the prison to the courthouse to testify: "Rose, natty-looking, stepped into the courtroom proper. It was the first time he has been seen since his conviction last June."[5] Boyer, now attempting to deflate the conspiracy charge, denied telling the royal commission that he'd been aware that Freddy was acting on behalf of the USSR when he described the RDX formula to him. Subpoenaed to appear, Freddy asked his lawyers Marcus and Cohen to inform the Crown that he "would only be too happy to testify." At the opening of the Boyer trial, as the jury was being selected, an unidentified young woman in a raccoon coat, described as obviously deranged, was taken shrieking from the courtroom by a couple of police constables.[6]

On 15 February 1946, the RCMP had raided Boyer's residence on Beaconsfield Avenue in Montreal. They found Boyer in pajamas, seized diaries, photographs and letters, among the letters one Boyer had written to the Under-Secretary of State expressing a wish to be sent to Russia as an observer of Soviet policies.

In April Freddy wrote to the Superintendent of Penitentiaries with a request to see his lawyer about "certain evidence" that had come to light in the Boyer trial. He had, he added, been held in isolation in the courthouse bullpen, never called upon to testify, denied cigarettes and reading material, simply escorted in the evenings back to Bordeaux jail. Both requests, to see Albert Marcus and Brais, were denied.[7] The following month, Fanny Rose, in a statement to the press, said that, based on the Boyer claim, Freddy was entitled to a new trial on the conspiracy charge

5. "Rose Appears Briefly at Boyer Hearing," *The Montreal Daily Star,* 24 March 1947.
6. "Boyer Now Denies He Knew Rose was Acting in the Interests of Russia," *The Montreal Gazette,* 29 March 1947; "Shrieking Woman Creates Scene as Boyer Case Opens," *The Montreal Daily Star,* 10 March 1947.
7. Correspondence, Fred Rose to Mr. G. Sauvant, Superintendent of Penitentiaries, Department of Justice, 19 April 1947.

"in an atmosphere free from the hysteria and prejudice that surrounded my husband's first trial."[8]

A 15 May 1947 note to the Deputy Minister, Department of Justice, from an "R.F." communicated doubt that Boyer's testimony at his own trial "could be of any assistance to Rose in any action that may be taken on his behalf. "That month, T. J. Bentley, a CCF MP, asked to see the correspondence between Freddy and the justice department.[9]

In May Freddy's brother Abe reported on a visit to him. He found his brother in a small cell "dressed in semi-military garb, with the prison number on his chest." He noted that Freddy was working in the penitentiary library and was in his free time "engaged in writing. He cannot, however, send out what he writes. This is against penitentiary regulations."[10]

In June the press began carrying stories of a Hollywood documentary film in the works about Soviet espionage in Canada.[11]

In July Fanny wrote to members of parliament asking why Freddy was, as of early May, not permitted to receive books sent to him, among them Arnold Toynbee's *A Study of History*.[12] Freddy, in a letter to the Superintendent of Penitentiaries, pointed out that there was in the prison regulations no reference to a Censorship Board: "You are no doubt aware of the fact that convicts spend about 23 hours a day in their cells on holidays and Sundays. Even on week days 18½ hours daily are passed in cells. If one wants to spend his time reading and studying, he should be encouraged and not hindered and contemporary history is as useful a subject to me as any trade book would be to another convict."

Books began to slowly find their way into Freddy's cell.

Despite the testimony of Kenneth Cheetham, in December Boyer was found guilty on the conspiracy charge. It was the third trial. The first had ended with a conflicted jury, the second terminated when a member

8. "Won't Let Rose See Lawyer," *The Daily Tribune*, 14 May 1947.
9. "Commons to See Fred Rose Letters," *The Montreal Daily Star*, 22 July 1947.
10. *The Canadian Jewish Weekly*, 22 May 1947. Freddy was apparently keeping a prison diary.
11. "Filming Spy Story," *The Windsor Star*, 18 June 1947. This might have been a garbled reference to preliminary discussion of the film about the defection of Igor Gouzenko produced in 1948 entitled *The Iron Curtain*.
12. "Fred Rose's Wife Voices Complaint," *The Montreal Gazette*, 7 July 1947.

of the jury fell ill. Boyer lost his appeal in the Quebec Court of Appeal. The Supreme Court of Canada refused to hear his case.[13]

Judged by the Remission Service of the Department of Justice to be "in a class not entitled to any preferred treatment" an application for clemency for Freddy was dismissed.

It was not very long before imprisonment began to take its toll on Freddy's health. A medical examination in March 1948 found that his diet was deficient in eggs, milk, fresh fruit, and contained excessive amounts of carbohydrates. In addition to the nutritional imbalance, he'd lost weight and was diagnosed with neuronitis, a form of vertigo, and glycosuria, the symptom of a possible kidney condition.

There would be medical examinations but little treatment. Dr. Gendreau, Deputy Commissioner of Penitentiaries, said in response to a recommendation for heat therapy that: "...no electric heating pads are provided in the penitentiaries. Heat might, however, be applied through the use of an infra-red lamp which is being used at the present time in the hospital at the Penitentiary. The convict might receive treatment for one or two hours a day under the lamp. Diathermy treatments (electronic heat therapy) are not given in the hospital. It would require the use of costly apparatus and for that purpose convict would have to be removed from the Penitentiary from time to time for purpose of treatment. This is not feasible."

The diet recommendation would be followed with the exception of chicken and fresh fruit; Freddy was promised the recommended doses of Vitamin "B."

In April 1948 Freddy was brought back to court to face the second charge, of having violated the Official Secrets Act. "I have," he said, "now been in prison for two years. I have spent six and one-half months in solitary confinement. My health is undermined, my family tortured. Then today I am suddenly surprised to hear that I am again going to be brought to trial." Freddy pointed out to Judge Wilfred Lazure that the decline in his health while in prison had required an examination by a medical specialist. The judge expressed an objection when Freddy wondered out loud whether it was going to be a regulation legal proceeding or another "Rose special." The judge assured Freddy that he

---

13. "Boyer Found Guilty on Conspiracy Charge," *The Montreal Gazette,* 8 December 1947.

was not responsible for the treatment he'd received, for anything that happened outside his courtroom. Joseph Cohen said he had expected the charge to be dropped.[14]

In June there was some correspondence between the RCMP and the federal citizenship branch over "whether steps [were] underway towards the revocation of naturalization in the case of Fred ROSE, ex M.P."[15]

In May Freddy was taken to the Ste. Anne's Veterans Hospital for further tests. The test results seemed inconclusive and he was ordered hospitalized for three days at the Queen Mary Hospital, also a veterans facility, in Montreal for the test results to be confirmed. The Crown announced that it was proceeding on the second charge, violation of the Official Secrets Act—3 George VI chapter 49.

Following a July interview with Freddy in the Warden's office at St. Vincent de Paul with Fanny present, Marcus pointed out that Freddy's physical condition appeared to be deteriorating. Marcus said that if the tests did not indicate his client *was* suffering from diabetes every effort ought to be made to determine the cause of his medical problems.

Freddy was kept in hospital under medical observation and treatment from 7 April 1948 to 5 August 1948. Further tests indicated he was not diabetic.

In August Freddy wrote to Fanny and daughter Laura. He was now, he said, working in the prison garden: "I work on flowers and help rid the grounds of weeds. My knowledge of flowers is limited to roses that are battling the elements to bloom again. The work is pleasant and not hard…. I'm back in my old cell. I replaced the books on the shelves, put up Laura's and your photographs and I was "home."

In a letter to the Commissioner of Penitentiaries describing his medical history since entering the prison, Freddy said he was told he suffered from sciatica, "a condition that has developed in the course of the past two years and which gets steadily worse. I can only see one satisfactory solution to my condition- that I be paroled to a city hospital for diagnosis and treatment. It will definitely not be done in a cell of stone and concrete and in an atmosphere that is hardly conducive to

14. "Fred Rose, Convicted Espionage Plotter, Asks if New Trial Is 'Rose Special'," *The Montreal Daily Star,* 4 May 1948; "Laying Rose Charge Now 'Abnormal,' Counsel Says," *The Toronto Daily Star,* 4 May 1948.
15. Correspondence, Commissioner, RCMP to the Under-Secretary of State, Citizenship & Registration Branch, Ottawa, 23 June 1948.

improvement.... I hope that this reasonable request will be granted, and that I will be given the opportunity to regain my health."

The prison authorities took note of the letters and arranged for another round of medical examinations.

In September Freddy was moved to Bordeaux for his court appearance on the second charge scheduled for October. The Commissioner of Penitentiaries told Freddy's lawyers that a request for further medical examinations from any outside party, i.e., the lawyers, would not be considered. The prison doctor found that Freddy was suffering from pain in his legs above the knees and prescribed a pain killer to be taken three times daily.

Freddy's lawyers, preoccupied with the September court appearance, soon learned that the trial was called off. Had it simply been a pressure tactic to get Freddy to abandon his demand for a new trial on the conspiracy charge?

Likely the most literate and articulate convict who'd ever graced the spaces of the prison, Freddy on 29 September 1948 again wrote to the Commissioner to inform him that prison authorities were misrepresenting his condition: "I realize that the international situation does not create the atmosphere in which I could expect much kindness, although I can hardly be blamed for it, being imprisoned since June 15th, 1946....not only is it impossible to cure my condition here but even useless to try to get an effective palliative to ease the excruciating pain in my leg."

Freddy repeated the request for access to medical care outside the prison system, offering to pay for all medicines prescribed by those doctors and any related medical services they recommended.

Deputy Commissioner Dr. Gendreau promised Freddy a further examination. In his report, Dr. Gendreau claimed the rheumatic pain Freddy was suffering from had greatly declined, that he only needed to follow the prescribed treatment for his condition to return to normal. The thing, he concluded, that had the greatest impact on Freddy's health was the prison environment. It is, said the doctor, more than likely that once he was free and out of prison his medical problems would vanish. It was, in other words, all Freddy's fault for having been a bad boy and winding up behind bars.

Following some back and forth another examination by Dr. Gendreau was scheduled to determine whether a consultation with an outside specialist would be considered.

Sleep problems developed. On 6 November 1948 the Acting Commissioner for Prisons in reply to a request for information informed Freddy's lawyers, Marcus and Feiner, that Dr. Gendreau, had examined Freddy and found no" detectable serious organic condition" that Freddy had agreed to take mild sedatives at night, that the doctor would continue to monitor Freddy's condition. Freddy had reported experiencing pain in the left leg, pain in the right heel, shooting pains in the hands when it rained. "I lost weight in 1947... Nothing can be done about the pain," Freddy said, "and it interferes with my reading. I keep a diary. It is the only way I can give vent to my frustration. You ask for something you get nothing."

An exasperated Dr. Gendreau suggested Freddy was making it all up: "The condition he complains of is entirely subjective. There are no objective findings. His complaints are probably of a rheumatic nature." Laura Rose, who'd visited her father regularly, told me prison staff recommended a change of climate!

Once again, Freddy's lawyers submitted a request to the Commissioner of Penitentiaries that Freddy be examined by his own doctors. Dr. Gendreau in a note to Deputy Commissioner J. McCulley repeated his earlier assessment that there was no detectable organic lesion, that Freddy's "physical appearance and demeanor are not suggestive of any illness."[16]

On 26 November 1948 a story appeared in the newspapers about a stabbing in the prison. The perpetrator, John Boyko, claimed Nick Tedesco, the dead victim, had attempted to convert him to Communism, that he'd seen Tedesco talking to Rose in the prison yard and that Freddy had told Tedesco that Boyko was a fascist. Said Boyko, convicted of the murder of his common law wife: "Tedesco is a rob man and a communist." In fact, the incident was the result of an argument about a quantity of tobacco Tedescso had stolen from Boyko.

For a time the local press weighed in on Boyko's side. Marcus phoned McCulley to say that the newspaper report reflected unfavorably

16. "Rose Faces 2nd Trial Next Month," *The Montreal Standard,* 28 August 1948.

on Freddy's record of good behavior, that Freddy should be permitted to see the report and offer a personal reply.[17]

The initial response was a no. Marcus and Feiner again requested that Freddy or his lawyers or Mrs. Rose be granted the right of a reply. Two days later, Freddy, in a long letter to the Commissioner, said he'd been questioned about the murder by two Provincial Police officers, that he'd known Tedesco casually but had never talked to him about Boyko or communism or fascism, that he'd never worked in the carpenter shop where the killing had occurred, that he had been asked by Boyko to interpret for him when he appeared before Warden Lebel to refuse the commutation of his death sentence and to request that he be hanged. It was, Freddy said, only fair that he be given the opportunity to defend himself against the raving of a twice-confessed killer, that he had seen a poem Tedesco had written in which he "expressed more human decency than the individuals who smear him in his death and who seem to delight in taking it out on people who are in no position to defend themselves."

The Commissioner told Freddy's lawyers it was "not permissible under the Regulations for Rose to make any statement to the public while undergoing imprisonment." In the first week in December a couple of Freddy's fellow convicts were questioned about the incident. They stated that they had never heard Tedesco and Rose discussing Communism "in any way, shape or form. It will also be noted from their statements hereto attached, they never heard TEDESCO talking about communism with BOYKO."

The December clemency request report said Freddy's conduct in prison was "very good" as was his industry, that he'd earned 175 remission days out of 180; "cannot say" was the answer to the question about whether he was likely hereafter to lead an honest life.

That month, Freddy was back in the prison hospital. Dr. Gendreau: "It is felt that convict Rose is at the present time receiving as much care and attention as his case deserves and that he has been placed in the hospital at the present time for the purpose of more accurate observation and is receiving treatment which is probably the only thing that can

---

17. "Police Say Lifer Killed Convict Because of Tobacco Theft," *The Montreal Daily Star,* 28 November 1947.

be done for him within the penitentiary. It is not felt, at the present time that his condition justifies outside hospitalization."

A question about Freddy's job in the library was raised in a story in *Le Devoir*. A memorandum from the Commissioner to the Acting Minister of Justice said that while the article contained certain allegations about Freddy's employment and treatment, he had not at any time been employed as or acted as the prison librarian, that his employment in the library was limited to "the mending and repairing of books under strict supervision of the Librarian and the disciplinary officers.... During the period April to August 1948 Rose was hospitalized in the Prison Hospital.... He was released to light duty in the prison yard...and resumed his employment in the Library on September 27th.... there is no evidence that he has attempted to spread communistic propaganda within the institution."

In an attempt to appeal the rejection of her husband's request for outside hospitalization, Fanny met with Joseph Jean, the federal Solicitor General. In December and January notes went back and forth from the Warden to the Commissioner to the Superintendent of Penitentiaries to the Solicitor General's private secretary.

In January 1949 the Prime Minister, Louis St. Laurent, received a letter from the Municipal Chapter of Montreal, Imperial Order Daughters of the Empire. The Order, claiming to be aware of the menace of Communist propaganda in Canada, wished to "protest vigorously the position Fred Rose, imprisoned Communist...holds in the library of the St. Vincent de Paul penitentiary....this man is given free rein and opportunity to practice his subversive tactics in a Government Institution in Canada. " An MP soon after raised the same question. The Minister of Justice, Stuart Sinclair Garson, undertook to assure the Order and others that Freddy's work in the prison library simply involved the repair of book covers, nothing more. The allegation, first made in December, 1948, was immediately denied by General R. B. Gibson, head of the Penitentiary Commission.[18] In March Social Credit MP Colon Low repeated the question and was told by the justice minister that "Fred Rose was serving six years for espionage"—not

---

18. "Charge Against Fred Rose Denied," *The Montreal Daily Star,* 20 December 1947.

strictly speaking what he had been imprisoned for—and was "employed in fitting and repairing covers for library books."[19]

The lawyer for Sam Carr, J. Herman, was granted a request to conduct an interview with Freddy.

Fanny cabled the Commissioner to again request her husband receive a medical examination. The warden was instructed to order one.

On 3 May Freddy was escorted to Bordeaux Jail to appear at the hearing of John Boyko, returning to St. Vincent de Paul four days later.

The May 1949 medical report repeated the finding that all of Freddy's complaints were *subjective*, that a physical examination discovered nothing that explained the pains he *claimed* to be experiencing. Moreover, Freddy had gained weight, 144 pounds upon admission, he was now 145. It "does not appear that his alleged aches and pains are as intense as it is claimed they are."

On 29 May Freddy wrote a letter of protest to the Commissioner. I'm not, he said, a "political babe in the woods…. My only alternative is to make it a public issue - nationally and internationally. I'll have my wife prepare a brief to the Human Rights Commission of the United Nations…. I hope that such action will not be necessary…"

Penitentiary officialdom seemed oddly determined not to allow Freddy to receive the benefit of a full medical examination from doctors outside the prison system. If, as they claimed, there was really nothing much the matter with Freddy an examination by a medical specialist outside the prison system would confirm that diagnosis and let them off the hook. Were they afraid an independent specialist would arrive at a different and contradictory medical assessment?

There was talk of parole, an option perhaps raised by Fanny. A report from the Chief of Remission Services said Freddy had earned 265 of 270 days.

In a 7 September 1949 report to the Warden the prison physician, Dr. Martel, again claimed to have found no objective symptoms, apart from an anal itch, "His present weight is 145 pounds and has not changed since his admission to the penitentiary. His general condition does not inspire any fear." Fanny, in a letter to MPs, said her husband's health had deteriorated, that he'd in fact *lost* ten pounds! Among those

---

19. "Fred Rose Binding Books," *The Ottawa Citizen*, 24 March 1949.

who responded to the letter, perhaps the only one, was the CCF's M. J. Coldwell, a man Freddy had in the past said unpleasant things about. Replying to a letter from Coldwell, the skeptical Commissioner ordered a further check on Freddy's weight. The examination found that Freddy did in fact *not* tip the scales at 145 as Dr. Martel had claimed, but at 135! As Fanny had claimed, Freddy had lost ten pounds. The Warden attempted an explanation: "This loss of weight however can be explained by the fact that throughout the hot summer months, this prisoner has done strenuous work, caring for the ornamentation grounds in the yard near the Hospital."

Feeling the parliamentary heat, the Commissioner investigated. How, he asked the Warden in a 14 October letter, was it that on 8 October Freddy weighed 133, and the 7 September report recorded his weight at 145 rather than 135: "A full explanation as to how this error occurred is requested by return mail, setting forth who weighed ROSE prior to the physician's report of September 7th, the date he was weighed, what record was made of his weight at that time, and on what information the physician based the statement as to weight contained in his letter of September 7th. Please state also the dates upon which ROSE has been weighed during the past twelve months and the weight recorded on each occasion"

Lebel, in an 18 October letter to the Commissioner, assumed responsibility for the weight error and provided the results of all the Freddy weigh-ins from the date of his admission in December 1946. Once again he attempted to explain the weight loss as a consequence of the work Freddy had done in the prison garden that hot summer and noted the caution forwarded to Dr. Martel: "The Physician has been duly warned to exercise the utmost care in future to ensure absolute accuracy for information transmitted to your office." Said Dr. Martel to the Warden on 25 October: "I may state that his physical condition is good even if his weight has gone down considerably due to the strenuous work he did this summer."

On 17 October Freddy wrote to the Commissioner to say that his wife had concluded from her meeting with him in late September that if there was confirmation that his weight had dropped to 135, "something could be done to get to the root of my condition." He recalled that on 6

October he weighed 133 pounds, a drop of two pounds since 18 August, that in an act of apparent vindictiveness, though he didn't use the word, on 14 October on orders from Dr. Martel and with no explanation, he was removed from the prison hospital and transferred to a cell in the Dome, a central area in the prison, an action he found "hardly reassuring." Dr. Martel told him that he had been removed from the hospital because he was not under treatment, that the cell in the Dome was no damper than the one in the hospital, which was untrue, and that he Dr. Martel had received no further instructions from the Commissioner since the news of the weight error.

Freddy reminded the Commissioner of the steadfast refusal of penitentiary officialdom to allow observation by a medical specialist at a city hospital and asked that the information on the weight error be forwarded to the Remission Service.

On 17 November 1949, Warden Lebel heard from Deputy Commissioner Dr. Gendreau: "It is felt that the convict Rose should be brought back to a hospital cell for the purpose of very accurate observation…. A very accurate record of his weight should be kept and this will help to determine whether or not his loss of weight was the result of his activities during the summer months or not." In other words from a cause other than Freddy's medical condition!

The next day the Commissioner wrote to Fanny Rose to say that Dr. Gendreau would be conducting an interview with Freddy the following week. A decision would then be made about arranging an examination by an outside specialist.

A Dr. Benjamin Levine, who had examined Freddy on 23 March 1948, wrote to tell the Commissioner of his concern and the concern of Fanny about Freddy's condition: "It appears he is suffering from symptoms referable to his urinary tract. Such as difficulty in starting his stream, excessive urination, frequency, low back pain, poor sleep, even with sleeping pills, a weight loss of eight pounds in the past year." Dr. Levine mentioned other symptoms and asked for the medical record of his examination at Ste. Anne de Bellevue Veterans Hospital.

A report arrived from Dr. Martel that disputed Dr. Levine's findings. It stated that Freddy's weight at the hospital was 144 pounds, that in

October 1948 his weight was 142, and at the time of the examination it was 144, with Freddy wearing "light clothes."

In a subsequent report, dated 1 December 1949, Dr. Gendreau said Freddy's weight was down to 131 pounds. In the report Gendreau switched the focus from Freddy's body to his mind. Freddy, he said, now seemed to be "losing some of his grip. He is not quite as talkative as formerly and does not seem to want to prove his point with the same determination as he did on previous occasions. Sometimes he begins to discuss a certain subject and he ends up shrugging his shoulders and saying: "Oh! Well, I don't want to discuss that anymore." Freddy, he said, told him he'd asked to be transferred from his library job because of the statement that he was "carrying on communistic propaganda" to garden work: "Convict has been back in the Hospital since Monday, November 21, 1949. When he was told that he would have to come back in the Hospital he first stated that he could see no reason as he thought he was not sick enough to be there." In the doctor's professional opinion if Freddy was not a mental case he was fast becoming one. His conclusion: "…there is nothing at the present time which can explain his continued loss of weight and before any further opinion is expressed or any conclusions reached it is felt advisable that a special examination be made… This could be done at Ste. Anne de Bellevue." Dr. Martel was asked to make the necessary arrangements. Freddy arrived at Ste. Anne de Bellevue on 5 January 1950 and was back in his cell on 12 January.

In February Warden Lebel received a request for an interview with Freddy from the editor of the British United Press, who was referred to the Commissioner. The record contains nothing on the outcome.

On 25 February 1950 the Commissioner wrote to Fanny, perhaps imagining M. J. Coldwell to be looking on, about the findings of the Ste. Anne de Bellevue tests. Claiming that while the tests were exhaustive it was nevertheless "impossible to account for his symptoms and weight loss on any definite organic condition." [*sic*] The consultant neurologist found "no definite organic neurological condition and the complaint of pain was possibly due to fibrositis." A recommended dietary modification involved a high vitamin and high caloric regimen. Three days later, there was a report from the Supervisor of Stewards that on 16 December Freddy, proceeding through the prison yard with another prison official, stopped him to say that he Freddy could see no reason for complaints about the food at the prison, "that a good many people do not eat as well on the outside."

On 1 March 1950 Dr. Martel wrote to the warden to say that though Freddy's weight was down to 129 pounds and he complained of nightly pain in his left leg and back "his physical condition is satisfactory and his moral [*sic*] good." It was in effect the response to a letter Freddy had written to the Commissioner on 26 February. Freddy, back in his prison cell, said that the physiotherapy he'd been promised had "so far failed to materialize. Six weeks have passed without action." Contrary to the recommendations, there had likewise been no change in his diet. Even, he said, "if I'd done all that I was charged with, something very far from reality, it should be remembered that I was never charged with having aided the enemies of the country.... I feel that some people, even when it comes to the matter of my health, confuse fact with fiction, cold war with heat treatment, medical attention with political expediency."

In a 6 March letter an irritated Dr. Gendreau asked the warden to get Dr. Martel to look into the physiotherapy question, to adjust Freddy's diet as the doctor saw fit, and to make his own copies of medical reports, not to request this service from the Commissioner's office because "there exists a sufficient volume of work here to keep the staff continually busy without the addition of copying such reports. Furthermore, the recommendations regarding treatment is something of immediate concern to the penitentiary authorities and not so particularly of this office which is mainly interested in seeing that treatment is properly administered."

On 26 June Dr. Gendreau wrote to the Commissioner to say that in an interview he'd had with Freddy on 26 April Freddy said he'd become aware that Sam Carr had been allowed to deduct the six months he'd spent in Provincial Jail from his sentence, that he Freddy was willing to give up release on medical grounds but was not accepting without a battle the same deal, that should the six months in Bordeaux, which he considered the worst six months in his life, not be deducted from his sentence, he would go on a hunger strike.

A couple of days later, Fanny wrote to the Solicitor General. In the letter she referred to the handling of Sam Carr's prison time and asked for clemency for Freddy to compensate for the time in Bordeaux Jail.

In early July Freddy wrote to Dr. Martel to tell him that the pain in his left leg had grown worse and was interfering with his sleep; he asked for his condition to be examined by a Dr. MacNaughton of the Montreal Neurological Institute, suggesting that the decision was his, Dr. Martel's, to make without the need to write to Ottawa. Dr. Martel forwarded the letter to the warden asking whether it might be sent on to Dr. Gendreau. Which it was. On 17 July the Senior Assistant Commissioner, G. L. Sauvant wrote to the warden with a no: "Convict ROSE knows that he was fully investigated and that this was done in a most exhaustive way. He already knows that all the findings were normal."

In December the warden passed on a copy of Freddy's written request to the Minister of Justice, Stuart Garson, that the time spent in Bordeaux be deducted from the time in St. Vincent de Paul.

On 27 June 1951 *The Globe and Mail* reported that Freddy would be released from prison on August 9th, that his six-year sentence had been reduced due to his record of good behavior, that he planned to live in Montreal upon his release. The warden told the RCMP that Freddy had had no visitors apart from his wife Fanny, daughter Laura, his brother Abe Rosenberg, a sister, a Mrs. T. Lecker, and his lawyer Albert Marcus, that he'd mixed very little with other prisoners, mostly keeping to himself.[20]

To the best of his knowledge, said the warden, Freddy never attempted to "promulgate his Communist ideals to other inmates." As Freddy's release date approached, the RCMP considered it necessary that "suitable arrangements be made for careful coverage of his movements after he gains his freedom." A rumor circulated that Freddy had spent a lot of time in the prison library and would soon begin work on a history of Canada. Stories began to appear speculating that upon release from prison Freddy would be deported.

---

20. "Rose to Live In Montreal When Released," *The Toronto Globe and Mail,* 27 June 1951; "Fred Rose," Special Branch, RCMP, 6 July 1951. Said a 11 July 1951 memorandum: "In view of the impending release of FRED ROSE from imprisonment, it is considered necessary that suitable arrangements be made for careful coverage of his movements immediately after he gains his freedom."

The morning of 9 August Freddy's brother Abe arrived at the prison in a taxi, along with Fanny and daughter Laura to take Freddy home. Six photographers were waiting to record the exodus. When Freddy protested this invasion of his privacy the warden suggested to avoid the press he leave by a side exit. Freddy told the warden he would have no objection to seeing the newspapermen at his home, that he had no grudge "whatsoever" against the penitentiary and would say so to the newspapers. His purpose seemed to be to reduce the expected public attention, the stoic party trooper's continuing and undying service to the cause. On the other hand, there were things to be said. Freddy had not been treated kindly by some members of the correctional proletariat. For a three week stretch, he was ordered to scrub and re-scrub a long prison stairway that was routinely given a quick swabbing. Prison authority doctors had claimed Freddy's worsening medical condition was something he imagined, at one point suggesting he was losing his marbles, refusing to allow an examination by specialists outside the prison system, lying about his weight loss, and when that was brought to light proposing that the decline in weight was due not to illness or institutional abuse but to summer work on the prison grounds.

At 10:45 a.m. Freddy was on his way home. The warden advised reporters that Freddy had been freed. Freddy told the reporters who visited his apartment later in the day that he wanted a full medical examination as soon as possible, adding that he was treated very well in prison, that Fanny and Laura saw him once a month, that he'd worked as a prison gardener in summer and shoveled snow from the exercise compound in winter. No comment was his reply to questions about politics. His hair seemed thinner, his moustache gone. He'd heard about moves to deport him, but preferred not to talk about the amendment to the Citizenship Act that might permit deportation of persons under circumstances similar to his but was not retroactive. Questioned about his plans he said he was still an electrician and was very happy to be reunited with his family that it was glorious to be out!

Said *Time* magazine, delighted to rub a little *schadenfreude* in the wound: "Rose was a changed man. Once a dapper, bouncy Communist with a glib party-line answer for every question, ex-Convict Rose was now a thin and wilted figure in a loose, yellow sport shirt, steadfastly silent on political questions and future plans."[21]

Only six days after Freddy's release, on 15 August 1951, Louis Joseph Daoust, who would do time in Alcatraz, transferred there from the United States Penitentiary in Atlanta, Georgia for the armed robbery of the Flagler Federal Savings and Loan Association in Miami, entered St. Vincent de Paul. In for up to 25 years on an armed robbery conviction, he was assigned Freddy's old book binding job in the prison library.

Different trajectories had brought these two men, who would never meet, into the prison's library to repair its books.

The report on Daoust received at Alcatraz from St. Vincent de Paul said, in part, that Louis was a 29-year-old penitentiary recidivist, that he'd never known his father that he was told by his mother that his father was still alive but the couple had separated a long time ago. He said he did not remember when his mother did not drink or did not have a stranger around the house. Louis was sent to live with his maternal grandfather, described as a sadist. His relationship with his mother was all but severed. At age 16 he had his first serious appearance in court for an attempted armed robbery. Louis said that he attended only three grades of public school before he was kicked out because he could not see.[22]

It was a time when the Roman Catholic Church, fierce enemies of the *red menace*, ran the schools. Louis said he began wearing glasses at the age of four but the glasses did not correct his vision sufficiently for him to see the blackboard, even from the front row of the classroom. These and related events in his life affected him very much creating much bitterness and resentment. He became very aggressive, "punchy," as he put it. In time he learned to change his attitude, he came to realize that his actions were causing him much grief. Louis did not learn to read and write in school but in later years taught himself to do these things. After he'd begun taking courses in philosophy, he could knowledgeably discuss Socrates and Plato.

In August 1951, days after Freddy had been released and had gone home, the RCMP received information that while in the joint he had

---

21. "Wilted Rose," *Time,* 20 August 1941.
22. Selected documents from the Alcatraz file of Louis Joseph Daoust, *National Archives and Records Administration.*

through the help of someone, the name has been redacted, been receiving "communist literature."[23]

Much was happening out in the world while Freddy was in stir.

In 1946–47, party stalwart Henri Gagnon, founder of the *Ligue des veterans sans logis*, led a squatters movement to obtain relief for homeless veterans returning from the battlefields of Europe. An LPP organizer, Gagnon was like Freddy an electrician by trade. A couple of barbotte houses had been seized. Toronto party people said this action would discredit the *ligue*. The squatters, men who had gone to war for the nation now desperate to find homes for wives and children, were accused of being dupes of Gagnon and his fellow Communists. The Toronto-based party intellectuals opposed the *ligue*. In their eyes the movement seemed an expression of the reactionary nationalism championed by Maurice Duplessis.

A major rift surfaced in the ranks. Québécois militants on one side, anglophone Toronto-based party heads, characterized as more comfortable attending cultural evenings than participating in street actions, on the other. Toronto seemed to desire a subservient Québécois franchise. At the December 1946 Provincial Executive meeting to discuss Freddy's fate, Henri Gagnon criticized English faction party organizers for their tepid support. Gagnon was being charged with conspiracy by the Duplessis government and needed help with his legal defense. The anglophones present were taken aback by Gagnon's statement. Harry Binder and another party member, Oscar Kogan, promised that the sum of $1,000 would be made available to Gagnon to assist with his legal troubles. Gagnon then thanked the party for contributing to the purchase of new furniture to replace household effects damaged as a result of his participation in the squatters movement.

The RCMP had been able to get hold of a detailed record of the proceedings as well as the subscription list of contributors to the Gagnon legal defense fund.

At a provincial party conference in Montreal in October 1947, Harry Binder, who had initially supported Gagnon and encouraged his takeover of the gambling venues, led a move to drum Gagnon and his associates out of the party. Others seeing the way the wind was blowing, got

---

23. Fred Rose, RCMP H. Q. File, 31 August 1951.

up and walked out. *Allez au diable, je pars*, said Evariste Dubé. The previous November, while Freddy was in Bordeaux Jail awaiting news of his appeal, Harry, at a closed party meeting in Montreal, had taken a different view: "The squatters' movement led by Henri Gagnon was the public expression of increasing understanding of the veterans and the role of our party."

Harry then experienced a change of heart. As Gagnon recalled: "Comrade Binder expressed the view that it was necessary to put an end to the *squatters* movement, that the seizure of the gambling houses by the veterans created public confusion and that the anti-vice angle prejudices the squatters movement. I was of the opposite opinion. I explained that the business with the gambling houses far from having a negative impact supports our cause. I was quite surprised by Harry's position on this, since the action of taking over a gambling venue was originally his. After a lively discussion, he allowed me to continue the operation." But not for very long. The party executive in Toronto claimed the "affaire des veterans" did more damage than good for the party. A rumor circulated that Gagnon was an RCMP agent. In August 1947 the *affaire* was over. In what has been described as a *reglement de contes*, a settling of scores between party cliques, Gagnon was driven out of the party for his participation in an allegedly "anti-Marxist nationalist faction."[24]

Decades later it seemed to a new generation of politicos that the Gouzenko business was to blame. Party faithful had become demoralized. If Freddy had been around and not in prison, things might have been different. The villain was enemy-of-the-people Igor, perhaps a knowing and willing agent of darker forces, whose revelations had generated the negative political climate.

On 9 August 1948 the Quebec painter Paul-Emile Borduas and fifteen other artists, inspired by the visual freedoms of European surrealism, published the *Refus global* manifesto. On one level, it was a bold public statement of the terms of a new direction in Quebec

---

24. Magda Fahrni, "In the Streets: Fatherhood and Public Protest," in *Household Politics: Montreal Families and Postwar Reconstruction*, University of Toronto Press, 2005. Robert Comeau and Bernard Dionne, "Henri Gagnon et la Ligue des Veterans sans logis (octobre 1946–août 1947) in *Les communistes au Quebec 1936–1956: Sur le Parti communiste du Canada/Parti ouvrier-progressiste*, les Presses de l'Unité, 1980. "Do the People Choose Their Candidates," *Combat*, 25 January 1947; Jacques G. Francoeur, "Reds Urged to Focus Attention on Veterans, Youth Groups, and Labour," *The Montreal Gazette*, 31 March 1947; "Harry Binder," RCMP memorandum, 8 November 1946.

painting. On another, it made no bones about the antagonism to be overcome. Said the Borduas text: "We are a small and humble people clutching the skirts of priests who've become sole guardians of faith, knowledge, truth, and our national heritage; and we have been shielded from the perilous evolution of thought going on all around us, as our well-intentioned but misguided educators distorted the great facts of history whenever they found it impractical to keep us totally ignorant....our institutions of learning, past masters of obscurantism, heirs to automatic, infallible papal authority, have found every means possible to organize a monopolistic reign of selective memory, static reason, paralyzing intention." It appeared to some to amount to a deter-mined anti-Christian campaign, in the words of Gerard Pelletier, on behalf of "the rule of instinct."[25]

The *Refus* seemed to take another step in the direction advocated by Judge Louis Boyer in his 1928 report on the Laurier Palace Fire enquiry. That document appeared to mark an important phase, perhaps the beginning, of the decline in Church authority in Quebec. There was, said the judge, every reason *not* to ban cinema attendance on the Lord's Day as demanded by the Church.

A year after the appearance of the manifesto Quebec's asbestos workers struck for better wages and improved working conditions. The strike, illegal and violent, in the town of Asbestos, ran for four months. The Johns Manville Corporation, an American firm, was the largest of the asbestos outfits. Church support for the companies was for a time divided; Joseph Charbonneau, Archbishop of Montreal, took the side of the strikers, as did other representatives of the clergy, among them the Dominican priest who founded the School of Social Science at Laval University, Georges-Henri Lévesque. When police threatened to open fire, the strikers backed down. Their leaders were arrested, some severely beaten. Though little was gained in the short term, the larger meaning of the strike, seen in the context of the *Refus global*, was that a different Quebec was emerging into the second half of the 20th century, a Quebec that little resembled the one envisioned by Fred Rose *or* Lionel Groulx.

---

25. Paul Emile Borduas et al., *Refus Global,* trans. Ray Ellenwood, Exile Editions, 1985. See too David Levy, "The Laurier Palace Fire," *The Montreal Star,* 8 January 1977.

"There is no secret and no defense." Albert Einstein

On 23 September 1949, Harry Truman went on American radio to announce that an atomic explosion had taken place in the USSR, three to five years earlier than projected. Eschatological closure, final and total, was now a practical reality. We walked, said John Foster Dulles, to the brink and looked it in the face. Nigel West's *Mortal Crimes: The Greatest Theft in History*, *Soviet Penetration of the Manhattan Project* explained how it had happened. It was not so much theft as a gift from scientists, party people involved in espionage, fellow travelers, people Lenin referred to as "useful idiots," men and women who said they were uneasy over the failure of the democracies to crush the Nazis, who'd managed to convince themselves that after Hiroshima and Nagasaki, the world would be a better place if Uncle Joe had the bomb too. "Our atomic monopoly," Manhattan Project director Robert Oppenheimer, Dr. Atomic, had told *Time* magazine in November 1948, "is like a cake of ice melting in the sun."

The forces of Chiang Kai-shek were defeated by Mao Zedong and on 1 October 1949 Mao proclaimed a People's Republic of China.

That same autumn, Joseph Albert Guay, jewelry salesman and resident of Quebec City desperately in love with a young waitress in divorce-proof Quebec made sure his wife Rita boarded a Canadian Pacific Airlines flight. J. Albert had arranged to place a few sticks of dynamite hooked to an alarm clock device on the aircraft. The aircraft was five minutes late in taking off. Instead of the explosion occurring over the St. Lawrence River and the evidence disappearing into the river waters the wreckage of the plane fell to the ground in a lumber industry region where the men who arrived at the scene of the crash instantly recognized the smell of dynamite. Shortly before the flight, Guay had insured his wife's life for $10,000. Twenty-two others died in the explosion. Guay claimed his two unwitting associates, a woman and her watchmaker brother, were knowing accomplices. All three were hanged. The woman, Marguerite Pitre, the last woman to be hanged in Canada, on 9 January 1953, her brother, crippled by a bone disease and escorted to the gallows in a wheelchair, on 25 July 1952, and Guay himself on 12

January 1951. *Au moins*, he declared looking on in the shadow of the rope, *je meurs célèbre.*[26]

In June 1950 the Democratic People's Republic of Korea *aka* North Korea, with the backing of the USSR and the People's Republic of China, invaded the Republic of Korea *aka* South Korea. Soviet diplomats at the UN walked out before the crucial vote, a gaff that opened the way for a United States-led United Nations force to move against the invasion. The military stalemate ended in an armistice in 1953.

In the spring of 1950, for not more than a few days, a rumor quickly denied by the party circulated that Fanny Rose would be the LPP candidate in a federal by election in Cartier.[27]

Michael Buhay, a prominent Party personality with election savvy, ran for the LPP in Cartier in 1947 after the seat was declared vacant.

With Freddy out of the game, the eyes of Cartier soon turned to party man Harry Binder. Of stocky build and unfazed demeanor, Harry, the Gagnon episode and other matters aside, was the model socialist flagbearer. He contested every Cartier election, federal, provincial, municipal. Harry's campaign theme was sung to the tune of *My Darling Clementine*: "A reminder, Harry Binder… dah-dah dah-dah, dah dah dah…" Dreadful sorry Clementine, thou art lost and gone forever…

Perhaps the espionage fiasco had left its mark. Harry never did fare as well as Freddy with Cartier voters. Harry is remembered by some as good-humored, by others as a hard-assed party man not at all as well-liked as Freddy. Years later someone who claimed to know Harry well described him as an unappealing person. In 1952, Harry managed to get himself elected to a minor municipal office but had to fight off the effort to deny him that modest prize on a trumped up pretext.

Born in Siberia, Harry arrived in Canada at age four in September 1917. Naturalized in 1930 in June he was appointed organizer of the Young Communist league in Hamilton, Ontario. In 1933 he became District Organizer for the Young Communist league in Saskatchewan. Harry was very active in the trade union movement and the party over the next 23 years rising in party ranks and holding a variety of positions. In 1940, while the Hitler-Stalin pact held, he was arrested for printing

26. James Quig, "He killed 23 people to murder his wife," *The Gazette*, 3 October 1981; Alan Hynd, "The Mystery of the Twenty-Three Murders," in *Great True Detective Mysteries*, Tempo Books, 1969.
27. "Party Issues Denial Mrs. Rose Will Run," *The Montreal Gazette*, 15 April 1950.

and distributing anti-war leaflets and did two years in the Kingston Penitentiary. In late 1942, he joined the Regina Rifles and served overseas till the war's end in 1945. In 1946, he was elected to the party's National Executive Committee.

Harry Binder also ran in federal elections in Ottawa West. The LPP candidate in the 1950 federal Cartier by-election, Harry placed second behind Liberal Leon Crestohl. The party sought balm in the statistics; Harry had captured 21.3 percent of the vote. In 1953, Harry's Cartier vote total dropped to less than a thousand votes.

A year or so after Khrushchev's 1956 denunciation of Stalin, an angry Harry Binder turned his back on the party and the city and moved to Toronto. He became a jeweler. One hears that speculation in gold made Harry a wealthy man. The son of a founder of the Communist party in Canada and himself a top organizer, Harry Binder toward the end spoke out against the great harm blind allegiance to Soviet communism had done. Communists, he said, especially in Poland, drew Jewish youth away and unavailable to battle the rise of fascism. Harry passed on in Florida at age 75 in December 1988.[28]

In the summer of 1948 the Department of Justice was again looking for a way to revoke the naturalization of Fred Rose. The Under-Secretary of State, E. H. Coleman, had advised Justice that instituting such a proceeding could only occur if Freddy's conviction under the Official Secrets Act was a conviction for treason or sedition. Justice wondered about an end run, an amendment to the Canadian Citizenship Act.[29] There the matter stood till Freddy found himself stranded in Warsaw.

---

28. Wiesbord; Harry Binder, selected documents, CSIS.
29. Correspondence, E. H. Coleman, Under-Secretary of State to Stuart Taylor Wood, Commissioner, RCMP, 12 July 1948; Stuart Taylor Wood, Commissioner, RCMP to F. P. Varcoe, Deputy Minister of Justice, 19 July 1948; F. P. Varcoe, Deputy Minister of Justice to Stuart Taylor Wood, Commissioner, RCMP, 21 July 1948.

X.

Out of Stir

Freddy walked out of the St. Vincent de Paul Penitentiary on that summer day in 1951 into a different time, a time of post-war affluence, of men in gray flannel suits, of rumors of flying saucers bearing aliens from perfect and merciless other worlds. While Herman Kahn sat at his desk at the RAND Corporation fine-tuning a scheme for waging nuclear war, radio broadcasts and newsreels reporting on the conflict in Korea, hardly let up on their shrill warnings about *the bomb* and the Russians and how the end of the world was just around the corner.

Freddy was now 44 years old, weighed 140 pounds, was described by prison officials as looking neither older nor younger than his age, of medium build, long of face, clean-shaven, balding, complexion fair, high receding forehead, eyes blue, wore no glasses, nose straight, mouth small, lips thin, nothing about his teeth, chin normal, ears protruding, short lobes, a wart on his back. Usual type of dress: beige winter coat, hat of light color. A good speaker, languages included English, French, Yiddish, German, and others. Had had a public school education, his finances "as far as it can be ascertained at present, FAIR."[1] Freddy may or may not have been aware that the Clark Street building he lived in was under regular surveillance. An RCMP report noted that although their car was parked a "reasonable distance from the Rose home, the residents of this Jewish district expressed their knowledge of the identity and nature of the duties being carried out by the members concerned." Residents, said the report, had been alerted by a *Herald* story: "It is to be appreciated that the subject resides in a district where conditions are not favorable to carry out such surveillance..." The surveillance was by order discontinued at 11:00 a.m. the next day.[2] In case fast access to Freddy was required, the RCMP's personal history file provided a description of his address at 4540 Clark Street: "A 3 storeys [*sic*] building (plus a basement where the janitor lives) of 16 apartments; subject occupies apt. 8 on the 2nd floor facing the stairs which lead to the door on Clark St. A side door in the kitchen opens on a fire-escape which leads to an Alley-Way leading to Clark St. or St. Urbain St."[3] Apparently, Freddy's father owned the building.

The day after Freddy was back home a *Globe and Mail* editorial proposed he be deported.[4] A popular concept but not something the government had the power to do. A week and some later a *Globe* editorial writer, perhaps the same one, had this to say: "Rose is so obviously undesirable in the highest degree, but he happens to be naturalized. The question that arises in his case is whether he can be 'de-naturalized'."[5] In 1952, Maurice Duplessis passed legislation to prevent Freddy from running as a candidate in the riding of Montreal-St. Louis, the provincial designation of Cartier. It would, said Duplessis, be unreasonable "if a man like Rose" ran in the next provincial elections. There was a comparable bill awaiting royal sanction aimed at Harry Binder to bar anyone with a criminal record from holding public office.[6]

---

1. "Fred Rose," RCMP report compiled following the release of Fred Rose from St. Vincent de Paul Penitentiary.
2. "Fred Rose," RCMP, Special Branch, Montreal, 15 August 1951.
3. "Fred Rose," RCMP, Personal History File, 30 April 1952.
4. "Deport Fred Rose," *The Toronto Globe and Mail*, 10 August 1951.
5. "The Law and Fred Rose," *The Toronto Globe and Mail*, 14 August 1951.
6. "Binder Not to Be Replaced Pending Appeal, Bill States," *The Montreal Gazette*, 19 January 1952; "Quebec Bill Bars 'Man Like Rose' From Legislature," *The Ottawa Journal*, 22 January 1952; "Another Clamp On Liberty In Quebec," *The Ottawa Citizen*, 22 January 1952.

"Gimme a chance," was the reply to a local reporter who asked what he was doing for a living. "I just got out. I would be basking in the sun, except there isn't any sun these days." He was, he confessed, having a tough time finding a job.[7]

With money borrowed from friends and supporters, Freddy became a partner in an electrical supplies business, Rameck Supplies Reg'd, specializing in lamps and modern lighting, located at 4525 St-Dominique Street in Montreal.

A fellow who'd worked with Freddy at Rameck told me the company was started by a one-time synagogue cantor who'd left the cantoral profession to join the party. Freddy did office work, odd jobs, some sales, made deliveries in the company vehicle. His carpenter father, angry at Freddy for having changed the family name and for taking up Marxism, was hired to do some carpentry work. The man remembers Freddy as a decent sort, even-tempered, a chain smoker. In all the time they spent together, most of it in the car on store errands, Freddy never tried to convert him to the cause. He recalled that Freddy seemed to be suffering from a nervous condition. He remembered regular visits to the shop by RCMP officers, who would show up under the pretense of being citizens interested in electrical equipment.[8] There was as well much surveillance of the traffic outside the St-Dominique Street premises, reports on the make and color and license numbers of automobiles parked outside the shop.[9]

Freddy had invested $6,000 in the business. Things didn't go well and he subsequently sold his share at a $4,000 loss.

In July 1952 the *Globe and Mail* illustrated a story about international espionage operations by the Communist network with a photo mosaic featuring Klaus Fuchs, Harry Gold, Julius and Ethel Rosenberg, Sam Carr and Fred Rose, apparently to associate Freddy with the better known atom spies.[10] In January 1953 Quebec seemed on the cusp of a labor crisis emerging out of the conflict between the province's Catholic unions and Maurice Duplessis's anti-union provincial government.[11]

---

7. "No Longer News, Rose Claims, But Things Are Tough," *The Montreal Gazette,* 4 September 1951.
8. Private communication. RCMP report on the finances of Rameck operations, 11 June 1952.
9. RCMP reports, 17 February 1953, 18 March 1953.
10. "In Red Spy Ring," *The Toronto Globe and Mail,* 2 July 1952.
11. "Quebec's Deep-Rooted Labor Conflict Moving Toward Crisis," *The Ottawa Journal,* 19 January 1953; "Union Asks Quebec Govt. To Settle Textile Strike," *The Ottawa Citizen,* 17 January 1953.

Freddy wasn't getting much help from the party. Years later Tim Buck would claim that prior to Freddy's arrest and trial he and the party had absolutely no knowledge of any party involvement in espionage. The party, he said, knew nothing about Freddy's association "with a Russian embassy official named Sokholovsky" [*sic*] who Freddy met regularly in Montreal, that the news came as a shock: "It wasn't until afterwords [*sic*] that we discovered that nine other people had been arrested ahead of him.... One or two were members of the Party. I didn't know them personally. The majority were not and were completely unknown to me, although I found out afterwords that Fred Rose knew all except one who lived in Montreal and one who lived in Ottawa."

Following his 1946 release on bail Freddy was, Buck said, called to a meeting in Toronto and told to "come clean." Buck seemed to have lost all recollection of his own trips to New York City, his meetings with Jacob Golos and Elizabeth Bentley, his fondness for Vat 69, his ordering of the Fred Rose Defense Committee off the streets of Montreal, that it was only a few years later that the party helped get an agent into the DeHavilland plant where the Avro Arrow was being assembled. Perhaps Buck thought these were memories he ought to keep to himself.[12]

Freddy had told a reporter that period politics were to blame for the guilty verdict. He denied he'd done anything wrong, and would not speak about his activities on behalf of the USSR. What Freddy, the ever loyal party man, never came clean about was the party's role in his departure. Out of prison he was barred by the party from taking part in politics. Laura Rose told me the Buck party pressed her father to leave the country, in effect drove him out. It was the way the party decided the question of what was to be done with him. There is in the official 1982 history of the CPC no mention of any of this. "Of course, they washed their hands of him," Laura said. The party's action left her father heartbroken.[13]

---

12. Tim Buck, *Yours in the Struggle*, NC Press, 1977, William Beeching and Phyllis Clarke (eds.). See also John Manley, "A Conscience for Canada," *Canadian Committee on Labour History*, 1978, on the unhappiness in the Party following the publication of the Tim Buck volume, an anthology of interview statements.

13. Private communication. See *Canada's Party of Socialism: history of the Communist Party of Canada, 1921–1976*, Progress Books, 1982, which has nothing to say about the Party driving Freddy out of the country.

Freddy was at the time living in Montreal, contemplating a bleak future. There was a report that after folding his business he'd drifted from job to job.

A May 1953 RCMP report noted that Freddy was upset and unwell and "very bitter about the Party casting him off even though he realized it would be bad for him to rejoin the Party." The Force thought it represented an opportunity to re-invent Freddy as Igor: "...close attention will be paid to the possibility that ROSE will reach a stage where his morals might provide an opportunity for an approach by our investigators."[14]

It was the year Josef Stalin died, apparently on 5 March though the date and the circumstances remain uncertain. It was a few months before the 19 June execution of Julius and Ethel Rosenberg.

Suffering from depression, Freddy spent time in the summer of 1953 in the Laurentian Mountains north of the city.

In August 1953 the RCMP were advised by the passport office that Freddy had applied for a Canadian passport for the purpose of visiting Czechoslovakia, that the travel document had been issued.[15]

On 8 October he sent this note to the passport office: "I wish to inform you that in the course of my visit to Europe I intend to spend about six weeks in Czechoslovakia. Having suffered from a constantly aggravating rheumatic condition for the past seven years, I hope to get some relief by taking treatment at the Piestany spas. In addition, I will attempt to make arrangements to procure the agency for certain Czechoslovakian products that may find a profitable market in Canada."

The RCMP were keeping close tabs on Freddy's plans, or thought they were. On 26 August 1953 they received a report that a tentative booking had been made for Freddy to leave Montreal on 7 September, then fly on to Prague on 9 September. A contradictory claim said that Freddy had slipped out of Canada on an ocean liner.

On 10 October 1953 Freddy boarded a KLM flight for Europe never to return, though that may not have been his plan when he left.[16] To be in effect driven from the country by the Party, by the press, by the

---

14. "L.P.P.—Secret Group—Montreal, "RCMP, "C" Division, Westmount, Quebec, 26 May 1953.
15. "Re: Fred Rose," "C" Division, RCMP, Westmount, P.Q., 19 August 1953.
16. "Re: Fred Rose," "C" Division, RCMP, Montreal, Special Branch, 14 October 1953.

government, to end up in Poland was, he wrote, "like going from one prison into another."[17]

The ever devious Tim Buck would go on to say that Freddy's departure for Europe was a mistake, that he was a victim of anti-Communist hysteria and the tenuous claims of Igor Gouzenko, "a man who hides his face in a paper bag."

The RCMP did observe that there was "no indication that the subject's trip is of a permanent nature."[18]

---

17. Laura Rose in an interview for the Francine Pelletier film.
18. "Re: Fred Rose," RCMP, Montreal, Special Branch, 2 November 1953.

XI.

Warsaw

Freddy arrived in Prague on 13 October suffering from arthritis and fibrosis. The next day he called in at the Canadian Legation to tell officials he intended to stay in the country for about six weeks, that his first stop would be the Piestany Spa.[1]

ROSE BATHING AT RED SPA, said one newspaper headline; EX SPY FRED ROSE GOES BEHIND CURTAIN, said another. Fanny tried to explain that Freddy had not "fled behind the Iron Curtain" but had gone to Europe for "business and health reasons", that in Czechoslovakia there were special mineral baths.[2] The reality was that the loyal political warrior had left the country because the Party had ordered him to. There may have been occasions when the couple simply didn't remember, told a different story so often they half believed it. Through it all, Freddy's medical condition continued to deteriorate.

Nothing came of Freddy's plan to establish an agency in Canada for a Czech electrical firm. It is not clear how serious an undertaking it ever

---

1. J. M. Teakles, "Registration of Canadians—Mr. Fred Rose," The Canadian Legation, Prague, Department of External Affairs, Canada, 14 October 1953.
2. "Didn't 'Flee' Says Wife," *The Ottawa Citizen,* 26 November 1953; "Rose Goes Behind 'Curtain'," *The Montreal Gazette,* 26 November 1953; "Rose Taking Czechoslovakia Health Care?" *The Ottawa Journal,* 26 November 1953.

was. There are few specifics. When the subject came up he would only say that RCMP harassment made him a business success long shot, that there were already in place regular channels for the Czech companies wanting to do business in Canada.

In constant pain, Freddy arrived in Poland 24 November 1953. The Polish Red Cross had arranged treatment for his sciatica, a condition he'd developed in prison. Treatment included cortisone and insulin shots. A couple of weeks later Freddy checked in with the Canadian Legation in Warsaw. He explained he'd been in Prague for medical treatment and was in Poland for health reasons, that in Canada he could not afford the treatment he required. He had not, he assured the officials, engaged in any political activity after his release from prison, that harassment by the RCMP and the regular appearance of newspaper stories referring to his conviction and time in prison had destroyed his business plans. Karl Gerhard, a *Gazette* reporter linked to a Nazi effort in the 1930s to acquire a piece of the island of Anticosti for use as a submarine base, would not, he said, leave him alone.

The Legation's report of the meeting was forwarded to the Under-Secretary of State for External Affairs in Ottawa. If, it said, "his health is, as he says, he is probably not of much use to the Party in Canada, particularly in view of his prison sentence. We gathered that he was contemplating staying in Poland."[3]

In Poland, Freddy got a job with the magazine *Polonia* editing English-language translations of Polish material. He explained to the Canadian consular official that there was no family for him to visit, that all his relatives in Lublin had been murdered by the Nazis.

Fanny and daughter Laura joined him in 1954. Said *The New York Times*: "Mrs. Rose and her 17-year-old daughter sailed from a Canadian east coast port last week after a round of farewell parties in suburban Cartier."[4] Freddy and Fanny were assigned a small Warsaw apartment above the old city square. In time, Laura returned to Canada.

---

3. J. L. Carter, "Fred Rose," Canadian Legation, Warsaw, Department of External Affairs, Canada, 15 December 1953.
4. "Rose, Canadian Spy, Reported in Europe," *The New York Times*, 25 November 1953; "Canadian Red's Family to Join Him in Poland," *The New York Times*, 5 April 1954.

There was no MP's pension. This arrangement for members of the House only began in 1952. By the time Freddy reached age 65, he was no longer a citizen.

Rumors circulated that Freddy and Fanny were not enjoying life in "Commie Territory" and wanted to return to Canada. Leon Balcer, a Progressive Conservative MP from Trois-Rivières, Maurice Duplessis's political base, put the question to the Minister of Immigration: Was there not a way to prevent Freddy from returning to Canada? Freddy and Fanny, said the minister Jack Pickersgill, were Canadian citizens. Much to his regret the government could take no action to block their return.[5] A March 1955 editorial in *The Globe and Mail* expressed opposition: "…if he is re-admitted to Canada, send him back to his Communist Utopia. If Poland should refuse him, let him sail the high seas forever like the Flying Dutchman. He is worse than worthless to this country."[6]

Before too long the minister put his officials on the case. In July 1955 the department sent this message to the Canadian Legation in Poland: "Fred Rose: Citizenship and Immigration would like to give consideration to the revocation of citizenship under Section 19(d) of [the] Canadian Citizenship Act. Would you please obtain authentic information when he commenced his residence in Poland and whether it has been continuous for a period of at least two years up to the present time."[7]

On 9 April 1956 Freddy received a letter from the Canadian Legation inviting him to come in for a talk. When the invitation was ignored, on 27 April the Vice-Consul visited his apartment. Freddy was out, likely at work. Fanny was given the disingenuous explanation by the official that she'd made the visit because she'd heard Freddy was ill and was for that reason unable to visit to the Legation. Wanting to avoid any sort of incident, Freddy phoned and said he would come in on 2 May.[8]

---

5. "Former MP Behind Curtain: Would Block Fred Rose Returning to Canada," *The Toronto Globe and Mail,* 4 March 1955.
6. "The Case of Fred Rose," *The Toronto Globe and Mail,* 16 March 1955.
7. From the Secretary of State for External Affairs, Canada to the Canadian Legation, Warsaw, Poland, 22 July 1955.
8. "Fred Rose," From the Canadian Legation, Warsaw to the Under-Secretary of State for External Affairs, Canada, 27 April 1956.

We are, Freddy told the Vice-Consul at the meeting, strangers here. We are not amongst our own. He explained that he'd arrived in Poland on a three-month visa that he had no intention of remaining in Poland, that he was not a Polish citizen and did not intend to become one. He would, he explained, like to return to Canada, but not if it meant he would be badgered by the press and the RCMP. The report on the visit noted that he spoke about Canada as "home." Mr. Rose, said the report, did not bring his passport with him. Then the deadly blow: "Mr. Rose *by his own admission* [emphasis mine] has lived in Poland continuously since November 1953. He has retained no tangible ties with Canada…"[9]

Freddy appeared to believe, incorrectly as it turned out, that his interests would best be served by offering Canadian diplomatic officials frankness and cooperation. Perhaps he did not know what the law said and might have received poor legal advice.

On 22 May 1956 Paul T. Malone, the Acting Under-Secretary of State for External Affairs informed the Deputy Minister, Department of Citizenship and Immigration, in confidence, that the Legation had Freddy's Warsaw address and concluded with this: "You will note that *by his own admission* [emphasis mine], Rose has lived in Poland continuously since November 1953. You may therefore wish to proceed with revocation."[10]

The same day a copy of the letter was forwarded to the RCMP Commissioner.

On 20 June Freddy received a Citizenship Questionnaire with a Notice of Intention to Revoke Citizenship. The covering letter advised that if he wished to take action to retain his Canadian citizenship he needed to ensure that the completed questionnaire reached the Registrar by 1 August. Freddy came in to see the chargé d'affaires. Could the submission date be postponed to 1 September to give him the opportunity to get his lawyer's advice on completing the form, and on whether or not he should oppose the revocation proceedings. If in the opinion of his lawyer an inquiry by a Commission might stir up unfavorable publicity around his name he would drop the challenge. Freddy said he

---

9. "Fred Rose," from the Correspondence, Canadian Legation, Warsaw to the Under-Secretary of State for External Affairs, Canada, 3 May 1956.
10. P. T. Malone, Acting Under-Secretary of State for External Affairs to the Deputy Minister, Department of Citizenship and Immigration, Ottawa, 22 May 1956.

cherished his Canadian citizenship very much and thought it unfair that it should be taken from him, that he had refused to become a Polish citizen, that he considered Canada home, that the only reason he'd come to Poland was because RCMP surveillance had made it impossible for him to earn a living to pay for treatment of the spinal arthritis condition he'd contracted while in prison. Treatment in Poland was without charge as were the extended sessions at the health spas.

A copy of the report was forwarded to the RCMP Commissioner. Ottawa advised the Legation in Warsaw that the 1 September deadline was agreeable.

Freddy, try as he might, was not always able to keep his cool in the face of the government's creepy eagle-scout maneuvers, which could result in yet another episode of the Freddy-is-crazy show. On 8 October 1956 the Consul in Warsaw, John Price Erichsen-Brown, in a letter to Ottawa, claimed Freddy threatened that at the citizenship hearing he would show that he was being persecuted by the Canadian Government because there was an election coming up the following year. I was, said the Consul, "startled when he went on to accuse the Canadian Government of having sought to bolster its case against him by getting a statement through the CBC." This had to do with a reporter named Wasserman in Warsaw with his wife, who had, Freddy said, gotten in touch with him. The Consul claimed that in his conversation with the Wassermans there was "no mention of Fred Rose at any time." Perhaps, he said, Freddy learned Wasserman was in town and "took the initiative in getting in touch with him, for what purpose I have no idea. It is possible that Rose's account of their interview, if they in fact met, has been deliberately distorted by Rose."[11]

In October Freddy had a Canadian visitor from Montreal whose name has been deleted from the record. In January 1957, there was a visit from his lawyer Albert Marcus.

In early February 1957 Freddy was interviewed by the Consul Erichsen-Brown at the consulate in Warsaw. He repeated what he'd said previously that his medical condition and financial problems were what had brought him to Europe that he was in poor health and flat broke.

---

11 J. P. Erichsen-Brown, The Canadian Legation, Warsaw, Poland to the Under-Secretary of State for External Affairs, Canada, 8 October 1956.

He'd originally arrived in Poland, he said, for medical treatment and to find an agency he could handle in Canada. The Consul replied that from the point of view of officialdom those matters were entirely irrelevant. Members of the Polish Red Cross were asked to appear at the hearing to confirm Freddy's statements about his medical condition and treatment. They said they did not see fit to appear in a foreign legation as witnesses, as did the clinic doctors. Written documents were provided.

Freddy said he began work at the *Polonia* publishing house 20 April 1954, that the work consisted of editing materials that had been translated into English for the magazine. The director of the publishing house likewise refused to appear at the Legation hearing but agreed to provide a written document.

When I came here, Freddy told the Consul, it was not "with the idea of staying, as you will see from this visa here, that it was merely a three month visa, the period that was felt would be necessary for treatment." Freddy pointed out that he was not a Polish citizen, that he was in Poland regarded as a Canadian citizen, that he did not possess dual citizenship, that while he'd been in Poland he was not a member of any party, that he'd kept out of politics.[12]

Freddy may not have understood that the purpose of the interview was to produce a document that had him stating *in his own words* that he had been out of Canada since the fall of 1953. In possession of that statement the government could proceed with the revocation of his citizenship.

On 11 April 1957 the Minister of Citizenship and Immigration at a meeting of the federal cabinet in Ottawa recommended exactly that, that "the citizenship of Fred Rose, now residing in Poland, be revoked since he had not maintained substantial connection with Canada within the meaning of the Canadian Citizenship Act. The objections of Mr. Rose to this action had been considered by a commission appointed in accordance with the law; and the commission found that Mr. Rose's citizenship was liable to revocation."[13]

---

12. Beryl Nation, Transcription of the interview conducted with Fred Rose by J. P. Erichsen-Brown, 2 February 1957; "Revocation of Citizenship of Fred Rose," Correspondence, the Canadian Legation, Warsaw to the Under-Secretary of State for External Affairs, Ottawa, Canada, 15 February 1957, transcript enclosed, forwarded to Ottawa by airmail.
13. From the minutes of a meeting of the Cabinet, House of Commons, 11 April 1957.

The prime minister, Louis St. Laurent, signed the order the same day. Freddy was advised of the ruling in a letter dated 15 April 1957 from J. E. Duggan, the Registrar of Canadian Citizenship. The RCMP were informed.[14]

Under the terms of the Citizenship Act, there could be no appeal. It seemed a deed of petty vindictiveness, the hounding of a man who had done his time, who was in financial distress, poor health and politically harmless.

On 6 May Freddy met with the Consul who asked him to return his certificate of citizenship and passport. Freddy said he possessed no certificate of citizenship and wished to hold on to his passport as it was the only document of identity he had, until his position was clarified. The letter informing him of the revocation order would, he said, assist him in obtaining a document of identity as a stateless person. The following day the Consul wrote to ask Freddy to surrender the passport, "technically" the property of the Canadian government, as soon as he had secured other documentation.[15]

The Consul was advised by the Under-Secretary of State for External Affairs that he "should take all steps possible to recover Mr. Rose's passport."

ROSE NO LONGER CITIZEN, said a *Gazette* headline on 26 June 1957. FRED ROSE LOSES CITIZENSHIP, crowed *The Herald*.

The Department of External Affairs expressed surprise that Freddy's lawyer was considering an appeal against the revocation of his citizenship; the Act did not allow for an appeal. It was decided not to ask for the assistance of Polish authorities in recovering the passport, that the Consul ought simply to continue to attempt to persuade Freddy to give up the passport. Why the urgency? The passport could be of no use to Freddy or anyone else. It was due to expire August 1958 and the particulars were on the Passport Control List. The Consul in a 19 August 1957 letter informed Freddy that the revocation proceedings were final and made another request for the passport. Freddy held on to the

---

14. J. T. Duggan, Registrar of Canadian Citizenship to Fred Rose, Esq., c/o The Canadian Legation, Warsaw, Poland, 15 April 1957.
15. J. P. Erichsen-Brown to Fred Rose, 7 May 1957.

passport and his name remained on the Passport Control List.[16] On 30 April 1958 J. E. Duggan wrote Freddy to remind him that the order revoking his citizenship was final, that it could not be rescinded because there was no procedure for doing so. Perhaps in reply to a request, he added that the Minister was not prepared to authorize Freddy's admission into Canada.[17] This may have come following a request from Laura Rose, who had written to the Canadian prime minister, John Diefenbaker, for permission for her father to attend her wedding. The request was denied.

Freddy was now a non-person both to the Government of Canada and the party he'd served.

Laura told me she at one point wrote to Prime Minister Pierre Trudeau asking that Freddy be allowed into the country to attend her daughter's birth. She received no reply. There were then any number of Nazi war criminals living here. Everyone knew this. Pierre Trudeau knew this. In his roles as justice minister and prime minister, he made sure no action would be taken to prosecute those people. A few years ago an Argentine friend told me there were more Nazis living in Canada than in Argentina. That turned out to be true. Nazis were welcomed into Canada. They weren't living in hiding. A private detective, Steve Rambam, found them in the white pages of the phone book. Freddy who'd done the time for his crime, such as it was, would remain *persona non grata*, never permitted to come home, not even for a short visit to participate in a family occasion in a land where Nazis lived in peace and comfort.[18]

In 1976, *Global TV* journalist Peter Desbarats wrote to Allan MacEachran, Secretary of State for External Affairs, about the possibility of Freddy receiving official permission to visit Canada. Nothing came of it. Desbarats told MacEachen he'd spoken to Laura about trying to arrange a TV interview. He wrote to Freddy who, as Laura predicted, did not reply to the letter.[19]

---

16. A. J. Hicks, Acting Under-Secretary of State for External Affairs, Ottawa, Canada, to the Canadian Legation, Warsaw, 6 August 1957; J. P. Erichsen-Brown to Fred Rose, 19 August 1957.

17. J. E. Duggan, Registrar of Canadian Citizenship, to Fred Rose, Esq., 30 April 1958, copied 2 May 1957 to the Commissioner, RCMP.

18. Ellie Tesher, "How Nazi War Criminals Got Into Canada," *The Toronto Star,* 12 November 1997.

19. Peter Desbarats, Ottawa Bureau Chief, Global TV News to the Hon. Allan J. MacEachen, Secretary of State for External Affairs, House of Commons, Ottawa, Canada, 16 July 1976.

The previous year Freddy received a visit in Warsaw from the Progressive Conservative MP Tom Cossitt who had also made friends with Igor.[20] In 1976, there was an attempt to promote a movement to bring Freddy back to Canada. But nothing came of that either.[21]

In 1977, a report circulated within the RCMP that seventy-year-old Freddy was surreptitiously returning to Canada: "Rose has been making semi-annual visits to Canada for a number of years to visit his family. [He] does this under the cover as a crew man from the Polish M/V *Batory* using false documentation."

A check early the following year concluded that given the state of his health and his failing eyesight it would have been unlikely.[22] Among Freddy's Canadian visitors were the sisters Dorothy and Betty Howarth. They found Freddy initially reluctant to talk about the past or what it was like to live in a Communist country. The subject of the socialist creed came up. What, he said, is the use of staying here? No matter how hard you work, you cannot make anything of yourself." The area Freddy lived in was close by the old Warsaw ghetto now the site of new apartment buildings.[23]

In May 1978, David Lewis paid Freddy a visit. He told the Department of External Affairs that Freddy was not in good health, that he was retired and living on a Polish pension, that Fanny was receiving a pension from Canada. Officials from Jewish organizations in Poland had helped Lewis get Freddy's address. Though the man had never moved, the embassy people told Lewis they had no idea where Freddy lived. A report about the David Lewis visit was passed on to the RCMP.[24]

The Poland Freddy settled in had endured much under Soviet rule. Poland's status as an enemy nation arose out of a long history of Polish-Russian conflict. While the Hitler-Stalin Pact held, 200,000 Poles were murdered. In April 1944 the Polish homeland army launched an uprising in Warsaw in the belief that an all-out Russian assault on Nazi positions

20. Visit of Thomas Charles Cossitt MP to Fred Rose, RCMP debriefing report, 15 January 1973.
21. "Re: Fred Rose," RCMP, 5 October 1976.
22. "Re: Fred Rose," RCMP report, 12 September 1977. Follow up reports 30 November 1977, 19 December 1977, 9 January 1978, 22 January 1978, 27 March 1978.
23. Dorothy Howarth, "Fred Rose, Now in Warsaw, Hungry for News From Canada," *The Ottawa Journal*, 23 August 1961.
24. "Visit to Warsaw by David Lewis—Contact with Fred Rose," Canadian embassy, Warsaw, Poland, to the Under-Secretary of State for External Affairs, Ottawa, 17 May 1978.

was in the works. Stalin held his military back, allowing the Germans to crush Polish resistance.

Freddy arrived in Poland in November 1953 during a period described as one of "full Stalinism." In time, the repression and violence of post-WWII Poland eased up, replaced by surveillance—of intellectuals, the Church, opposition movements—managed through an elaborate system of informers, eavesdropping techniques and the scrutiny of correspondence. In 1956, the regime tried a carrot. Those who cooperated with information on colleagues, friends and family members might receive a one-time-trip-out-of-the-country passport.[25]

A 1956 issue of *Polonia*, the publication Freddy worked for, tried to show a happy face. WE ADVANCE FROM A FORWARD POSITION, said the lead article's headline. The "Polish industry has fulfilled the Six-Year Plan with a surplus and carried out the tasks presented in this plan, although delays, weaknesses and incompletely realized tasks were revealed in some sections." Included in the issue were pieces on modern architecture, Polish poster art, semi-conductors, the music of Chopin, and Poland's chances in the Melbourne Olympic Games.

Poles were able to celebrate the traditional Catholic holidays, Christmas, Epiphany. But billy clubs were kept at the ready. Street demonstrations were swiftly dispersed to prevent a recurrence of a workers' revolt like the one that occurred in Poznan that year.

Following the 1967 Six-Day War, Zionism rose to the top of the Polish enemies agenda. In virtually Jewless Poland an anti-Semitic campaign grew with wildfire swiftness.

In December 1970 workers' protests triggered by a rise in food prices on the Baltic Coast resulted in the killing of several dozen people. The regime responded to strikes in 1976 with arrests, fines, prison, some killings. The reaction to the human rights movement was otherwise restrained. Poland had become financially dependent on the West.

When the British journalist Timothy Garton Ash arrived in Poland in 1980 he kept hearing the word *Yowta*. It was the Polish pronunciation of Yalta, as he put it, "the first fact of life in contemporary Poland" where in February 1945 Stalin sat down with Churchill and Roosevelt

---

25. Andrzej Paczkowski, "Poland, the 'Enemy Nation'," in Stephane Courtois, Nicolas Werth, Jean-Louis Panne, Andrzej Paczkowski, Karel B. Artosek, Jean-Louis Margolin, *The Black Book of Communism: Crimes, Terror, Repression*, trans. by Jonathan Murphy and Mark Kramer, Harvard University Press, 1999.

and promised free and open elections in the occupied Polish Republic.[26] Strike action spread. The attempt to repress *Solidarity,* the Polish trade union movement resulted in killings, arrests, the burning of union buildings. Martial law declared in 1981 was suspended in July 1983. In August 1988 the government announced it would enter into negotiations with *Solidarity.* It was not something Freddy, felled by heart trouble in March 1983, lived to see.

In 1978, two years before the founding of *Solidarity*, the journalist and poet Ryszard Kapuscinski published a book about the collapse of the Haile Selassie regime in Ethiopia, *The Emperor: Downfall of an Autocrat.* Drawing on fact and invention, Kapuscinski described how over a period of a decade and a half the great contradiction between the reality of the Benevolent Majesty's oppressive and corrupt government and how it represented itself became clearer, how as the gap narrowed the staying power of the regime shrunk to nothing. Any Pole who read the book understood the message: Communist governance in Poland would before long be a thing of the past.

In Warsaw Freddy found himself cut off from the political waters he'd splashed in most of his life, cut off too from friends and family. Health issues mounted, both his and Fanny's. Prospects for a return home grew ever dimmer.

There is the claim that Freddy was contributing material to *The Canadian Tribune* under the *nom d'exil* George Lambert. The tone and wording of a 1967 piece, "Poland and Peace" does sound like him. The article included a photograph of workers in the Gdansk shipyards: "The shipyards in Gdansk [formerly Danzig]," says the caption, "are a busy place. Its workers point with pride to the fact that they have produced 361 ships in the past five years."[27]

Between 1953 and 1982, Freddy wrote dozens of letters home. Few seem to have survived, apart from the ones written to Bella Brenton and Lea Roback, a well-known and tireless party worker who'd spent the better part of a lifetime in the political trenches.[28] Laura told me Bella,

26. Timothy Garton Ash, *The Polish Revolution: Solidarity 1980–1982,* Jonathan Cape 1983.
27. George Lambert, "Poland and Peace," *The Canadian Tribune,* 24 April 1967.
28. Correspondence, Fred Rose to Bella Brenton, Lea Roback and Laura Rose, 28 October 1953 to 8 July 1982.

the wife of Frank Brenton, a close political associate, was the person Freddy considered his best friend in Montreal.

Freddy sent out 80 end-of-year UNICEF cards. Other letters may have survived, stashed in drawers, packed away somewhere. Unfortunately, Bella's letters to Freddy seem to have disappeared. Bella, who escaped Montreal winters in Mexico, was once or twice called on to assist with the legalities of Fanny's citizenship status. Lea was on the point of retirement. Bella and Lea were acquainted. Bella visited Freddy and Fanny in Warsaw several times.

The prison diary Freddy kept has apparently been lost; the letters may fill in for a vanished memoir.

Freddy spent much of his time in Warsaw reflecting on the past, on the current world scene, on events in Poland and other parts of the Soviet empire, on the dire circumstances he and Fanny now found themselves in. The letters find him clinging to the belief that the socialist vision could be salvaged, that the breakdowns and excesses were the result of the wrong people in positions of authority.

A born talker, Freddy was never completely comfortable communicating with his friends this way. After fifteen years of letter writing he told Bella he found the mail an unsatisfactory medium for exchanging views.

Unlike the Rosenberg letters, Freddy's letters didn't on the surface seem intended to serve a larger purpose. Perhaps they were what they appeared to be, correspondence with friends to whom Freddy might pour out his heart, accounts of the couple's daily Warsaw routine, family matters, opinions, among them that "the world is in a mess."

Totalitarian regimes rarely favor action for its own sake. Could it have been that the purpose of the letters to Bella was to tell Polish authorities he was relaying approved thoughts back to Canada so that he and Fanny might continue to receive much needed medical assistance? It was a time when the USSR and the Poles and the others had begun to feel increased concern about international opinion.

On one occasion Freddy found the cashews missing from a parcel Bella had sent, maple sugar scattered over the wrapping. The parcel had been opened, searched, the nuts but not the sugar stolen? Were there any letters that were held back? Did Freddy need to be careful about what he said?

The letters are a chronicle of physical and emotional distress. They contain no references to the Party or to tracts of socialist theory, in any event not Freddy's thing. Freddy was a pragmatic guy, a schmoozer, a street organizer. Might there have been things he wanted to say but did not? In the socialist world of incompetence and scarcity, things often didn't work out as advertised. Almost to the end, he tried to maintain the view that the grim conditions in Soviet socialist Europe would improve, that they were improving.

Polish travel documents Freddy obtained identified him as a stateless person which required him to pay in dollars for travel outside Poland. Did he refuse to become a Polish citizen? Was Polish citizenship an option? Stateless and passportless, travel was limited to Warsaw Pact nations—East Germany, Czechoslovakia, Bulgaria, Hungary, Romania, the USSR. Travel to any Western European country or to Cuba or Angola or The People's Republic of China was probably out of the question.

There is no reference in the letters to world events he surely would have taken a great interest in: the JFK assassination, Prague 1968, the removal from power of Alexander Dubček, *Solidarity*'s Lech Walesa, the 1978 accession to the papacy of the Polish-born Karol Wojtyla, Pope John Paul II, the 1981 assassination attempt on the Pope, shot while driving through St. Peter's Square in Rome by Mehmet Ali Ağca.

In East Berlin Freddy had observed people better-dressed. He found the shops in the GDR well-stocked, had the impression that prosperity declined as one traveled east. There were more automobiles now riding the streets of Warsaw, though when it came to economic matters, the Germans seemed more flexible than the Poles. There were no references to East Germany's Stasi or related agencies in Poland or elsewhere.

Canadian visitors included party man Stanley Ryerson, David Lewis, Bella, Laura, Pierre Richer, a Parti Québécois member. There was no mention in the letters of Eric Adams or David Shugar, both of whom were thought to have settled in Poland.

When Freddy arrived in Czechoslovakia in the fall of 1953 seeking treatment for his medical condition he was absolutely alone. There he sat in Frantiskovy Lazne, a town in the Cheb district of the Karlovy Vary region in West Bohemia, awaiting word from Fanny and Laura. He wrote Bella that he planned to see Prague, then visit Lublin, Poland, the city of his birth and the Majdanek death camp "where millions were slaughtered including many of my relatives." In the same letter he mentioned a visit to the site of the Terezin concentration camp: "I came away with a sad feeling mainly because it is so soon forgiven and forgotten." These are the sole references in the letters to the Holocaust. Absent too are references to the seizure by Polish citizens of Jewish property and possessions. This might have been in compliance with post WWII Soviet policy that discouraged references to Holocaust-related matters. The mention of the visit to Majdanek seemed intended, at least in part, to point a finger at Nazi excesses and away from Soviet oppression.

Freddy struggled to cope with the trauma of his exile. "You realize," he said in an early letter, "that I prefer to keep out from a discussion on Canadian politics. It's wiser that way. I'm not close enough to the scene—neither there nor here." This in reply to a letter about a New Year's Eve celebration in Montreal: "I would have loved to have been with the group of friends at your place.... On such occasions I get a special yen for my old pals." Along with the nostalgia is the effort to cheer himself up, to try to see the bright side of his predicament, to feel some optimism about conditions in Soviet Europe—Germany, Romania, Hungary, Bulgaria, Poland and the USSR itself, places he would visit. There is this in a letter written in the fall of 1958: "From year to year I find change for the better in the USSR." He enjoyed, he said "walking through the streets of Warsaw and watching the new buildings going up." He spent a month at a seaside resort in Romania where he found "new cities, new industries, lovely housing developments." No mention of Nicolae Ceauşescu.

Fanny joined him in 1954. A key concern of the couple was for daughter Laura, her visits and letters eased the pain of separation. Freddy expressed great regret at not being permitted to travel home in October 1958 for Laura's wedding. There were no restrictions on Fanny's travel; she was able to travel to Montreal and back by ship, *The Batory,* later on LOT, the Polish airline. There is no reference in Freddy's letters to the revocation of his citizenship, only the observation that he had become a stateless person.

At one point, after a few years on the magazine job, he tells Bella he is considering taking a half-time job: "I find it too hard to sit and edit poor translations eight hours a day." He feels that office friction has contributed to his run-down condition: "People pay with their health for conscientiousness… There is more and more work to be done, a limited number of people to do it." He welcomed an office re-organization that would give him less to do.

There seemed to be something of a departure from the cracked-eggs-to-omelet man Freddy had been. "My own troubles," as he put it in June 1963, "have taught me tolerance and understanding." He had become more introspective: "Dreams and reality have generally little in common. We had created in our minds an idyllic picture, and some of us tend to get disillusioned because things didn't work out the way we wanted them to. The fact is that our thinking was based not on fact but on fancy. We tended to generalize, and therefore couldn't see the specific situations existing in the various countries. Least of all we mis-understood the make-up of human beings, their peculiarities (the result of their environment), the deep roots of habits and traditions, the fact that socialism got its start in backward countries—in every respect, that the war wreaked havoc in these parts (not only material destruction but moral decline), etc. Centralization, which was imperative at one stage, including during wartime, became a hindrance later on. Habits formed during that period are hard to break…. People everywhere want the things that make life more pleasant and they judge the system not on the basis of some dogma but rather by what it gives them. The Chinese still have to learn that—I mean the leaders…. Westerners who have had a life of plenty tend to judge harshly the people in this part of the world."

Over the years, Freddy and Fanny both experienced declining health. Freddy suffered from glaucoma and cataracts, requiring surgery, as well as severe back pain, for which he took pills. There was surgery for a ruptured appendix. Medical care was provided by the Polish state. At one point a bout of dysentery put him in hospital for three weeks. In 1963, Fanny had to deal with colitis and an ulcer condition and spent the better part of a month at a medical facility in southern Poland.

Warsaw weather had much the same unpredictability as Montreal weather. Rainy periods made it hard on his arthritis.

There was travel to the hot springs in Karlovy Vary in Czechoslovakia and the mineral baths of Carlsbad for treatment, exercise, and massage. There were repeated trips to Sochi on the Black Sea, where Stalin had vacationed, the location of numerous sanatoria. Russian workers and others came to Sochi for the sulfuric springs that were supposed to cure arthritis.

Khrushchev escaping his removal from power with his life in 1964 seemed yet another sign of slow but steady progress, a lesson for the Chinese who, Freddy thought, were committing all the sins of the Communists of the past. There was nothing said about Khrushchev's denunciation of Stalin.

In the mid-sixties Freddy returned from a trip to Lublin where he'd seen a new housing coop project: "Time and intelligent guidance are bound to overcome the negative aspects. All we need is peace in the world...right now, in addition to the war in Vietnam, the situation in the Middle East doesn't look too good. Israeli leaders are playing a dangerous game; they're staking everything on American support."

Israeli leaders are playing a dangerous game; they're staking everything on American support.

Parisian friends had just returned from China: "It's easy for well-to-do people to fall for the ultra-revolutionary line of the Chinese. Whatever may be wrong with some of the practices of the USSR and the other countries in this camp, the Chinese cannot alter the situation with their violent attack on the camp. Mao has split the internationalist movement and among others the poor Vietnamese are paying for it...this action is criminal and no "leftist" phrases can hide this fact... I'm a humanist.... I've learned a lot from the fourteen years I've spent in this part of the world, enough not to fall for revolutionary rah-rah or any cult whether the name is Stalin or Mao or whatever... To the well-to-do it's a sort of hobby, a game, but reality is anything but a game... What's happening between the USSR and China is shocking...regrettable and painful."

Freddy believed Mao's madness was the cause of the rift with the USSR which in turn was responsible for the American acceleration of the war in Vietnam. Mao, Freddy believed, was the villain of the piece. He'd betrayed the socialist dream, "that made sense and still makes sense for war is unthinkable and unity and united action are imperative if man is to keep pace with scientific and technological development.... Of course the Chinese can talk so irresponsibly because the possession of the A- and H- bombs by the Soviet Union has saved them from nuclear aggression. I don't doubt their great achievements... but Mao's policies smack a bit too much of Stalin's blind spots. The big leap didn't bring the expected results and instead of aggressive language Communists would be expected to analyze the results and draw the necessary conclusions. There are no miraculous short cuts."

That may have been the current Soviet line. There is the standard Soviet criticism of nationalism and ethnic causes, the odd equation of Mao's bogus socialism with the nationalism of Israel and Quebec, as if there was some sort of unspoken alliance between Maoists, faux socialists and the ditzy rich.

In Sochi in 1968, he and Fanny met the composer and conductor Aram Katchaturian who offered them passes for a Leningrad Symphony concert of his music.

Freddy applauded the 1968 Tet offensive, calling it "a remarkable demonstration of human determination and endurance." In the same letter he expressed disappointment over events in Cuba: "The trials and sentences in Cuba are disturbing—the cult of Castro is obviously no better than any other cult. I don't know what Fidel expects to achieve, but I can see nothing good in store for the Cuban people as a result of his actions."

Freddy heaped equal praise on the USSR's Luna and Soyuz space programs and the 1969 American moonshot: "The moon landing was a great feat. It was shown live on TV here—blast off to the splash-down."

December 1969, in a card to Lea: "I'd like to start working on an autobiography—maybe it will be published some day—and 1970 is the year to begin."

In Poland in 1970, there had been "...no respite from the strikes—when some are settled others break out.... The leaders of the new unions have been using their power to demand bigger and bigger wage increases at a time when there are food shortages and economic difficulties."

Anxious for the sight of a silver lining, Freddy observed that there were now 56,000 automobiles in Warsaw, surely he believed another sign of progress. He applauded the demonstrations in the United States opposing the American invasion of Cambodia.

By the mid 1970s Warsaw had a very modern central railway station in the heart of the city. But a few years later: "the authorities are grappling with a meat shortage, importing large quantities... Big meat eaters, the Poles apparently hate going without their morning sausage."

There was bad news from Quebec: "The FLQ shot its bolt with the kidnappings and murder of Laporte—a sign of desperation and weakness. I guess Lévesque will cash in on the situation—the violence of the FLQ and the drastic means resorted to by Trudeau and Bourassa. Events in Chile and Bolivia have shown the fallacy of extremist action a la Mao, Guevara, Castro.... What a long way the old province has traveled. From one time docility to kidnapping and murder. Too bad that the acts of frustration on the part of a small group of confused individuals brought Quebec into the limelight ...and defaced its image... Maoism, anarchism or ultranationalism is hardly the answer to Quebec's problems..."

In a reference to executions in Sudan, Freddy said he had little faith in military dictators. In an end-of-year 1970 greeting card: "What a year it has been. Endless strikes, shortages of food... Fanny gets up at 5 a.m. to stand in line for bread." A couple of months earlier he'd written that much progress was being made in the GDR.

Early in the new year, 1971, there was more trouble: "...prices have risen, meat shortages, grumbling." Strikes broke out on the Baltic coast, demonstrations by strikers resulted in bloodshed. At this point, Freddy didn't see the strikers as entirely responsible. The new political leadership met with shipyard workers.

A year later, things in Poland seemed to be improving. It's like Canada! Fanny exclaimed. Not exactly said Freddy, but better than it had been.

Freddy was pleased to hear of Richard Nixon's plans to visit China; he hoped the *rapprochement* would not be used against the USSR. He seemed to feel a certain fondness for the American president who he credited with bold foreign policy moves claiming that the Nixon administration had recognized the realities of international developments and acted accordingly. As for Watergate, Freddy thought Nixon was certain of victory in the 1972 election and didn't need the bugging operation but had fallen victim to the corrupting influence of power. He felt much anger at the massive bombing of Cambodia in the spring of 1973 that ended in August, calling it an outrage. It will, Freddy said, "be interesting to see what happens in Indochina in the next few months." In April 1975 Pol Pot led the Khmer Rouge into Phnom Penh and the North Vietnamese marched into Saigon.

Freddy was certain Pierre Trudeau would retain his majority in the 1972 Canadian federal election and was surprised by the loss of support.

In December 1972 Freddy's glaucoma was more or less under control. We're getting older, he observed, and we feel it, not only in our bones.

In a letter to Lea, 16 September 1973: "The situation in the world is gradually improving, and in Europe it is very evident… Technically a lot of progress has been made in Poland. The events in Chile and the death of Allende is a reminder that not all is as yet well."

In August 1975 Freddy and Fanny had a visit from "a friend of the Carrs," presumably Sam Carr. He doesn't say any more, no who. Freddy's eye trouble now made letter writing difficult. Unable to read, he turned for comfort to music, Dinah Shore a favorite. Lea sent him a Felix Leclerc LP. French-Canadian LPs, he said, "bring Quebec closer…"

That month, he received a pack of *Gazette* clippings, material that provided the sequence of events of 1945–1946, the sensational headlines, Gouzenko's "rehearsed" remarks. Another pack arrived in September. By April 1979 he had completed 130 typed pages of his memoir. Not clear how much more he was able to do, given the difficulties with his eyesight.

In February 1976 colitis, ulcer and kidney trouble put Fanny back in hospital. There were x-rays, blood tests. The couple needed to rely on friends for shopping: bread, butter, cheese, eggs. There was a meat shortage.

With the murder of the Israeli athletes in Munich in 1972 in mind, Freddy expressed the hope that the Olympics scheduled for Montreal in the summer of 1976 "will pass peacefully without any terrorist attacks."

Later that year, perhaps a reference to the PQ election victory on 15 November 1976: "The English-speaking community in Quebec appears to be fairly nervous about the developments in the province...some people planning to leave..."

Never a fan of nationalisms, not in Israel not in Quebec either, which he believed were inimical to the interests of the working class.

On Jimmy Carter winning the 1976 American election: "...an ambitious small-town politician and a reactionary Pole are a dangerous combination." The reference was to ex-McGill University graduate Zbigniew Brzezinski.

Freddy was deeply unhappy about his treatment in "the old man's book," one-time party head Tim Buck's posthumous 1977 publication *Yours in the Struggle: Reminiscences of Tim Buck*. The book was a collection of edited CBC interview transcripts published without the blessing of the party. Freddy, who might not have known this, had apparently received a pre-publication copy from someone in Toronto. Didn't say who. Buck had been removed as party chief in 1962." When I read the chapter of interest to me I was awfully mad," said Freddy. "The whole thing is a malicious fabrication, the result of an imagination run wild. Why did he do it? With every passing year he was becoming more and more bitter. He wasn't used to opposition of the type he was confronted with in Montreal in 1956 and obviously resented his replacement as chief in the early sixties. According to him there was no one who could take his place...a megalomania."

In 1977, a cataract was found in Freddy's right eye, his vision was worsening, he would need surgery. In July 1979 he was in hospital for four weeks. In early 1980, a routine cardiogram indicated emerging cardiac trouble.

There were in Warsaw acquaintances, perhaps colleagues, neighbors. Social events. Freddy enjoyed the Warsaw visits of the Moscow Art Theatre, the Budapest Ballet, the Mosieve Company, the Leipzig Philharmonic, Italian, French, and American cinema, the American film

Who's Afraid of Virginia Woolf, Russia's *The Cranes Are Flying:* "...a very fine war picture, extremely human, without slogans or heroics."

The couple owned a TV set, watched a fair amount of TV, one evening Fellini's *La Dolce Vita.* Freddy with his electrician's skill was able to convert their phonograph player to stereo. Listening to music at home and attending concerts were sources of comfort. Apart from his fondness for the voice of Dinah Shore, he listened to the classical repertoire, and the music of Quebec. He'd picked up a slide projector in Dresden. For reading there were Penguin paperback mysteries, newspapers and magazines. He received *Maclean's* magazine, had a subscription to *The Financial Post* he didn't want renewed. At the office there were copies of *The Nation, The Herald Tribune, Time, The New Statesman, The New York Times* and the *Times of London.* He'd acquired a copy of Andrew Collard's *Montreal Yesterdays.*

In 1980, after receiving news of the death by cancer of Canadian friends, Freddy wondered why billions were being spent on weapons of annihilation and relatively little on combating cancer and heart disease: "The international situation is very discouraging. A new arms race has been started by the decision on the production and deployment of intermediate nuclear missiles in West-European countries."

The deterioration that socialist Poland had begun to experience in 1956 was now gathering momentum.

The memoirs had occupied Freddy's attention for a decade. Hampered by failing vision and severe back pain, Freddy said he nevertheless was trying to "do as much work as possible." Perhaps the option of taping the recollections for transcription did not occur to him. It did seem from the way he spoke of the project that the work would be more autobiography than political tract. He'd now been in Poland for almost twenty years mulling things over.

In the fall 1980 a wave of strikes in Poland resulted in an atmosphere of tension. As his health deteriorated, so did domestic political conditions. As Freddy put it, he and Fanny were no longer young and energetic. Nevertheless, he pressed on with the memoirs: "I'm continuing to write but I still have a long way to go..." Work was proceeding "more slowly than I expected." Back pain limited the effort to two hours daily.

As Freddy's health declined and socialism seemed to be collapsing all around them he couldn't help but notice, as he sadly observed, that the couple's chances of ever returning home to Canada were remote. In 1981, he observed in a letter to Bella that after a brief period of calm the strikes continued. The Polish parliament had appointed the Minister of Defense, Wojciech Jaruzelski, to the premiership. Not mentioned in the letters by name Jaruzelski "appealed for 90 days without strikes....so far the response of the *Solidarity* leadership has been negative, heedless of the dangers involved, of the tragic consequences..." Freddy again reminded Bella that he had been "trying to write my story and have done quite a lot but I still have a long way to go."

As the situation worsened, Freddy began to side with Polish official-dom against *Solidarity* and the unions. In his view, corrupt officials who betrayed socialist principles were to blame for the problems Poland was experiencing. There had been as well an absence of common sense: "In the drive for speedy industrialization, the old leaders often forgot about the needs of the workers...housing, social facilities in the old factories, the health service, a just wage system, a better supply of goods..."

By the summer 1981 the end seemed near: "...the economic situation is steadily becoming worse. At our age and with our poor health it was all a little too much for us, especially for Fanny. She had the responsibility of standing in endless lines to get the essentials—bread, butter, cheese, cereals, meat, etc. Most of those items are now rationed.... The terrible mess here is the result of mismanagement, corruption, demoralization on the part of the former party and government leaders, which in turn influenced their subordinates....the whole party and nation are paying the price for the misdeeds of unscrupulous individuals."

There were now even longer food lines awaiting Fanny, who was herself not well: "...the mere idea of going out to shop is frightening. She doesn't have the energy to stand in endless lines. All this shouldn't have happened to us at our age."

As the couple struggled to get by amidst the social disintegration, work on the memoirs seemed mostly what kept Freddy mentally afloat. In a response to Bella having raised the issue of the couple returning to Montreal, Freddy said it was too "painful to write about."

In a letter to Laura he asked her to show Bella, he spelled out his assessment of the couple's predicament: "Due to the present state of our health we're in no position to move anywhere, least of all to Canada. I'm not a Canadian citizen—I'm a stateless person—and in 1957 the Department of Immigration informed me that I would never be allowed to enter the country. In 1965 or 1966 there was a Canadian parliamentary delegation here which included David Lewis, the NDP leader. He came over to visit me, and just before leaving our place he asked me if I would like him to speak to the Minister about permission to visit my family. 'Go ahead and ask him,' I said. 'A few years ago he was here again and dropped in to see me. He told me that he had spoken to [Jean] Marchand and the latter told him that it should be possible to arrange.' But the next day Marchand, the Minister of Manpower and Immigration, informed Lewis that the RCMP said no and he could do nothing about it. Perhaps Marchand had been advised that there was no upside, that allowing Freddy to return even if only for a brief visit would result in a bad press, political damage.

"However, aside from these technical obstacles there are more important difficulties. What should we live on? Fanny's pension of $168 plus a pension that I might get would hardly cover our expenses. The medicines we need would take a substantial part of our income. What about rent and living expenses Laura is in no position to help us financially, and we don't want to be a burden on anybody.

"Here our pensions cover all expenses. We get free medical care and medicines are free of charge, including eye drops which Laura used to send me at $27 for a tiny bottle.

"Of course there are disadvantages being far away from our family and close friends. As we get older and weaker we feel the lack of that more and more and there's nothing we'd like more than to be among our own. But we must look at things realistically."

Marcel Fournier, a Quebec sociologist, spent an afternoon with Freddy and Fanny in Warsaw in November 1982. Like the Howarth sisters, he found the address in a phone directory. It was a few weeks before the imposition of martial law. Freddy, whose stay in Poland was negotiated with the Polish embassy in Canada, did not then have much to say about *Solidarity*. It seemed to Prof. Fournier that he was reluctant to speak critically of the Polish authorities. In a 1980 letter he'd expressed disappointment with the turn in Poland away from socialist goals to *Solidarity's* clerico-religious and nationalist values. The long lines at the shops, the menace of civil war, the threat of Soviet military intervention left him saddened and distressed. But that was not to see the role of the USSR in totally negative terms. Fournier recalled a lively conversation with the couple. Though he had little enthusiasm for Quebec nationalism, Freddy spoke positively of René Lévesque. Freddy, Fournier wrote, didn't seem to him unwell, didn't give the impression he saw himself as a retired person whose end was near. He was keeping in touch with events in Quebec by correspondence with Montreal friends and the receipt of books on Canadian topics. Freddy knew about the November 1976 election victory of René Lévesque's *Parti québécois.* Looking back, Fournier observed, the 1943 and 1945 election victories in cosmopolitan Cartier were ideological triumphs, the 1943 by-election win "an important victory for Quebec's communist militants."[29] One is left to wonder how well Freddy would have done if he'd campaigned in Cartier strictly as a Polish socialist.

Among Freddy and Fanny's Warsaw visitors was Merrily Weisbord, a long-time family friend, who wrote about a 1978 visit: "He is physically ailing, but mentally and emotionally undaunted. We cover the early history of the Communist Party in Quebec. He will not discuss: Euro-Communism, the Soviet government or the Canadian Communist Party after 1946. "I don't know, kid. I was already in the coop at this point." I ask questions of him and his wife. Why don't they talk? Why haven't they come back to Canada? They smile at my enthusiasm. Fred has twice been refused permission to visit Canada. They are not physically strong enough to "join the battle." It is a young person talking to an old, old world."[30]

Edo Tarlo, a woman who'd worked on Freddy's election campaigns said she returned from her Warsaw visit depressed by what she saw:

---

29. Marcel Fournier, "Fred Rose: Notes pour une biographie," in Robert Comeau and Bernard Dionne (eds.), *Le Droit de se Taire: histoire des communistes au Quebec, de la Première Guerre mondiale a la Revolution tranquille,* VLB, Etudes Québécois, 1989.
30. Weisbord, *The Strangest Dream.*

"I'm glad I saw Fred before he died. We talked. We listened to Dinah Shore and I felt a great warmth for him."[31]

In those last years word came from Warsaw that Freddy was un-happy with life there and yearned to return to Canada. A virtual prisoner in Oz, Freddy understood that there would be no return to Kansas. He struggled to fend off the reality of the nightmare socialist Poland had become. Making the rounds of Vancouver and Toronto and Montreal in those long ago heady times, addressing the laboring crowds gathered at rallies, talking the talk of the dawning of a workers' state was one thing, this Polish reality he was trapped in quite another.

Freddy was gone when in October 1984, as part of the crackdown on Poland's *Solidarity* movement, the priest Jerzy Popieluszko was kid-napped by Polish secret police, beaten to death with a wooden club, his body dumped in the Vistula River. The only thing unusual about the incident was that public outrage forced Communist authorities to arrest and try his killers. The officials who'd ordered the crime were acquitted. Jaruzelski, perhaps aware that the game was virtually over, would claim that he was a decent fellow simply trying to maintain order in the face of growing labor unrest, thus hoping to dissuade Leonid Brezhnev from sending in the tanks as he had done in Czechoslovakia. One is left to wonder. Brezhnev was seriously ill and would be dead within a month.

---

31. Correspondence, Eda Tarlo to Francine Pelletier, undated.

XII.

Igor's Exile

"The legend says that a flock of clamorous geese flew up from their nests and woke the sleeping Roman soldiers, thus saving Rome. I feel that is what we did in 1945—awoke democracy. History does not mention it, but I suspect that to celebrate the victory, the Roman soldiers served roast goose. That is the state which we have been living in since 1945—roasted..."

Svetlana Gouzenko
in a letter to Harry Chapman Pincher, 17 April 1983,
from a memoir-in-progress entitled *Roman Goose.*

"He wanted all the Charles Atlas body-building equipment."

Roma Joy, wife of RCMP Officer Don Fast.

Igor Gouzenko was born in 1919 in a village outside Moscow. He was, someone said, what you got if you called central casting and asked them to send up a Russian. Recruited by the KGB for training in coding, in obscuring the content of telegraph messages, in 1943 Lieut. Igor Gouzenko was posted to Ottawa with his wife and infant son to do military encryption work in the Soviet embassy for the GRU.[1]

Svetlana Gouzenko told the journalist John Sawatsky that her husband made the decision to defect after hearing about the defection of

---

1. Igor Gouzenko, *This Was My Choice*, J. M. Dent and Sons, 1948, published in America that year as *The Iron Curtain.*

Victor Kravchenko in 1944 and the positive reception Kravchenko received in the United States. This would have been three months *before* Igor learned of the recall notice.[2]

Kravchenko was an engineer employed by *Amtorg*, the Soviet government purchasing commission in America. On 4 April, the day after he defected Kravchenko took his story about the depravities of the Soviet system to *The New York Times*, a tactic Igor would attempt to copy. Soon the news was in all the papers. It was discussed at the Soviet embassy in Ottawa. It was, Svetlana recalled, decisive, it meant that it was possible to make the break. Said a Russian-language review of Kravchenko's *I Chose Freedom* (1946), published in the United States: "The wider the circle of those whom Kravchenko's book will convince that one cannot remain silent, the more successful its undoubtedly historic mission will be. It will accomplish this mission if it will force a sufficiently wide circle of Americans to want to know the truth about Russia."[3]

Igor as a young man joined Komsomol, the Soviet Youth League. For a time he was prepared as an adult to play the compliant Soviet technocrat. But that didn't last. Unlike Kravchenko, Igor had early on lost his ideological faith. He was not the committed revolutionary who suffered the trauma of an abandoned vision. He did not, as Kravchenko did, feel the pain of disillusion. "Something precious within me," Kravchenko said, "is dead." There was now for Igor only the shared awareness of menace. The words of Kravchenko could have been his own: "...agents, if ordered, will strike me down."

There is in Igor's story likewise little to compare with the anguish of Walter Krivitsky. While the Spanish Civil War raged on Krivitsky said he watched in despair as Stalin drove a knife into the back of the Loyalist government, the Moscow purges transported to Spain, Stalin's looting of the gold in the Spanish treasury and extending the hand of friendship to Hitler even as he ordered the execution of the great generals of the Red Army.

Igor's autobiography, *This Was My Choice*, was written partly in

---

2. John Sawatsky, *Gouzenko, the Untold Story*, Macmillan of Canada, 1984.
3. Victor Kravchenko, *I Chose Freedom: The Personal and Political Life of a Soviet Official*, Charles Scribner's Sons, 1946; J. Denke, "The Truth About Stalin's Russia," *The Socialist Courier*, May 1946 (translated from the Russian). See also Gary Kern, *The Kravchenko Case: One Man's War on Stalin*, Enigma Books, 2007.

English, partly in Russian, ghost edited and patched up by Montreal sportswriter Andy O'Brien. The book depicts Soviet society as "a dreamland of unreality," brutal, oppressive, cynical, a regime that employed fear and food deprivation to keep the population in line. Without *blat*—influence—one was virtually doomed. It was a life from which Igor was spared by his aptitude for absorbing technical knowledge. As the account of his life in the USSR makes clear, Igor had good reason for hating Stalin, for seeking to escape the Soviet paradise, for endeavoring to inflict as much damage as he could on Uncle Joe. A particular sore point, to which Igor devoted the better part of a chapter, was the abusive treatment of WWII Russian army veterans. A wave of arrests greeted those so-called unruly men who spoke publicly and openly of the horrors of war. The Soviet press carried stories of a drive against hooliganism. Nobody, Igor wrote, was sure what the term meant, but everybody knew it applied to the veterans.

Igor described the astonishment of Soviet embassy staff in Ottawa at the support the USSR received from Canadian Jews. Russian Jews made up a large percentage of the inmates in some Gulag camps. During the war, the shooting of Jews at the front was common. In the summer of 1945, as the war was winding down, the Central Committee of the Party issued a directive that Jews were to be removed from positions of responsibility. The directive was kept secret so as not to alienate Jews abroad sympathetic to the Soviet state, who were generally ignorant of the savagery with which Jews in the USSR were treated.

Igor regarded Freddy, linked to thirteen of the people investigated by the royal commission, with special distaste as a Stalin pawn. He wondered how a man who'd worked for the USSR since his late teens and who possessed an arrest record could have been elected to parliament. Freddy, said Igor, was among those most prominently mentioned in the Soviet documents, a man who had passed on to Stalin military information obtained from Canadian army officers who'd served in the war.

Igor was aware that in Canada he was a target of KGB assassins: "I understand that I need to be careful, and I am." As well, he needed to be cautious about what he remembered in the post-defection interrogation sessions, that he needed to distance himself from the embassy's espionage activity, to make it clear he was but a simple technician whose information came entirely from his decoding work and embassy gossip. A potentially tricky balancing act. On the one hand, the bearer of bad news, but at the same time leaving little doubt that he was just that, in no way ever a participant, that he was close enough to the espionage scheme to be credible but far enough away to be innocent of any direct involvement. He needed to project an image of himself as pure and self-less, a *Stakhanov* of truth in a world of liars and dupes. Igor exploded at being referred to as a spy in a TV interview.[4]

In telling his story, Igor mentioned the July 1944 recall notice but said nothing about GRU unhappiness over his behavior or about the mishandled documents. In his October 1945 statement, Igor described his reason for defecting as other than self-interest, that he was happy he'd found the strength within himself to take that step and warn Canada of the Soviet danger.

Hollywood was anxious to bring Igor's story to America's movie screens. In 1948, the year of publication, Igor's book was made into a motion picture, *The Iron Curtain*, directed by William Wellman. Igor received a writing credit. Dana Andrews and Gene Tierney were cast as Mr. and Mrs. Gouzenko, June Havoc as an embassy temptress. All the names except Igor's were changed. Like Igor, the character in the movie defects after hearing that he is to be sent back home. Here his visit to the newspaper follows the trip to the Minister of Justice. The Fred Rose character, named John Grubb, is linked exclusively to embassy staff but not to Igor. The film was not a big hit. Igor appeared in the epilogue of a smaller-budget 1954 made for TV re-make as himself.

On 16 July 1946, the day after the final royal commission report was made public, Igor and the Canadian prime minister had their first and only meeting. Without mentioning Victor Kravchenko by name Mackenzie King asked Igor if he'd read the Kravchenko book *I Chose Freedom* (1946). Igor said he had, that he was working on a book of his own. In the prime minister's eyes Igor was no longer the dubious figure he'd once been but "a clean cut young man with steady eyes and a keen intellect."[5]

Igor Gouzenko remains a figure of controversy. If one believes the

4. *This Hour Has Seven Days*, CBC-TV, 13 March 1966.
5. Mackenzie King, *Diary*.

information he turned over to Canadian authorities dealt a blow to Soviet ambitions, he was a good guy, a brave idealist who risked his life to rescue the West from the brutal ambitions of Stalin. If that information is judged of limited or exaggerated usefulness, Igor becomes a lesser personality whose motives and personal shortcomings need to be the focus. There are claims the man was an out and out stooge, if not of the RCMP then of Great Britain's MI5, knowingly involved in a calculated scheme to launch the Cold War, trigger an arms race, and let loose the forces of reaction.[6]

As we know, the first thought of the prime minister, the man who looked into Hitler's eyes and saw Joan of Arc, was, knowing nothing and caring nothing about the circumstances of Igor's desperate action, to return him to the Soviet embassy. Norman Robertson appeared to have been determined to hold onto Igor and used the RCMP to do that. The RCMP did what they were told but hardly ever thought much of Igor, no more now than then.

In 1999, Andrew Kavchak, a federal government lawyer, approached the City of Ottawa and the federal government with a proposal to acknowledge Igor's heroism. Kavchak's paternal grandfather was among the Polish officers murdered by the Soviet army in the Katyn forest in 1940. As Kavchak explained to me, it was important that the tribute happen if possible while Svetlana was still alive. He soon however found himself in a bureaucratic swamp. The City of Ottawa said yes, then no, then yes. The Department of External Affairs was opposed, concerned that the commemoration would create a diplomatic embarrassment for members of the Russian embassy. The department was unmoved by the argument that the USSR no longer existed, that the Cold War a thing of the past, that the event to be celebrated had taken place over a half century earlier. Finally, *Heritage Canada* agreed, which persuaded the city of Ottawa to go ahead. The city's plaque went up in Dundonald Park, the park facing the nondescript apartment building at 511 Somerset in June 2003. A federal plaque sits alongside it, put up in the spring of 2004. Too late for Svetlana, who died in September 2001. A year later there was a ceremony on the anniversary of her death in Mississauga,

---

6. Knight, *How the Cold War Began*; Kristmanson, "Pulp History: Repossessing the Gouzenko Myth," in *Plateaus of Freedom*.

Ontario. The family decided to have a public memorial service at the gravesite, previously unmarked. The event was announced in the press. The family had lived incognito for decades. The stone that was unveiled bore the name GOUZENKO. The official spokesperson dispatched by the federal government was Senator Laurier Lapierre, who at one time had attempted to rough Igor up in a TV interview. Said the City of Ottawa plaque: "This panel is placed...in recognition of the courage of Igor Gouzenko and his wife Sevtlana for their historic flight to freedom in Canada on September 5, 1945." Not long after the plaques were in place Kavchak got a call from someone at Canada Post who in the 1980s had submitted a proposal for an Igor stamp. The proposal went nowhere, perhaps the timing was wrong.[7]

In yet another example of the curvature of ideological space, we find KGB and GRU assessments of Igor near identical with that of the RCMP.

In a memoir, KGB man Vitalii Pavlov began his verbal attack on Igor by tipping his cap to the competing spy agency, the GRU. Our results, he said, meaning those of the KGB, could not be compared with the successes of the GRU which contributed Soviet victories over Germany and Japan. In other words, Igor had betrayed a great patriotic service, one that had done much to win the war against the enemies of the west. Igor's document theft produced ammunition for the anti-Soviet campaign organized by the British and the Americans. I cannot, Pavlov said, believe the widespread myth that Gouzenko made the decision to betray his country on his own. It is difficult, he went on, not to see the involvement of the CIA Pavlov may have been referring to the American wartime Office of Strategic Services (OSS), immediate forebear of the CIA not created until 1947. Perhaps Pavlov was counting on his readers not knowing that. Perhaps he didn't know it himself. An ex-RCMP man, who had met Pavlov in Moscow, told me that by the time Pavlov got round to writing his book his memory was in poor shape. An exemplary Soviet polemicist, Pavlov was not one to let the facts get in his way. It was, he claimed, the goal of reactionary circles to damage Soviet-Canada relations that had widened during the

---

7. Andrew Kavchak, private communication. See Andrew Kavchak, "Remembering Gouzenko: The Struggle to Honour a Cold War Hero," *The Mackenzie Institute*, April, 2004; "The Cold War's Ottawa Spark," *The Ottawa Citizen,* 13 April 2004; Jeff Sallot, "Remembering a Soviet Defector," *The Globe and Mail,* 31 May 2003.

war. Igor, he said, was an unfriendly loner who shut himself off from his Russian colleagues, as did his wife. The account of his defection was mostly written for him, though some things were left that make clear the negative side of his personality: how he'd managed to avoid military service during the war, that he was a pathological coward and an —asshole! By defecting he heartlessly betrayed his mother and his sister. Evidently a *tovarich* with a limited gift for irony, KGB man Pavlov said he was especially unhappy over the human rights violations perpetrated by the royal commission, whose witnesses were forced to testify after detention for a long period in isolated cells without lawyers.[8]

Oddly, Pavlov inserted a quote from British journalist Harry Chapman Pincher's *Their Trade is Treachery* (1981), who he referred to as a former British agent, to the effect that these acts of treachery such as the one committed by Igor are accompanied by depression, feelings of guilt, panic, general sadness and fear of punishment, often alcoholism, as the traitor attempts to blunt his feelings. Occasionally there is suicide. You can't, Pavlov said, but agree with Pincher that their feelings of unworthiness are what fuel their petty hostility to Russia. An outstanding investigative reporter, Chapman Pincher, who began his career as a scientist and had worked on secret weapons research, assured me he was never a British agent. Moreover, it is strange that Pavlov would have picked Harry of all people, one of Igor's staunchest supporters, to back up his attempt to shred Igor's reputation.

Curiously, the RCMP's Igor was not much different from Pavlov's. The RCMP in fact hardly ever had any more affection for Igor than did the KGB. In *The Horsemen*, a volume of recollections, Clifford Harvison, who became RCMP Commissioner, said Igor was "...a courageous man who risked his life to do a great service for Canada and the Western world..." But, he went on, Igor was not a humble man, his motives for defection included vanity, that he seethed with resentment over the failure of his Soviet superiors to recognize his talents and to promote him to a higher military rank justified by those talents. Defectors, said Harvison, have unusual personality traits.[9]

---

8. Vitalii Pavlov, *Operation "Snow": Half a Century at KGB Foreign Intelligence,* Geya, 1996.
9. Clifford W. Harvison, "Igor Gouzenko and Soviet Espionage," in *The Horsemen,* McClelland & Stewart. 1967.

The unofficial RCMP view today is that Igor didn't defect for ideological reasons and didn't have that much information. According to a former RCMP counter-intelligence specialist familiar with the Force's Gouzenko file: "[Igor Gouzenko] really didn't know a hell of a lot of anything, he knew very little...how much could a 24-year-old Soviet embassy cipher clerk have known, apart from the content of the cables he encoded and de-coded and the scuttlebutt he heard around the embassy...he was not a trained intelligence officer, and while the documents were good stuff his contribution, though helpful in decrypting GRU messages, was overstated." As for Igor's book about the defection and events leading up to it, the RCMP assessment is pretty much of a piece with that of the KGB: "...he didn't even write that friggin book!"[10]

Evy Wilson told me that while her father was in what amounted protective RCMP custody he was given the nom de defection *Zradce*, a Czech term meaning Iscariot, traitor, quisling, double-crosser.

In 1975, the Gouzenko affair resurfaced in the Canadian parliament and in newspaper headlines in connection with an allegation that money earmarked for the Gouzenkos had been diverted into the pockets of RCMP officers, that the information he'd provided hadn't been used effectively, and that contrary to what was said by the Force the Gouzenkos had received no financial help from Canada. Igor believed the RCMP had planted stories about him with journalists that resulted in a negative press, that in January 1954, members of the Force had attempted to assassinate him, that he was at one point involved in a wild car chase with an RCMP officer at the wheel, that a few months before the Fidel Castro victory in Cuba, a senior member of the Force urged he emigrate to Cuba.

In 1981, a royal commission inquiry reported that RCMP files on Igor contained statements of ridicule, that Igor was identified in the files as a nuisance and a "troublemaker."[11]

For Igor these things could only have one explanation: the Soviets had managed to penetrate the Force.

The notion that Igor was a lackey of MI5 or the RCMP may have originated with Tim Buck who was questioned by a reporter in early

---

10. Private communication.
11. "Certain R.C.M.P. Activities and the Question of Governmental Knowledge," *Commission of Enquiry Concerning Certain Activities of the RCMP, Three reports*, Government of Canada, 1979.

April 1946 for his thoughts on whether Freddy would be convicted. As you already know, he said, "his actions have no connection with this party. I cannot speak for him. So far as the evidence submitted is concerned, he will be convicted but on the other hand it will take more than Gouzenko's testimony and all the documents Gouzenko claims to have taken, as proof. This man...worked with the RCMP while he was in the employment of the Soviet government, for almost six months." Buck went on to claim that Igor never carried those documents under his shirt and that it must have taken a truck to carry all the papers away—or that if he did carry them away in his shirt, it took him a very long time.[12]

Whatever the shadings of the Gouzenko personality, it does not appear in any way to extend to the information he provided. In a recently published work that re-visits the Hollis question in greater detail, Chapman Pincher reminds readers that the information Igor turned over concerning GRU agents proved to be entirely accurate, including the lead to the bogus Witczak and GRU use of Canada to run operatives into the United States, that unlike many defectors Igor did not seek to impress his hosts with invented details. No defector, Harry was assured by the FBI, had ever supplied such a haul of information.[13]

September 1945 was considered the blackest day in GRU history. KGB head Lavrenti Beria rated the Gouzenko revelations a tremendous blow to the USSR's plans. Gouzenko's defection, he said, had caused great damage.

Said KGB man Pavel Sudoplatov in his memoir *Special Tasks*: "I remember that the defection of the Soviet code clerk Igor Gouzenko in Canada in September 1945 had deep repercussions. He gave the American and Canadian counterintelligence services clues to our agent networks in the United States and Canada during the war. More important, he revealed a list of key scientists we had targeted for development."[14]

The exposure of Zabotin's GRU network resulted in internal organizational casualties, among them the director of the GRU, a Lieutenant-General who had had a private line to Stalin's office and the right of

---

12. "Re: Labour Progressive Party, Ottawa, Ontario," RCMP report, "A" Division, Ottawa, 2 April 1946.
13. See Harry Chapman Pincher, *Treachery,* 2011.
14. Pavel Sudoplatov and Anatoli Sudoplatov, with Jerrold L. and Leona P. Schecter, foreword by Robert Conquest, *Special Tasks: The Memoirs of an Unwanted Witness—A Soviet Spymaster,* Little, Brown and Company, 1994.

direct personal access to Stalin without appointment.[15]

A half century later, the GRU would not respond to questions about Igor.

Some elements of Col. Zabotin's Canadian network may have remained in the shadows. In 1989, there was a report in *The Globe and Mail* about a forthcoming publication titled *The Passions of Atomic Hell* by a Soviet author, Stanislav Pestov, contending that there were a number of Canadians in a spy ring with the code name *Bek* supervised by Col. Zabotin, involved in Soviet A-bomb espionage, who were never identified. The book, excerpts of which were published in the Soviet newspaper *Argumenti i Fakti*, provided no sources.[16]

The reporter Peter Worthington had urged Igor to work on a memoir of his thirty years in Canada. Not clear if he ever did. Igor left a thick unfinished manuscript of another fictional opus, *Ocean of Time*.

Igor, who had escaped his Soviet masters in the age of radio, was in Canada when television arrived. In 1966, a white-hooded Igor agreed to be interviewed on the CBC-TV news magazine show *This Hour Has Seven Days*. The questions of interviewers Laurier Lapierre and Patrick Watson, especially those from Lapierre, were less than friendly. Were you, asked Lapierre, sent here because you were a Soviet agent? Exasperated, Igor tried to explain the Soviet technique for dealing with defectors: "First of all they want to smear, to destroy name and then kill quietly and nobody cares what happened."

Igor first appeared on Canadian television in 1958 in a black hood on the CBC's *Front Page Challenge*. Presumably, the point of the hood was to tell viewers KGB assassins were on his trail. His TV appearances in a hood and his demand for bodyguard protection may have encouraged the suspicion that he was unstable.

There are claims that Igor was an unpleasant fellow whose chronic money problems led him repeatedly to attempt to squeeze journalists in exchange for the limited information in his possession. John Sawatsky in *Men in the Shadows* quoted a retired senior RCMP officer who told him that: "Gouzenko was not a true lover of liberty. He was a thoroughly

---

15. Alexander Foote, *Handbook for Spies,* Doubleday, 1949. Foote, born in Yorkshire, England, was a Soviet espionage radio operator.
16. Jeff Sallot, "Canadians Who Aided Soviet A-bomb Not Caught, Book Says," *The Globe and Mail,* 14 October 1989.

ignorant Russian peasant...an unsavoury character." Svetlana Gouzenko said she knew the source of that statement, that it was someone associated with the Soviet agent Kim Philby.[17]

The late Gordon Lunan claimed Igor had little to offer by way of information about Soviet espionage activity because that activity was being run by party animal Col. Zabotin, a man of unfocused interests, that Freddy was not up to much, that Boyer's RDX secrets were hardly secret and the value of Nunn May's nuclear information was limited, that it was ideological hysteria that made Igor, that his self-interested and manipulative claims ignited a witch hunt that destroyed many innocent people, damage Igor seemed to care nothing about, that his personal habits were piggish. In restaurants he ordered three meals at a time which he ate with knife, fork, and hands indiscriminately. He sometimes defecated standing up at other people's toilets. He occasionally beat his wife.[18]

In a 1987 interview with the CBC Svetlana Gouzenko said that during the 1946 royal commission enquiry and the trials that followed the family in fact received no money, only food and shelter at Camp X, that they were totally dependent on the RCMP. The RCMP claimed otherwise, she said, but she and Igor were not even provided with I.D. documents, which created difficulties in dealings with banks. Despite the 1975 claim that the Gouzenkos were being looked after by the government, all the money they ever had, she said, was money Igor earned from his writing, *This Was My Choice* and a prize-winning fictional work, *The Fall of a Titan* (1954), which paid for everything they bought and owned. She suspected RCMP officers of pocketing sums of money intended for the family, that the Force's smear campaign involved Soviet agents. Is it possible, the interviewer asked, that Igor received a large sum of money but then gambled it away without telling her? Was the diabetic Igor an alcoholic? There was a claim that the Canadian government had spent $7 million to settle Igor down only to discover that Igor was a drunk who would go out and blow hundreds of thousands of dollars. One, replied Svetlana, would have to drink the Pacific Ocean out to do that. With Kim Philby in mind, Svetlana thought the gambling and

17. Svetlana Gouzenko, CBC interview, 1996.
18. Lunan, *The Making of a Spy*.

boozing allegations were "the work of Soviet agents and lots of useful idiots who repeat [these things]. Canadian security was run by British intelligence which was at the time in reality a branch of the KGB."[19]

The Gouzenkos were certain the espionage information they'd passed on to Canadian authorities represented only the tip of a larger iceberg, that the Soviet government had numbers of people working for them in the media and in government, which was to say that, contrary to Beria, the damage Igor's revelations had done to Soviet operations in Canada was minimal, that the royal commission findings and the indictments and trials and prison sentences had hardly left a dent in those operations.

The Gouzenkos's Canadian existence was less than happy. The family's need to hide out from the KGB in a pseudonym and the constant fear of assassination put ordinary citizenship beyond their grasp. Their life in Canada recalled the warning Walter Krivitsky received from Basov, the Soviet goon he ran into in Horn and Hardart's in Times Square: "You will not be able to live by yourself in a world in which you have never belonged."

In his book about the role of the GRU in getting Stalin the bomb, Vladimir Lota referred to Igor as *the Scorpion*. There is little doubt that for many years Igor remained near the top of the KGB hit list.

The Gouzenkos were puzzled by the apparent inability of Canadian authorities and the press to comprehend the fear that they could be tracked down by KGB assassins, that their children might be kidnapped, a dread that, rightly or wrongly, became the explanation for whatever went wrong in their lives. Though Igor earned sums of money from his writings, he wasn't much good at knowing what to do with it, as he himself readily conceded.

The more he found that terrible things were being said about him in books and newspapers and magazines, insinuations that he was a professional alcoholic living the sweet life who had bilked the Canadian government out of millions of dollars, the more convinced he was that Soviet hitmen were getting closer. It was all proof that key people in the Canadian government, including members of the cabinet and senior

---

19. *The Gouzenko Affair*, CBC Archives. Apparently Philby made only occasional visits to Washington, about three in all. He had after he advised Moscow of the Gouzenko defection little to do with Igor. He was by 1953 long gone from Washington and SIS. Private communication.

officials, belonged to Soviet cells. Igor after all came from a world that placed no stock in coincidence, where next to nothing was permitted to happen by chance.

In 1953, he decided to take his fight into the courts. The notion that he could through litigation defend himself from slander might have been inspired by Kravchenko's 1949 victory in a Parisian courtroom over a French Communist Party-orchestrated attack that had appeared in the party periodical *Les Lettres Françaises.*[20]

In three different cases, in 1953, 1958, and 1959, Igor received an apology and a money settlement. In 1964, Igor approached Toronto lawyer Alan Eagleson to act for him in a suit against *Newsweek* magazine. Eagleson in a telephone conversation recalled Igor presenting himself as a quiet, naïve fellow who didn't understand what was happening to him. Igor, Eagleson told me, seemed to have limited assets, at least insofar as he wanted to spend his money on litigation. As it happened Eagleson's schedule didn't allow him to take on the case. I was, he said, busy with hockey players.[21]

The *Newsweek* case was turned over to an Eagleson associate and eventually handled by a third lawyer who, after the case was lost, was sued by Igor for incompetence. In the suit, Igor alleged that the lawyer had been bought by the magazine and had come under Soviet influence. On the other hand, Igor had refused to provide the lawyer with modest payments for his services which led to delays. At one point Igor had apparently failed to deliver on an agreed upon fee for services, $200 and four of his paintings.[22]

During the 1968 Liberal leadership campaign Igor circulated a pamphlet, *Memorandum—Trudeau,* claiming Pierre Trudeau might be a possible Castro agent. He sued *The Toronto Star* when the paper published an editorial critical of his action. The six-person jury refused to rule on whether the editorial was defamatory.[23]

Igor pursued claims over negative allegations in David Martin's

20. *Kravchenko versus Moscow: Report of the Famous Paris case,* Wingate, 1950.
21. Private communication, Alan Eagleson, 28 August 2005.
22. See Gouzenko v. Harris, Luck, Thurston and Conrad, Ontario Supreme Court (High Court of Justice) Goodman J., Heard 4, 5, 6, 9, 10, 11, 12, and 13 June 1975. Igor believed he had been libeled by stories in *Newsweek* magazine, February, 1964, Maclean's, September 1964, stories in *The Toronto Telegram* and *The Globe and Mail,* January 1965, and *The Toronto Star,* June 1968.
23. Peter Worthington, "Gouzenko's Lost a Libel Suit," *The Toronto Sun,* 15 October 1974.

Wilderness of Mirrors (2003), June Callwood's *Portrait of Canada* (1981) and John Sawatsky's *Men in the Shadows* (1980). Gouzenko, Callwood wrote, "who appeared at news conferences with a brown paper bag over his head, seemed erratic and unstable." Defectors, said Sawatsky, "often have trouble adjusting to their new circumstances." Sawatsky related Igor's difficulties to others, among them the 1978 defection of Arkady Shevchenko, a Soviet official at the UN. Shevchenko had fallen in love with an attractive young woman he spent considerable sums on, a woman he met via an escort service he found in the Yellow Pages. Martin quoted an unnamed chief of the CIA's Soviet Bloc desk: "There is no such thing as a normal defector. He defects for a series of reasons usually having to do with serious psychological problems. There is something wrong with him in the first instance. The fact is that the guy is sick and temperamental.[24]

Igor died before the suit naming Sawatsky reached the courts. The same fate overtook the Callwood litigation. Igor's litigiousness, Sawatsky speculated, was not motivated by money. Igor imagined himself to be a historical figure and discovered he was able to bully the media into protecting that concept he had of his importance. Igor's explanation was that it was crucial to defend himself against calumny if he wanted to stay alive.

Igor and Svetlana Gouzenko settled in the Toronto suburb of Mississauga with their children as Stanley and Anna Krysac, a Czech term meaning *rat*. Knight thinks this cover name was John Leopold's idea. Things did not go well. There were money problems, debt, family friction. As time went on, the allure of Canadian reality began to fade.

Was Igor, as he believed, the target of a campaign to blacken his reputation, that once discredited he could be assassinated with little public notice taken? Again and again Igor returned to the courts to confront negative stories in the media. The hostility in the *Seven Days* interview, coming twenty years after the defection, might for Igor have seemed evidence of Soviet influence.

What appeared to Igor to be the RCMP's refusal to act on the information he'd provided only amplified his apprehension. On the other

---

24. Sawatsky *Men in the Shadows;* David Martin, *Wilderness of Mirrors,* Ballantine Books, 1981; Sawatsky, "Libel Suits and More Libel Suits," in *Gouzenko: The Untold Story.*

hand, that the KGB wanted him in their sights was not something he imagined.

Igor was never convinced that he and his family were entirely secure, safe from the KGB, that his revelations of Soviet influence had eliminated that influence, or that an ordinary Canadian existence could be theirs.

In 1975, he told a reporter that the Russian espionage operation in Canada was much, much larger than the activity he exposed in 1945. I was, said Igor, able to tell only about persons working for the Soviets in military intelligence here—and that was only one of nine rings we were operating in Canada.... I was unable to learn and reveal the true identity of some persons who were working here for Soviet military intelligence—I only knew their code names. What Canada in his view now needed was another Gouzenko.[25]

The apparent indifference of Canadian officialdom appeared to the Gouzenkos to be the work of Soviet-controlled operators, the slander directed against them engineered by Canadians in league with Moscow plotters. They may have been unaware of an RCMP operation dating from the early 1950s code named *Featherbed*, a scheme to identify former Canadian party members who held senior positions in government and might be Soviet agents. *Featherbed* looked into the 1945–46 leads Igor had provided but failed to turn up a single solid case of either direct Soviet influence or espionage.[26]

None of that altered the fact that Igor was ever a target of KGB hitmen. He was seen with the Conservative MP Tom Cossitt at a hockey game featuring the Soviet national team. Cossitt had asked Solicitor-General Warren Allmand to increase Igor's $800 a month pension. In rejecting the request, Allmand said the Trudeau government believed it had been more than fair. A Soviet agent befriended Cossitt in the hope of learning Igor's whereabouts. When that scheme failed, the KGB in their frustration planned to look for a way to discredit Cossitt who died

25. Robert MacDonald, "Gouzenko Talks: So Many Spies We Need Another Gouzenko," *The Toronto Sun,* 21 May 1975.
26. Reg Whitaker, "Spies Who Might Have Been: Canada and the Myth of Cold War Counterintelligence," *Intelligence and National Security* 12:4, October 1997. Sawatsky found that at one point there were 262 names in the file which, in its early days, included Under-Secretary of External Affairs, O. D. Skelton. Norman Robertson was among those suspected.

before the endeavor got started.[27]

Igor knew that men selected for service abroad needed to have at least one living parent in the USSR who would function as an unofficial hostage to ensure good conduct and one's return. Interviewed for the last time in 1996, Svetlana said that Igor was tried in absentia and sentenced to death. The family learned through a series of unlikely coincidences involving family members who'd survived Siberian labor camps that Igor's mother had died under interrogation, Svetlana's father and mother were arrested and sent to Gulag for six years. A sister was arrested, her two-year-old child abandoned. For years the Gouzenkos lived in fear that their children would be kidnapped. A bomb had been placed in their mailbox.[28]

A couple of years before his death Igor sat down with another reporter to review the 35 years he had spent in hiding in Canada. He was sixty-one years old, worn out from the experience and suffering from diabetes. He recalled that at Camp X Svetlana was pregnant and had no winter clothes. A security guard gave her a coat that belonged to his mother-in-law that he charged to the Canadian government. Canadian authorities turned all their belongings left in the Somerset Street apartment over to the Russians—including family photo albums. The family lost a 300 acre farm outside Toronto because they were without the documents to refinance the mortgage.[29]

A half century after the defection the Gouzenko conundrum had lost little of its intrigue. At an April 2004 conference in Ottawa a point heard over and over was that it was common knowledge that Stalin wanted a bomb of his own and had set about in the mid 1940s to get one. Clearly, Georgi Malenkov had put party operatives active in North America to work on the project. In 1943, a letter from a disgruntled Soviet employee made it clear that the USSR was deeply involved in nuclear espionage. On the other hand, the Soviets, anxious to spruce up their image with Canadians, regarded the CPC as an inept partner in the task.[30]

---

27. Christopher Andrew and Vasili Mitrokhin, *The Sword and the Shield: The Secret Mitrokhin Archive and the Secret History of the KGB*, Basic Books, 1999.

28. Svetlana Gouzenko, CBC interview, 3 May 1996.

29. John Picton, "Igor Gouzenko: My 35 Years in Hiding," *The Toronto Star*, 11 September 1980.

30. J. L. Black & Martin Rudner (eds.), *The Gouzenko Affair*, Penumbra Press, 2006.

It ought not to have come as a big surprise that while the arrests and trials that followed Igor's revelations about Soviet espionage caused much pain they resulted in relatively few convictions; the principals, the Russians, Col. Zabotin et al., could not be arrested and brought to trial, let alone questioned.

The Gouzenko family today claims to be in possesion of a trove of material they are guarding from hostile eyes, including the manuscript of a Svetlana Gouzenko memoir and dozens of containers of material Igor amassed on Soviet espionage schemes, some of it in *braille,* little if any of it ever made public. Whether the material constitutes new information from unnamed sources or a reiteration of the familiar is uncertain. Did Igor, exasperated by what seemed to him RCMP contempt and believing he needed to turn up the heat, spend the years obsessively re-working a basic stock of material to construct a more convincing case?

The family appears to want to secure the material for publication on their own behalf by a high profile publisher, perhaps unaware that the Cold War game is now mostly done. It does seem that whatever information of substance Igor was able to garner from his experience in the USSR and his work in the embassy, found its way into his books and interviews and depositions and trial testimony. It is likewise unlikely that Svetlana's memoir would have much more to tell us than she told CBC interviewers. On the other hand, we ought not to entirely discount the possibility that the couple managed to somehow squirrel away hitherto unrevealed GRU secrets.

Great stores of KGB material have entered the public domain from one-time Soviet intelligence honchos Pavel Sudoplatov, Vasili Mitrokhin, Oleg Gorievsky, Alexander Vassiliev, and others. A new batch has recently been advertised: one Pavel Stroilov claims to have 50,000 pages of unpublished, untranslated top-secret Kremlin documents that appears to be of little interest to the CIA or anyone else. Dissident Vladimir Bukovsky, who spent twelve years in Soviet prisons and psychiatric hospitals, claims to have smuggled out a massive amount of archival material offered to uninterested publishers.[31]

A replay of Igor at *The Journal* or bad timing?

---

31. Claire Berlinski, "A Hidden History of Evil: Why Doesn't Anyone Care About the Unread Soviet Archives?" *Documentation Center of Cambodia,* 2010.

While GRU files remain for the time being inaccessible. There are on the other hand numbers of unread GRU cables gathering dust in the files of American intelligence agencies.

One consequence of the Gouzenko affair was its negative impact on post-war discussions between the Allies and Soviet leadership, in particular on international atomic energy talks.[32]

The question keeps surfacing: Did Igor's revelations kick off the Cold War, the arms race, and the assault on Canadian unions and cultural institutions? Could all that have really begun the evening of 5 September 1945?[33]

The official US government view we know is that the Cold War began with the Japanese signature on the Instrument of Surrender aboard the battleship *Missouri* in Tokyo Bay, 2 September 1945.

At war's end the USSR and the United States stood eyeball to eyeball in Berlin. Would Stalin direct his armies westward, and if he did would Truman use the Bomb?

When in 1781 the American president John Adams sent his son John Quincy to St. Petersburg to assist envoy Francis Dana, America was much feared as the command centre of world revolution. Young Adams was a fluent speaker of French. Dana spoke neither French nor Russian, the languages of Catherine the Great's court. It was Dana's task to persuade Catherine to admit the United States into the League of Armed Neutrality, formed by Russia to protect neutral shipping from the British navy. Dana was denied admission to the court: "In so far as the separation of the American colonies from the mother country was concerned, Russia and Catherine II [the Great] were unconcerned, but with regard to the revolutionary example that the Americans might pro-

---

32. Paul Dufour, "Eggheads and Espionage: The Gouzenko Affair in Canada," *Journal of Canadian Studies,* Vol. 16, No. 3 & 4, Fall-Winter, 1981.

33. The Gouzenko literature is voluminous. See Harvey Klehr, "Spy vs. Spy: What Igor Gouzenko Taught the West," *The Weekly Standard,* 18 December 2006; "A Glimpse Inside the Spy Scandal That Rocked Ottawa," *The Ottawa Citizen,* 23 April 2006; Jim Creskey, "The Man Who Launched a North American Inquisition: The Ottawa Defection of Soviet Diplomat-Spy Igor Gouzenko," *Embassy, Canada's Foreign Policy Newsweekly,* 26 October 2005; John F. Fox, Jr., "Impact of CORBY on FBI-Counter Espionage and Security Relations with Canada." Paper presented at the Igor Gouzenko Conference, Carleton University, Ottawa, April 2004; Laurence Hannant, "Igor Gouzenko and Canada's Cold War," *The Beaver,* October/November 1995; John D. Holding, Q.C., "Reflections on Igor Gouzenko," *The Advocates Society Journal,* October, 1985; Christopher Young, "Gouzenko Case Began Cold War," *The Ottawa Citizen,* 8 January 1985; Robert Fulford, "Gouzenko's Legacy," *Saturday Night,* October 1982. There is as well a large literature of works by and about Soviet defectors.

vide, there undoubtedly was concern. Francis Dana believed, with reason, that Catherine would not recognize the United States during her lifetime. In fact, Russia did not recognize the United States until early in the 19th century..."[34]

A decade later Catherine sent her army into Poland to crush an attempt at establishing a Polish-Lithuanian American-style constitutional democracy.

The first volume of Alexis de Tocqueville's 1835 bestseller *Democracy in America* concluded with the vision of a divided planet amounting to a prophesy: "There are at the present time," he wrote, "two great nations in the world, which started from different points, but seem to tend towards the same end. I allude to the Russians and the Americans....each of them seems marked out by the will of Heaven to sway the destinies of half the globe.[35]

The Spanish-American War (1898–1901) transformed America into a Pacific power and a geopolitical rival to imperial Russia. Suspicion of Russian intentions led to American support for Japan in the 1905 struggle between the Russians and the Japanese for control of North Asia. Said Theodore Roosevelt, the American president: "No human beings, black, yellow or white, could be quite as untruthful, as insincere, as arrogant—in short, as untrustworthy in every way—as the Russians."

Then too, resentment against the West dating from the Crimean War continued to stain the Slavic consciousness.

Animosity between competitors for Asian trade advantage was in place when in April 1917 Vladimir Illych Lenin climbed up on an armored car in the Finland Station to address a Petrograd mob. Cheered on by men recently returned from exile and prison, Lenin told them they were the advance guard of an international proletarian army, that the collapse of European capitalism was at hand, a revolution that did not need bourgeois democracy. Within a few months the Bolsheviks were Russia's rulers.

In vain did American president Woodrow Wilson dispatch troops as part of an expeditionary force to drive the Bolsheviks from power. At the conclusion of WWI the collapse of the imperial monarchies—in

---

34. In an email from Anne E. Bentley, Massachusetts Historical Society, 25 February 2008.
35. Alexis de Tocqueville, *Democracy in America*, trans. George Lawrence, Perennial Classics, 2000.

Russia, Germany, Austria-Hungary, and Ottoman Turkey—was evident. As the writer Adrian Weale put it: "...a new menace had arisen. The Bolshevik faction of the Russian Communist Party had succeeded in seizing power in Petrograd by a bold coup d'état...and even as civil war raged within their own country, provided inspiration for similarly minded groups throughout Europe. Revolution was in the air." Among those who in November 1918 took notice and were appalled by the fact that Jews, Social Democrats, and Bolsheviks had become Germany's new masters was the young army officer Adolf Hitler.[36]

In the decades that followed the fear, reasonable or unreasonable, that revolutionary upheaval flowing out of the USSR would bring havoc to the settled societies of Europe, Asia and the Americas grew.

Interviewed in 1969 for the Marcel Ophuls film *The Sorrow and the Pity*, a French citizen who'd joined the Charlemagne Division of the Waffen SS and fought the Soviets on the Eastern front in the last months of WWII said that democracy offered no idealism for the young Catholic members of his generation. France in the years leading up to the war was torn between two radical ideologies: Bolshevism and National Socialism. As Catholics, he explained, we wouldn't choose the Communists, so we chose the other revolutionary party. Bolsheviks and Jews were interchangeable: "Don't forget that my entire youth took place in an atmosphere which was rife in violent anti-Semitism." Claiming to have been swept up in the tide of history, he pointed out that for the youth of his time, the Nazi Nuremburg rally seemed like a Catholic mass. Moreover, there were reports during the civil war in Spain of nuns being massacred by Republican volunteers. Of the seven thousand young Frenchmen who put on German uniforms and headed east, only three hundred returned.

At the time of the February 1945 Yalta meeting, Stalin commanded the largest army in Europe, 12,000,000 troops in 300 divisions. Poland was occupied and Soviet forces poised for the final assault on Berlin. The USSR had, as if in fulfillment of an Old Testament curse, become an empowered global foe. On the one hand the focus on the Bolshevik menace limited the attention of the democracies in the years between the wars to the rise of Nazi Germany. On the other, the view in Great

---

36. Adrian Weale, *Renegades: Hitler's Englishmen*, Weidenfeld & Nicolson, 1994.

Britain, France, and the United States that Hitler was the man to destroy Bolshevism, had in effect given Stalin, who would otherwise have remained a minor oriental despot, the opportunity to march the Red Army into the heart of Europe.

As Germany neared defeat, the foreign minister Ulrich Freidrich Joachim Wilhelm von Ribbentrop prepared a statement diplomats of the Reich were instructed to relay to the British and the Americans: Germany's war had been a crusade against Jew-inspired Bolshevism, that Nazism had a positive attitude to Christendom, the Jews a domestic affair—which, if Germany doesn't want to fall to Communism, must be solved in Germany.[37]

For a time Churchill toyed with a scheme code-named *Operation Unthinkable* that imagined allied divisions joining the remnant of the Nazi army in a counter-offensive to drive the Russians out of Poland. For good or ill, nothing came of it.[38]

"We are in the midst of a cold war which is getting warmer," one-time FDR advisor Bernard Baruch told the US Senate in a speech in 1948. The term, apparently coined by George Orwell though some credit has gone to Soviet propagandists, was first used by Baruch during a congressional debate the previous year.

"The real winners of the Cold War," said Eli Rosenbaum, director of the US Justice Department's Office of Special Investigations, "were Nazi war criminals." Nazis welcomed into cold warrior ranks by US forces in Europe included Klaus Barbie, chief of the Gestapo in Lyon, France. The thing about Barbie, a C.I.C. agent pointed out, was that he didn't need to disguise his background, the Americans knew exactly who and what Barbie was, which didn't prevent Barbie from obtaining a red de-Nazification stamp on his I.D. card and the I.D. cards of all his Nazi chums and black market colleagues.[39]

In one account, Col. Nikolai Zabotin was said to have died of a heart attack a few days after his arrival back in Moscow to answer questions. In another he was quietly executed with a bullet to the back of the

---

37. Robert J. Hayok, *Eavesdropping on Hell: Historical Guide to Western Communications Intelligence and the Holocaust, 1939–1945*, National Security Agency, 2005.
38. Max Hastings, *Winston's War: Churchill, 1940–1945*, Knopf, 2010.
39. David Blansky, "Exclusive Interview with Eli Rosenbaum, Head Nazi Hunter," April 2002; see too Allan A. Ryan, Jr., "Klaus Barbie and the United States Government: The Report, with Documentary Appendix, to the Attorney General of the United States," August 1983.

head and shipped home in a box; in another he was pushed off a Russian freighter into the indifferent waters of the Pacific Ocean; in another, an inquiry ordered by Stalin found the colonel guilty and both he and his wife and small son were dispatched to Gulag; in yet another, he received a medal for devoted service.

Evy Wilson told me her father opposed the execution of Julius and Ethel Rosenberg, believing Soviet authorities cared nothing for the couple and would press their lackeys in the West to turn the couple's deaths into propaganda.

In 1998, a former Soviet defense expert, Aleksey Arbatov, conceded that the Soviet empire was created and built for the arms race, confrontation, and even war with the rest of the world.

It would have been unlikely for Igor to have ever considered a return home to Russia or even a brief visit back to a world he knew, a world he'd been born into, where he'd spent his childhood and his youth.

Some years before his death by cardiac arrest on Friday 25 June, 1982, thirty-nine years to the day after he'd arrived in Canada, diabetic Igor had gone blind. In the end, it was a pathological mistrust of physicians *not* the KGB that did him in, an apprehension he shared with his old antagonist Josef Stalin who, as his own end approached, came to embrace the truth of the Jewish doctors's plot he'd invented and insisted on being treated by veterinarians.[40]

Harry Chapman Pincher's *Their Trade is Treachery* (1981) made the intriguing case that the MI5 man the British sent to debrief Igor, Roger Hollis, was apparently a GRU agent.

Hollis had been dispatched to Ottawa on the recommendation of Kim Philby officially preoccupied with KGB business in Istanbul and eager to keep an eye on the reports coming in from Ottawa from British intelligence officers Peter Dwyer and John-Paul Evans. Philby, as observed by his Soviet controller Boris Krotenschield, was "a bit agitated" by the news of Igor's defection.[41]

40. Jonathan Brent, Vladimir Naumov, *Stalin's Last Crime: The Plot Against the Jewish Doctors,* HarperCollins Publishers, 2004.
41. Gentikh Borovik, *The Philby Files,* Little, Brown & Company Limited, 1994, Introduction by Phillip Knightley.

Apprehensive that the Gouzenko revelations might lead to his own unmasking, Philby saw to it that it was not the more adroit Jane Archer, the MI5 Krivitsky debriefer, who was dispatched to Ottawa to interview the Russian. Hollis, who joined MI5 in 1938, was named director-general in 1956, retiring in 1965.

About Hollis Kim Philby had this to say: "My opposite number in MI5 was Roger Hollis, the head of its section investigating Soviet and Communistic affairs. He was a likeable person, of cautious bent.... Although he lacked the strain of irresponsibility which I think essential (in moderation) to the rounded human being, we got on well together and were soon exchanging information without reserve on either side."[42]

Hollis arrived in Ottawa September 19, 1945, but did not see Igor on that first visit. The Gouzenkos were being moved around to evade KGB assassins. Hollis finally met Igor during his second visit on 21 November 1945, somewhere in Ottawa.

Here is Igor's account of the interview as described to Chapman Pincher: "He was only about 40, but was so stooped that he approached me in a crouching way as though anxious that his face should not be seen. I was surprised by this man. Who seemed almost afraid to talk to me, asked me very little when I told him that the GRU had a spy inside MI5 in England, known by the code name Elli. We talked in English but for such a short time that we did not even sit down. He took very few notes, if any, and behaved as though he wanted to get away from me as quickly as possible."[43]

Hollis, as Chapman Pincher has pointed out, had a spine curvature.

It may be understandable that when Igor visited *The Ottawa Journal* in an agitated state and virtually incoherent the night editor sent him packing. But why would a British intelligence official who had crossed an ocean to question a Soviet defector not handle the encounter with greater patience and curiosity?

In 1952, at the request of MI5, Igor drafted a memo to the RCMP in which he reminded both services that in 1945 he'd told Hollis there was

---

42. Kim Philby, *My Silent War: The Autobiography of a Spy*, Modern Library, 2002. The dedication in the original published in Great Britain in 1968 said: "To the Comrades who showed me the way to service," a dedication removed from the 2002 edition. For a more complete picture of the Hollis-Philby relationship see Chapman Pincher, *Treachery*, 2011.
43. Chapman Pincher, "In a New World," *Treachery*, 2011.

a Soviet mole in the senior ranks of MI5 codenamed Elli, that he'd learned this from a Lieut. Luibimov, a colleague in GRU headquarters in Moscow. Igor came to fear his reference to Luibimov might have gotten the man shot.[44]

In 1972 an MI5 man later identified as Patrick Stewart involved in the *Fluency* committee's investigation of Soviet penetration of MI5, met Igor in a room at the Royal York Hotel in Toronto and showed him a typewritten report that purported to be Hollis's account of the 1945 interview. Igor said he did not know the identity of the man he'd met in 1945, that Hollis had been introduced to him as "a gentleman from England," standard British intelligence debriefing practice. He remembered that this person had spent only three or four minutes with him, and here was a lengthy report brimming with nonsense and lies, full of statements he'd never made including the claim that MI5 had a man inside the Kremlin. Whoever wrote that report, Igor told the fellow, had to be working for the Soviets.[45]

In the spring of 1981, following the publication of *Their Trade is Treachery* Margaret Thatcher, the British prime minister, rose in the House to offer what appeared to be an unimpressive defense of Hollis, simply stating that no evidence had been found to incriminate him. Thatcher must have understood that she was either covering up the actions of a spy or worse perhaps defending the reputation of an absolute incompetent. Hollis had passed on in October 1973.[46]

In 2006, quite by chance, I met a nephew of Hollis at a literary event in London. When I put the question to him he insisted the claim was without merit, "It's not true," was how he responded.

The controversy persists, in part because the Hollis report remains a thing of legend, apparently having disappeared from both MI5 and CSIS/RCMP files. Could it have been among the many thousands of MI5 files that were destroyed or marked for destruction since 1992 because the agency claimed to have run out of shelf space? On 29 December 2010 I wrote to the Security Service *aka* MI5 requesting a

---

44. Chapman Pincher, "Blind Eye to Elli," Treachery, 2011.
45. John Sawatsky, "The MI5 Interview," in *Gouzenko: The Untold Story*. I have it from a confidential source that Patrick Stewart, was at the time confined in a wheelchair, that the individual who met Gouzenko in the Royal York Hotel was probably an Art Stuart, an MI5 man based at the time in Washington whose name the Russian heard as *Stewart* and about whom little is known.
46. Margaret Thatcher, House of Commons Statement, 26 March 1981.

copy. Their reply, dated 21 January 2011, referred me to Christopher Andrew's authorized history of MI5, *The Defense of the Realm*. In my follow up of 8 February 2011 I pointed out that Andrew, who characterized Igor as a drunk who varied his stories as it suited him, made no reference to the Hollis report or to Igor's puzzled reaction to it.[47]

There has to date been no reply to the second letter. In June 2005 the RCMP responding to my request for the report said they were "unable to locate any information relating to [my] request." A subsequent request made in January 2011 to *Library and Archives Canada* (LAC) produced this response: "This is regarding your email dating from January which asks if Library and Archives Canada (LAC) would have a report written by British Official Roger Hollis who had interviewed I. Gouzenko in 1945. You thought a copy may have been sent to the RCMP. In response, I have searched our more available databases and finding aids but was not successful in locating such a report within the time that we are able to spend on any one request. I consulted the indexes to presentations, witnesses etc. in the finding aid for the Royal Commission into the event (FA-33-52), as well as checking our Archives Search database. If a copy of the report was passed to the RCMP, it may well be found within the voluminous Canadian Security Intelligence Service fonds, or collection (Archival reference (R929-0-4-E). Unfortunately given resource constraints, we are limited as to the time we are able to spend on any one request, and to do an extensive search of this fonds would greatly exceed this limit."

In other words LAC is not prepared to say they have or do not have a copy of the Hollis report in their files, only that if I wished to keep looking that was my choice.

The smoking gun, confirmation of Hollis's GRU connection from an authentic GRU document or a credible GRU source, has yet to materialize. But as intelligence professionals are fond of reminding us, the absence of evidence is not evidence of absence. GRU records have for the time being been closed on Vladimir Putin's orders. A one-time official who writes under the name Vladimir Lota was allowed access to complete his book about the role of the GRU in acquiring atomic bomb

---

47. Christopher Andrew, "Counter-Espionage and Soviet Penetration: Igor Gouzenko and Kim Philby," in *The Defense of the Realm: The Authorized History of MI5*, Allen Lane, 2009. See too Paul Monk, "Christopher Andrew and the Strange Case of Roger Hollis, *Quadrant* (Australia), April 2010.

secrets. Lota, who would not respond to Chapman Pincher's letters, has now himself apparently been locked out.

Igor's claim of a mole inside MI5 code named Elli has never been challenged. This England was rotten with Soviet stooges—Philby, Maclean, Burgess, Blunt, Cairncross, to name a handful whose identities are not in doubt. The arrows all seem to point in Hollis's direction. Thirty years after the publication of *Their Trade Is Treachery* no other serious candidate has been identified.

The Hollis business was likely to have heightened Igor's suspicions. He knew that Krivitsky had met his end by gunshot in a Washington, D.C., hotel room. In an incident reported in the press in the fall of 1956, Victor Kravchenko, going by the name Peter Martin, shot and wounded an intruder in his East Side Manhattan apartment. In February 1966 Kravchenko was found dead at his desk of a gunshot wound to the head, whether a KGB *wet job* or a suicide has never been definitely established.[48]

So it was that the intelligence officer British authorities assigned to interview Igor Gouzenko, the man instrumental in bringing down Fred Rose, was himself quite probably a Soviet operative.[49]

48. Joel Seldin, "Kravchenko Confirms He's 'Martin,' Tells of Battle With Intruder," *The New York Herald Tribune,* 22 October 1956; FBI memorandum to the Director, 4 July 1966, "Victor A. Kravchenko was found shot to death in his New York City apartment 25 February 1966." See too Kern, *The Kravchenko Case.*

49. See the Peter D. Stachura review: *Chapman Pincher, Treachery, Betrayals, Blunders, and Cover-Ups. Six Decades of Espionage, Mainstream Publishing,* in Glaukopis, July 2011.

XIII.

Adieu Comrade, said the Fat Lady: Traitor, Pariah, Ex-Citizen...

More fuller-brush man than deadly espionage operative, Fred Rose hardly rates entry in a club that includes Richard Sorge, Kim Philby, Anthony Blunt, Klaus Fuchs, Theodore Hall, "the boy who gave away the bomb," and others. Freddy was at best a competent recruiter of men and women who didn't appear to need much coaxing.

Nearing the end of his life Freddy was brought face to face with the collapse of the Leninist vision he'd lived by. In Canada he might have been spared. The party would have remained ever marginal to the nation's politics and Freddy's ideological fantasy would have endured as a lofty aspiration without serious test or challenge. In his beloved USSR he might have been a candidate for an execution.

Suffering poor health, failing eyesight and in some despair Freddy, the Bolshevik streetman unpracticed in the *talmudics* of discovering in Marxian texts new readings that pointed the way out of the ideological gloom, undertook no hermeneutical u-turns, no re-interpretations of *Das Capital* to explain why things had gone so wrong in the socialist states. No citations from Louis Althusser or Antonio Gramsci or Walter

Benjamin. There were only the painful lessons of Krivitsky and Kravchenko. In those final Warsaw days Freddy became in some ways a personality wracked by disillusion not all that different from the Igor who'd fled the Soviet embassy. Igor blind, Freddy near blind—the two might have passed each other on an Ottawa street with no sign of recognition.

Nikolai Bukharin, said Nadezhda Mandelstam, "clearly saw that the new world he was actively helping to build was horrifyingly unlike the original concept. Life was deviating from the blueprints, but the blueprints had been declared sacrosanct and it was forbidden to compare them with what was actually coming into being…. A man who knew you cannot build the present out of the bricks of the future was bound to resign himself beforehand to his inevitable doom and the prospect of the firing squad."[1] It is unlikely that Freddy, trapped in Warsaw Pact Warsaw, would have been much inclined to run his weakened eyes over the pages of Nadezhda Mandelstam's account of a terrorized socialist paradise ruled by fearful, abusive bureaucrats who wielded absolute and absolutely arbitrary authority, men who had driven her husband, the poet Osip Mandelstam, to his death. Tim Buck had attended Bukharin's trial. The guilty verdict, Buck claimed in a pamphlet, was fully justified: it was the conclusion of a legitimate campaign to beat back a decade of internal subversion plotted by Bukharin and Trotsky in an "alliance with Fascism."

The future clear, the past anyone's guess. With a scissors taken to a photo one might travel back in time, alter an occasion, eliminate a participant, make everything come out differently. Dubček in the photo today, gone tomorrow. Party faithful were inclined to speak with care or guard their silence. Among the stories Elizabeth Bentley told was one of a female party member who'd attempted suicide and wound up in the psychiatric ward of a New York City hospital. For all that, she refused to tell the examining psychiatrist anything about the organization that had driven her over the edge. I never talked, I never talked, she proudly repeated!

---

1. Nadezhda Mandelstam, *Hope Against Hope: A Memoir,* 1970, trans. from the Russian by Max Hayward, Atheneum, 1976.

Apparently Lenin attempted to put the brakes on Russian anti-Semitism, but the contagion was back in vogue when Stalin took over. Accusing fingers were pointed at Jews involved in the cultural sphere and in political positions, Trotsky among them. Fabricated charges of fascism and espionage punished by imprisonment and death. At the Twelfth Party Congress held in Moscow in 1923, as Lenin lay dying, Stalin proposed a threefold division of the Soviet people. In it Jews comprised an element of the population to be destroyed. Though there were many Jews in key positions in the Kremlin and the party, the Soviet version of the *Internationale* meant that party Jews were not to go to the aid of Jews, and generally did not.

In preparation for life in the worker's state Jews needed to shed their Jewishness, Judaic caterpillars to be transformed into Marxist-Leninist butterflies, the final solution as conceived on the left. But would that have been enough? Recall the fate of the Spanish Marranos. Like the heads of the Inquisition the Communist leadership would be inclined to seek out and always find something not quite right about these cosmopolitan apostates. Attachment to the precepts of Marxism-Leninism would never be sufficient, on occasion irrelevant.

The late Russian film historian Rashit Yangirov told me that in the 1920s the authorities encouraged the development of the cinemas of the autonomous republics such as Chuvash, Tartaria, and Daghestan, and supported the production of Yiddish-language films. Before long they decided that ethnicity interfered with class consciousness. In the 1930s the movement was crushed and its administrators shot on trumped up corruption charges.[2]

The ever-devoted Litvin-Witczak found no welcome mat upon his return to the USSR. Jews were now much out of favour. In the spring of 1953, as the anti-Semitic campaign of party and state peaked, Litvin was removed from active army duty and fired from the Military Diplomatic Academy of the General Staff.[3]

In the 1930s and 1940s, the much-acclaimed Soviet commitment to establish a Jewish autonomous republic in Birobidzhan in Soviet Asia created much excitement among the members of the Jewish left in

---

2. In conversation.
3. Gruntman, "The New Life of Comrade Litvin."

Canada, among them Joshua Gershman. In April 1945 in the course of the federal election campaign, Jewish LPP candidates, Freddy included, were speaking positively about the establishment of a Jewish state in British mandate Palestine, a very different thing.

In November 1945 a Canadian Birobidzhan Committee was formed to be headquartered in Montreal. One of Freddy's brothers was a leading member of the Canadian Birobidzhan Committee. In February the Committee held its initial Montreal meeting. Could $200,000 be raised to equip a Jewish vocational institute there? Among the 200 delegates, Freddy said he hoped to see in Birobidzhan "a monument from Canadian Jewry." In 1946, the Canadian Birobidzhan Committee announced that there was in the Jewish family room for Zionists and non-Zionists, that they did not see a conflict between Birobidzhan and the Zionist project in Palestine. The RCMP were keeping a watchful eye. They concluded, based on a report in the February 1946 *Canadian Jewish Monthly*, that a "large number of Jewish organizations have answered the call of the Canadian Biro-Bidjan [*sic*] Committee to come to the conference called to raise means for the settlement of Jewish orphans in Biro-Bidjan. Among the organizations which have responded are: The United Jewish People's Order, the Association of Russian Jews, The Association of Roumanian Jews, The Jewish Polish Association, The Furriers' Union, The Amalgamated and Bakers Union, and the Wintchewsky [*sic*] Schools."[4]

Enthusiasm for the autonomous Birobidzhan republic, said scholar Henry Srebrnik, was a product of the "misplaced hopes of desperate people," a doomed from the start con job, whatever hope it might have inspired finally dashed with the murder of Shloime Mikhoels, chairman of the Jewish Anti-Fascist Committee. Mikhoels and the poet Itzik Fefer had visited Montreal in the summer of 1943 with accounts of the slaughter of Europe's Jews. The Committee was formed in the USSR in 1942 to generate support among Jewish communities in the west, a scheme apparently brought to KGB chief Lavrenti Beria by Henryk Ehrlich and Victor Alter. It involved Soviet actors, poets, painters,

---

4. Henry Srebrnik, *Jerusalem on the Amur*, 2008; On 25 February 1946, the RCMP's "O" Division in Toronto reported on a story published in the *Canadian Jewish Monthly* a few days earlier about a conference on the project held in Montreal.

scientists.[5] After the war, Holocaust information was repressed, the committee shut down, its leaders murdered, according to one guess, because of their ties to the West as the Cold War re-focused attention on competing global interests.

In time a Communist as devoted to the cause as Joshua Gershman, editor of the CPC's Yiddish-language newspaper, and a founder of the Communist affiliated UJPO had had enough; he departed the party after 54 years of extraordinary dedication and a record of exemplary service to the labour movement.[6]

For Freddy's Quebec devotees, Fishel Rosenberg was but a child of Polish immigrants, son of a Polish carpenter father, an immigrant radical adrift in the true north. Thus is Freddy's Jewishness airbrushed away, like the Kirilenko presence in a photo, all the better to construct a narrative in which the hostility to the man can be read pure and simple as establishment antagonism to socialism. A point of view Freddy shared with government prosecutors. In this version, the party's role in Freddy's departure for Europe can be ignored and Freddy's experience of struggle and disappointment pressed into a reassuring ideological shape.[7]

There are those who today will point out the great popularity of the man named Fred Rose among Quebec's francophone socialists, how he towered over the depravity of Stalinism, that one can make too much of the *alleged* Soviet espionage network that operated in Canada during wartime, that perhaps Freddy was not even the Soviet agent the evidence makes him out to have been, that Lenin in fact was a far less brutal leader than liberals and conservatives now claim, that he allowed internal party debate, at times finding himself on the losing side of central committee votes. Little is said of the murders of Isaac Babel, Vsevolod Myerhold and Osip Mandelstam and millions of others. Josef Stalin might have been a terrible guy, but that was something the left were the first to draw the world's attention to. On the other hand, his victory at the battle of Stalingrad rescued civilization from Nazism. Then too,

5. Srebrnik, "Such Stuff as Diasporic Dreams Are Made On: Birobidzhan and the Canadian-Jewish Communist Imagination," a lecture at the University of Calgary Institute for the Humanities, 2001.
6. Gerald Tulchinsky, "Family Quarrel: Joe Salsberg, the 'Jewish' Question, and Canadian Communism," *Labour/Le Travail*, 56, Fall, 2005, pp. 149–173.
7. Comeau and Dionne, *Les communistes au Quebec 1936–1956*.

Freddy's lawyer, Joseph Cohen, might have for some reason thrown the case. Was there not direct British involvement in the Gouzenko defection? Isn't the speed with which the American media seized on the Gouzenko revelations to attack the USSR highly suggestive? Fred Rose was guilty of nothing, his trial in effect a "show trial" mounted for strictly propaganda purposes, etc.[8]

My letters to the Communist Party of Canada inquiring about the lost memoir have gone unanswered. Laura, who told me the document wound up in party hands after her father's death, may be the only person to have read it. It was, she said, "a kind of autobiography, but a very short one, summarizing his life...he did write about that time, having met with a party person and that person suggesting that he leave.... I thought, he wrote, my heart would break. And for my father to say that ...it still amazes me. I never heard him express himself in that manner."[9]

The prison diary too seems to have disappeared.

In 1972 Freddy learned that Raymond Boyer had published a book dealing with his prison experience, *Barreaux de Fer, Hommes de Chair*.[10] I'd love, said Freddy in a letter to Lea Roback, to see Boyer's book to compare my impression with his. Not clear if he ever did. He said nothing more about Boyer in the letter. If anyone was responsible for his having spent those years in prison it was Raymond Boyer whose silence might have spared him that ordeal as well as his own imprisonment. Freddy's friends and political associates tend to speak of Boyer with a certain fondness and regard Igor as the chief villain of Freddy's tragedy as did Freddy himself.

Out of prison, Boyer abandoned chemistry for criminology. Boyer's post-prison career included a post as a research associate in criminology in the Institute of Forensic Psychiatry, McGill University, a leading role in the prisoners' rights organization the *Ligue des Droits des Detenus*, and work on behalf of political refugees, especially Chileans in flight from the Pinochet regime. Boyer helped support an art gallery that exhibited the work of the incarcerated, the *Galerie Maximum* run by Pierre Paul Geoffroy, a man who'd done time for FLQ activity. It opened in 1983

---

8. Private communication.
9. Laura Rose interview for the Francine Pelletier film about Fred Rose.
10. Raymond Boyer, *Barreaux de fer, hommes de chair*, Editions de jour, 1972.

on Mount Royal Avenue in Montreal. The *galerie* organized an annual competition for *le Prix Raymond Boyer*, awarded to the artist who produced the best work of prison art.[11]

In 1981, Boyer introduced Claire Culhane at the launch of a French translation of her book about a hostage taking in a British Columbia penitentiary, *Barred from Prison*. The FLQ's Paul Rose, who wrote the preface, was released from the Cowansville medium-security prison for the occasion on condition he not make any public declaration. Rose inscribed copies, said nothing. Boyer lauded Ms. Culhane's courage for speaking out for prisoners's rights.[12]

Boyer, who had entered St. Vincent de Paul on 21 December 1948 to serve nineteen months of a two-year sentence, found it inexplicable that one of the prison regulations said it was strictly forbidden for inmates to have knowledge of those regulations. A copy of the "Loi des penitenciers" circulated in secret meaning its contents could not be employed in an inmate's formal complaint.

A few months after he'd been inside, Boyer was approached by a fellow cell block inmate named Butch, a tough anglophone from the Eastern Townships, with an offer to murder Boyer's ex-wife Anita. A favor for a pal. Butch had learned from a radio news item that Anita had divorced Boyer and remarried. Due for release, Butch, who assumed Boyer hungered for revenge, thought it wouldn't be much of a problem because there was nothing linking him to Anita. Fifty dollars would cover the cost of travel and necessities. Anita had married yet another Communist millionaire, Fredrick Vanderbilt Field, and was living in the United States. Boyer found it difficult convincing Butch that he'd agreed to the divorce and was not troubled by Anita remarrying. Butch found Boyer's attitude excessively gallant.[13]

---

11. Ian Ferrier, "Convict art reveals the human side: Gallerie Maximum gives prison artists chance to show what they can do," *The Gazette*, 22 February 1985; John Kalbfleisch, "Prison Didn't Diminish Spy's Passion for Justice," *The Gazette*, 18 March 2001. The Prix Raymond Boyer was awarded under the auspices of ARCAD (Association de rencontres culturales avec les detenus).

12. "Rose release conditional on his silence," *The Globe and Mail*, 23 September, 1981.

13. Fredrick Vanderbilt Field, *From Right to Left: An Autobiography*, Lawrence Hill & Company, 1983; "Mexico: Red Haven," *Time*, 9 September 1957. Field in 1945 held a meeting in his Manhattan apartment for a group of American party members, that included Elizabeth Bentley, to discuss a party business matter that included Elizabeth Bentley. In his autobiography Field refers to his brief marriage to Anita Cohen Boyer: "Anita and I had exactly one more or less normal year together." A woman who was acquainted with the Boyers thought Anita's relationship with Field began before Raymond Boyer was sent to prison.

Boyer's ex-wife, Anita Cohen, was the daughter of a New York cantor. They'd married in 1940. To please his father-in-law, Roman Catholic Boyer converted to Judaism. When *The Gazette* suggested that Jewish Anita had turned him on to Communism, Boyer in a fury denounced the paper as an anti-Semitic rag.

It would seem unlikely that in his time inside he and Freddy would not have encountered each other, up close or at a distance. Freddy didn't say if this ever happened. There is in Boyer's account of his time inside no mention of Freddy or why he himself was in prison, only a blurb on the back cover of his book to explain.

"No former prisoner," said fellow St. Vincent de Paul inmate Ben Jauvin at the Chapelle du Bon Pasteur memorial service for Boyer in 1993, "did more for us ex-convicts to put us on the way back into society. For him, prison was like a military college, except that you found there a better class of people."

Many old-line Cartier party members have since passed on, their children themselves now aging adults. A woman who did secretarial work in Freddy's campaign office says she is able to recall very little. Her daughter remembers sitting on Paul Robeson's knee at a rally in Montreal, Robeson among Freddy's big fans. Laura's ex, a prince of the high school basketball court, was not happy about my phone call. He would not say what he remembered about his one-time father-in-law, only that he did not now wish to be in any way associated with him. Laura, he said, "was just a pretty girl." Did he think I was suggesting the marriage was ideologically motivated?

A half century later some of Freddy's former comrades contend that Stalin's pact with Hitler was a brilliant strategic gambit. Party people, who long ago disavowed the party, will insist they saw no reason Freddy was sent to prison, that the Russians were wartime allies, that it was the Red army, Russians *not* Communists who bled and died in the war to defeat the Nazis.

A woman who belonged to Norman Bethune's highrent Montreal circle made a face but said nothing at the mention of his name. In 1976, the Chinese government gave the city a gift the city reluctantly accepted, a white stone statue of Bethune. It stands at a downtown Montreal mini-park space in a small, grassy triangular spot where pigeons and seagulls have at it and students and homeless alcoholics gather. One cold winter day, an admirer climbed up and placed a warm red tuque on Norman's head.

Irene, a Norman Bethune acquaintance and once a woman of stunning good looks, reminded me that in sifting through the debris of the period, the fragmented record of things done, the incomplete recollections of things said and not said, one might fail to grasp the atmosphere of the time, the aspiration for a better society, a better life.

"It begins with logic and ends with the firing squad." I was talking to the great Yugoslav film director Dusan Makavejev. That's it, he said unhappily. It was 1978. Yugoslavia was still Yugoslavia. Despite everything, the man was a Balkan socialist, and a Balkan socialist he would remain, the way a Catholic who knows all about sacerdotal abuse could never be anything else.

The world of Cartier was a transient world with no other fate than to be abandoned at the first opportunity. The war in Europe had done in Freddy's scheme to build a toiler's Jerusalem among Cartier's balcons and escaliers. By the time Freddy got out of prison in 1951, Depression days that had boosted party membership were history. So who now needed Freddy or the party?

The Cartier depicted in Freddy's election pamphlets as a downtrodden, disease-ridden zone of shoeless children, foul-smelling courtyards, and overcrowded, dilapidated dwellings with ancient plumbing would be left behind, the people's paradise Freddy was striving to turn Cartier into sought elsewhere.

Numbers of Cartier's garment factory drones had become entrepreneurs. Anyone, Russell Goldberg tailor to the seriously affluent told me, who had gone into any business in 1939 emerged well off in 1945. Money had been made. The bubbling over of ideological passion had cooled, in its place a steady exodus out of the hood into the city's split-level bourgeois precincts, the mini *goldena medinas* north and west- Snowdon, Outremont, Hampstead, Westmount, the Town of Mont Royal, and beyond. Could Freddy in going-to-the-dogs Warsaw have even tried to wrap his mind around the fact that it was the involvement of the USSR in the war to crush the Nazis that gave the citizens of Cartier this good life they would not otherwise have had?

Eagerly, not to say happily, and perhaps foolishly, one joined the exile from the world of one's childhood. The children of transplanted residents took to sneering at Cartier as *the slums*. Gentile DPs - displaced persons—labeled *hunkies*, congregated in Hungarian restaurants and social clubs on the Main. The *yid* escapees from Nazi death camps who had begun to settle in the district were ridiculed as *mockies* for their accented speech. Those numbers included black-coated shtreimeled *hasids* who brought with them an altogether different idea of heaven. I recall a gentle, unassuming, saintly fellow whose wife and all of whose children had been murdered in Europe. Disadvantaged newcomers rarely receive a warm welcome, not slave plantation arrivals and not Nazi lager inmates either. The *mockies* were no exception. Here is Primo Levi remembering Auschwitz: "Rarely was a newcomer received, I won't say as a friend but at least as a companion-in-misfortune; in the majority of cases, those with seniority (and seniority was acquired in three or four months; the changeover was swift!) showed irritation or even hostility. The 'newcomer' … was derided and subjected to cruel pranks…"[14]

Citizens of Cartier who never had much money now had a lot of it. People who never dreamed of owning cars, now owned them. Happy days were here at last. The year the war ended saw the opening of *Ruby Foo's* on the Decarie strip serving pricey Lobster Cantonese, a once forbidden dish, to the city's new elite. It had been the location of a failing ice cream parlour named *Gallaghers*. The mob ran the strip. There was no Ruby Foo. Nick Pileggi told me there had been an eatery in New York where bookmakers and gamblers hung out called *Ruby Foo's*, perhaps the inspiration. Someone who'd worked at the restaurant, a produce and meat buyer, said it was an institution, like a city, a "high class place," the brainchild of a rackets man named Leo Berco/Bercovich, whose cousin Louis was the shooter of gambling czar Harry Davis. There was a strict dress code, jacket and tie *de rigueur*. The place to be seen on Saturday night among the city's elite. The space could accommodate 400. The waiters wore red jackets with black lapels, in summer white jackets with green lapels. There was a roast beef wagon. A pastry section in the huge kitchen. I was told that after a trip to Hong Kong, Bercovich and the

---

14. Primo Levi, "The Gray Zone" in *The Drowned and the Saved*, trans. Raymond Rosenthal, Summit Books, 1988.

other bosses added a *duck a l'orange* dish to the menu, imagining the dish to be Chinese. I've asked rabbis to explain the extraordinary appeal of Chinese food to Jewish *fressers*. None could.

Driving out to *Ruby Foo's* to stuff oneself with oriental specialties was a measure of how much things had changed. Financing for the restaurant came from a thriving wartime gambling scene, in particular the city's barbotte establishments. Inconspicuous at a table in the restaurant wearing one of Russell's monogrammed tailor-made shirts sipping a ginger ale sat casino-man Meyer Lansky who was heard to rate the kitchen facilities at *Ruby Foo's* outstanding, the best anywhere...

One or two people close to Freddy would claim he did it for humanity. He of the roving eye, short-assed spiffy dresser who called all the girls sweetheart. Comrade Rosenberg, did you posing in the shaving glass see Bogart-Moses or was it just the voice of Uncle Joe you heard in the burning bush?

In August 1946, when Freddy's application for bail from Bordeaux Jail was going nowhere, a Port Arthur, Ontario, resident who identified himself or herself only as a "Labor Well Wisher" wondered in a letter to the *Port Arthur News-Chronicle* whether anyone could "show how the spy system...was connected in any way with the labor movement."[15]

Marxism-Leninism did not represent a late in life born-again conversion. Nor was it the case as it was with some Eastern Euopean intellecttuals of an ideological epiphany experienced at the point of a gun. Freddy had evidently been persuaded as a young person studying Marxism that this was History's only alternative. Thus besotted, he was drawn to the party the way others were drawn to other careers and professions, the medical profession, the stock market. We don't know what Freddy knew about the terrible things that went on in the Ukraine during Stalin's imposed famine, the millions starved to death.

Freddy, who betrayed the labour movement and played fast and loose with the Cartier electorate, was himself betrayed—by his Soviet comrades, by the Party, by political associates. The USSR posthumously rewarded Kim Philby with a stamp Joseph Brodsky guessed was for pointing the way to the Middle East.[16] There would be no stamp for

---

15. "Advice for Labor," *The News Chronicle* (Port Arthur, Ontario), 19 August 1946.
16. Joseph Brodsky, "Collector's Item" in *On Grief and Reason*, Farrar Straus & Giroux, 1995.

party-man Freddy who, to paraphrase V. I. Lenin, was supported by his comrades the way the rope supports the man who is hanged.

Mackenzie King escaped his colloquy with *the great beyond* onto the plain-speaking rose-tinted Canadian fifty-dollar bill where he may be found among the themes of Canadian human rights history and a quotation from the Universal Declaration of Human Rights.

Alas for Freddy, who passed on far from home, a mostly forgotten figure, there would be no official remembrance. Said *The Gazette* on the occasion of his passing: "Mr. Rose protested his innocence of treason to the end, and given the anti-Russian paranoia of the post-war years, it's just conceivable there is less to his guilt than met the court's eye... Whatever the real Fred Rose, he stands for most who remember his name as a symbol of corrupted idealism and betrayal."[17]

In March 1966 Freddy was scolded in an RCMP document because he "did not visit Canada to attend his father's funeral."[18] Perhaps the Force had forgotten that his citizenship had been revoked. The year of Jacob Rosenberg's death his son would not have been permitted to enter Canada for any reason.

Did Pierre Trudeau, as one hears, refuse to allow Freddy himself to return home to die? It was otherwise for dead Freddy. I assume, said a spokesman for the Department of External Affairs, "that there's no problem bringing the body in."[19] Freddy was cremated in Poland, his ashes shipped back for a burial in the Kehal Israel Cemetery in Dollard des Ormeaux.

I made, said Freddy, one mistake in my life and I paid for it. The mistake was not Freddy's alone, it was the larger resolve of the left to play sidekick to totalitarian gangsterism.

Over lunch in the extraordinary dining room of the Hotel Metropol in Moscow my dear late friend Rashit recalled how incomprehensible it was that while times were near unbearable in Moscow, Americans gathered in summer camps in the Catskills where they played at being Communists.

---

17. "Fred Rose 1907–1983," *The Gazette,* 17–18 March 1983.
18. "Fred Rose, Poland," RCMP, "C" Division, Montreal, P.Q., 18 March 1966.
19. "Rose May Be Buried in Canada," *The Globe and Mail,* 18 March 1983. The Fred Rose story continues to inspire much nostalgia. See Henry Srebrnik, "The Return of Fred Rose (on the Centenary of His Birth)," *Outlook,* Vol. 45, No. 5, Sept./Oct. 2007.

The end of the Cold War loomed when Fishel Rosenberg died in Warsaw in 1983 at age 76. It was a little over a decade since Nixon's meeting with Mao in Beijing. Now Mao was gone, China ruled by Deng Xiaoping, at one time abused by Gang of Four delinquents. Deng never did see any great role for party-line ideology in implementing Zhou Enlai's four modernizations. By a callous irony, Freddy ended his Polish days in the days of the Polish pope, the Poland of Lech Walesa's *Solidarity*, Uncle Joe long dead, the Soviet Union enmeshed in a disastrous war in Afghanistan.

Acknowledgements

For information in-emails and/or conversation I am indebted to Gary Kern, Nigel West, John F. Fox, Jr., Dan Mulvenna, Amy Knight, Mark Kristmanson, Hayden B. Peake, William McMurtry, Alan Eagelson, Gordon Lunan, Andrew Kavchak, Laura Rose, Irene Kon, Evelyn Pomerantz, Eddie Cartile, William Weintraub, Kirwan Cox, Harry Gulkin, Russell Goldberg, Bernard Shapiro, Harvey Yarosky, Nick Pileggi, Gerald Tulchinsky, John Haynes, Gerald Ottenbreit, Jr., Evy Wilson, and Silvia Friedman.

Research support was provided by Nathan Wong, Janice Rosen of the Canadian Jewish Congress, and Shannon Hodge of the Jewish Public Library.

My son Joshua helped with the selection of photographs and illustrations, my son Vanya with computer problems.

I remain much indebted for invaluable assistance to Francine Pelletier; Diana Gibson of the Library and Archives Canada; Benoit Morin of the Westmount Public Library; Judge Fred Kaufman; Robert Israel; Barbara Kincaid, General Counsel, Court Operations Sector, Supreme Court of Canada; and my old high school pal, Justice Morris J. Fish.

Ian McKay, of Queens University, generously provided comments on an early draft.

Germaine Lacasse read a later draft for historical accuracy.

All aspects of the Gouzenko affair were discussed at great length with Harry Chapman Pincher. Harry and Billee and their chocolate lab Tom welcomed Jeannie and me into their home for drinks and lunch and animated conversation.

My publisher Robert Miller never failed to offer reassuring calm.

Bibi and Franklin helped keep me sane.

Above all, this work would not have been possible without Jeannie.

Index